When
Workers
Fight

WHEN
Bruno Ramirez

Contributions in Labor History, Number 2

WORKERS FIGHT

THE POLITICS OF INDUSTRIAL RELATIONS IN THE PROGRESSIVE ERA, 1898-1916

GREENWOOD PRESS
WESTPORT, CONNECTICUT · LONDON, ENGLAND

Library of Congress Cataloging in Publication Data

Ramirez, Bruno.
    When workers fight.

    (Contributions in labor history ; no. 2 ISSN 0146-
3608)
    Bibliography: p.
    Includes index.
    1. Industrial relations—United States—History.
2. Trade-unions—United States—History. I. Title.
II. Series: Contributions in labor history ; no. 2.
HD8072.R34   331'.0973   77-83895
ISBN 0-8371-9826-7

Library of Congress Catalog Card Number: 77-83895
ISBN: 0-8371-9826-7
ISSN: 0146-3608

First published in 1978

Greenwood Press, Inc.
51 Riverside Avenue, Westport, Connecticut 06880

Printed in the United States of America

10 9 8 7 6 5 4 3 2 1

CONTENTS

PART 3: THE CRITICAL YEARS

PREFACE

My interest in industrial relations was provoked by the lively historio-
graphical debate that has been going on for some time concerning the
character and significance of the progressive reform movement. When I
decided to write about this topic, I was convinced, as I still am today, of
the pivotal importance of the so-called "Progressive Era" as a formative
period for American labor, business, and reform ideology and policy.

Both the merits and the limitations of the existing literature encouraged me to undertake this work and to add to the current debate my own
historical findings and interpretative hypotheses on the relationship between capital and labor in the light of the broader reform movement. My
attempt to approach industrial relations not as a mere by-product of industrial development but as a central basis for business, government, and labor
intervention has necessarily led my inquiry to span several areas that are
normally considered to be the domain of specialized historical disciplines.
From a methodological point of view, this had the advantage of challeng-
ing a certain division-of-labor attitude prevailing in the historical profession and of permitting me to combine a synthesis approach with one of
detailed historical analysis. On the other hand the disadvantage is, of
course, that readers may feel—and perhaps rightly so—that some of my
interpretative hypotheses may appear to be insufficiently supported by
my historical findings and that my omission of certain "facts" or "developments" may weaken my overall conclusions.

Another consequence of this approach has been that the chronological framework that generally underlies this work has not always been

strictly maintained. This is particularly true in Part 3, where my concern to pursue a number of central themes in a more analytical manner has necessitated a certain chronological overlapping in my exposition, which I hope will not be too distracting for the readers.

Many friends, including both scholars and nonscholars, who read earlier drafts or portions of the manuscript encouraged me to make this work available in published form. Their encouragement has helped me to overcome my hesitations and to reach the conclusion that despite its limitations, this work offers a valid and useful contribution to the understanding of the period in question. I wish to thank all these friends, and in particular Gisela Bock, Paolo Carpignano, Bruno Cartosio, Ferruccio Gambino, and Peter Taylor.

I am especially grateful to Professor Kenneth McNaught, who was my supervisor at the University of Toronto and who offered exemplary encouragement and assistance. I also wish to express my deep gratitude to David Montgomery for his valuable criticisms that made me aware of some of the limitations in my work and for at the same time encouraging me to pursue my efforts further. Similarly, Milton Cantor's acute criticisms were instrumental in improving the quality of the manuscript in preparation for its publication. I only regret my inability to do full justice to these criticisms.

I owe a great debt to Judith Fiorito Ramirez, my wife and companion for many years, both for the material support and encouragement she gave me, especially in the earlier stages of this work, and also for her valuable comments and criticisms that improved considerably the style and the substance of the manuscript.

Of course, I am solely responsible for the views expressed in this work.

The staffs of the various libraries mentioned in the bibliography made my research less arduous than it might have been. Similarly, I wish to thank the staff of Greenwood Press for their competence and kindness. My thanks also go to Alina Gildiner for her willingness to type the final version of the manuscript under conditions of hardship and to Miriana Kaludjerovic for having put up with me during many moments of tension and frustration.

Finally, a word on financial support. Except for a much appreciated small grant from the University of Western Ontario that helped me cover typing and duplicating costs, I was unable to obtain any financial support for reasons that may only be clear to the connoisseur of the bureaucratic mind. The only benefit I am accruing from this is that it now makes my task of acknowledgment a very small one.

When
Workers
Fight

INTRODUCTION: INDUSTRIAL RELATIONS AND THE SEARCH FOR ORDER

In 1898, as the United States was beginning to recover from one of the largest and most severe depressions of its history, the newly elected President, William McKinley, appointed a commission whose task was to investigate the industrial and labor conditions of the country. McKinley's concern about industrial conditions in America was more than justified. The expansion of the American productive apparatus—already underway—had to rest on an accurate knowledge of changing economic and social conditions. A decade and a half later, the need to appoint another similar commission arose again. Unlike the earlier commission, the appointment of the new one was dictated by compelling factors: the fifteen-odd years that had lapsed had seen industrial conflict and violence escalate at a fearful rate, leaving deep marks on American society and calling for immediate solutions.

Apart from the immense historical value of their findings, the two investigating commissions stand as important marks to delineate a crucial chapter in the history of capital-labor relations. If, in fact, the long economic upswing that followed the depression of the 1890s brought prosperity and growth, it also ushered in a new age of confrontation between those two ancient foes of (capitalist) industrial development. The history of this confrontation runs as a constant thread throughout the Progressive era and to a large extent characterizes that period. One can hardly think of any contemporary observer who was not familiar with that tortuous issue known as the "labor problem." True, many would often depict and explain it in simple terms, quickly assigning blame to one of the parties involved. But the labor problem that confronted Progressive America precluded any such hasty judgment. This was true for contemporary observers, and it is equally true for historians who have since attempted to reconstruct its contours. The history of the labor problem in the Progressive era is not only a history of fierce and often brutal confrontation; it is also a history of repeated attempted solutions, of mediations by reformers' groups and by public agencies, of businessmen's strategies, of workingmen and women organizing and reorganizing their strength.

It is in this context that collective bargaining acquires a fundamental historical significance. This study focuses on collective bargaining because it emerged as the one solution to the labor problem that was believed to be in keeping with the ideal of a democratic institutional framework to which large sectors of the reform movement aspired. Collective bargaining, it was believed, would provide an equitable and secure basis through which American capital and American labor would solve their common problem and further their common interests. Its importance in the eyes of its advocates lay not only in the economic function that it would resolve but also in the political role that it would play in the context of the often unpredictable forces operative in the country. Prominent figures as diverse in their social background and functions as Marcus Hanna, Ralph Easley, John Mitchell, and John Commons—to mention just a few—were all firmly committed to this belief.

Yet collective bargaining was by no means the only solution. Other alternatives were sought and enforced (such as welfarism and scientific management), sometimes coexisting with collective bargaining, more often directly undermining it. Their history has to be explored not only because they gave rise to distinct forms of industrial and labor relations but also because they effectively prevented the extension of collective bargaining to other sectors of industry, thus contributing enormously to its decline. Their history is also important because it casts much light on the ambiguous and often contradictory stance of many prolabor reformers. In an age in which the ideal of science emerged as a powerful cultural and productive force, it was not easy to resist forms of industrial and labor relations that purported to embody the most advanced scientific criteria of social organization. Therefore it is not strange to see reformers such as Louis Brandeis— to cite just one example—caught in the dilemma between industrial efficiency on the one hand and industrial democracy on the other. If Brandeis's dedication to furthering both fronts of social progress was unquestionable, not equally unquestionable seemed his ability to reconcile two forms of labor relations—scientific management and collective bargaining—that to the average working man of those days appeared in sharp contradiction.

The chronology traditionally attached to collective bargaining is also in need of reexamination. After experiencing a sort of golden age during World War I, collective bargaining collapsed in the postwar months. Yet its fate cannot be seen strictly in terms of war mobilization and reconversion. No doubt the industrial policies that were designed to deal with the domestic effects of the war had a direct and immediate bearing on collective bargaining. But the decline of collective bargaining must be explained in long-range terms. Its roots go back to the prewar years when a number of factors emerged that seriously weakened its base and circumscribed its effects. This study will explore those factors and contribute to an explanation of the decline of collective bargaining that goes beyond the episodic treatment of capital-labor relations.

Any historical study of industrial and labor relations presents peculiar methodological problems. Such an investigation cannot dispense with a certain rigor in analyzing the structure and operation of given forms of industrial organization, but it is essential to transcend these areas and view them in the broader context of changing economic and political conditions. This is especially the case since they were the expression of power relations between capital and labor.

The historical study of industrial and labor relations has found itself caught in a sort of methodological limbo. Traditional labor historiography has more often than not shied away from these areas, being concerned primarily with the study of trade union organizations and their historical evolution. The same can be said of the field of business history, although as the works of Robert Ozanne, Hugh Aitken, and Stephen Scheinberg, to mention just a few, show, there has been an increasing tendency among business historians to focus on industrial and labor relations.[1]

Among historians who have tried to cast new light on the nature of progressivism and in the process revise traditional interpretations, industrial and labor relations have received marginal attention and have often gone unnoticed. Robert Wiebe's influential interpretation of the role of businessmen in generating reforms in the Progressive era is a notable illustration.[2] Businessmen's attitudes toward labor and their attempts to deal with it are a central theme of his study. However, the emphasis that he places on organizations as weapons to bring about reforms and social change leads him to reduce the labor problem to a mere confrontation between organizations. Apart from the limited understanding that such an approach yields for a period in which organized labor was but a small fraction of the entire labor force, one hardly gets the impression from Wiebe's study that labor—organized or unorganized—was a reality with which businessmen had to grapple in their daily operations and which therefore demanded specific policies and strategies. As far as labor is concerned, Wiebe's conclusions on the progressive character of businessmen's politics are based more on their ability to mobilize themselves than on the specific content of their labor policies.

James Weinstein's study of the U.S. corporate elite in the Progressive era shows much more awareness of the reality of industrial and labor relations and of the political implications surrounding them.[3] Partly, this results from the fact that central to his study is the National Civic Federation—the organization that more than any other devoted itself to industrial relations issues. Weinstein's approach—which reflects a methodology which was common among New Left historians throughout the 1960s—leads him to place his whole focus on the ideological content of corporate politics and reforms. However successful Weinstein is in his goal of differentiating corporate liberal reformism from socialist politics, his study fails to see industrial and labor relations as a result of corporate strategies and as a reflection of changing capital-labor power relations.

Gabriel Kolko's *The Triumph of Conservatism* needs a lengthier comment, both because of the central place it occupies in revisionist historiography and because of the direct impact it had in the elaboration of the present inquiry. Kolko's distinct contribution has been that of looking at progressivism "in the context of the nature and tendencies of the economy," thereby making it possible to distinguish the mere intellectual dimension of Progressivism (the social values it propounded, its ideology, its rhetoric) from its attempt to deal with the "operational realities" that the new era imposed on the leaders of the nation.[4] One such reality that Kolko singled out as underlying the period was the reality of a market characterized by unregulated competition—typical of a phase of capitalist development where "new competitors sprang up, and [where] . . . economic power was diffused throughout an expanding nation."[5] The attempt to rationalize the market and bring about stability and predictability in the economy is therefore, according to Kolko, the fundamental theme that runs throughout the Progressive era and that ultimately characterizes its political dynamics. Kolko saw as protagonist the key business interests of the country who, after failing through strictly economic means (the merger movement), resorted to political means (federal regulation of the economy).

Kolko's detailed analysis of the most important legislative measures designed to regulate the economy is of fundamental importance not only because it shows the crucial role big business played in initiating and promoting those measures but also because it reveals the changing function of the state in an expanding and modernizing economy—from a role of mere mediator between contending interest groups to one of active regulator of the economic process and guarantor of its stability. The expression Kolko has coined to describe this process, "political capitalism," as truistic as it may sound (one can hardly conceive of a form of capitalism that is not political), synthesizes the trends that were occurring in those years: rationalization of the economy, consolidation of economic power, legitimation of emerging power relations.[6] It also deals with the fundamental question of the relationship between the dominant centers of economic power and "the basic legislative structure" that emerged as a result of the reform impetus of those years.[7]

In one important sense, however, Kolko's analysis appears partial for it fails to take into account a whole sphere of economic activity—production —that was a central focus in the process of economic rationalization that went on during the Progressive era. According to Kolko the main source of economic instability was the peculiar competitive nature that the American market exhibited around the turn of the century—a condition that called for economic as well as political rationalization. Kolko's explicit usage of the term *rationalization* evidences his concern to exclude areas of business activity such as "the improvement of efficiency, output, or internal organization of a company."[8] Yet it was precisely at this level of economic activity—the organization of production—that lay a major source of economic unpredictability and instability. As Thorstein Veblen saw with extreme perceptiveness, in the age of the machine process rationalization and planning of production became as necessary as planning in the sphere of distribution and exchange. The opposition—organized or unorganized—of the workers, the need to make the most efficient use of the available labor resources, and the need to gain competitive advantage by securing more favorable wage policies were all imperatives that made industrial and labor relations a central focus of business activity throughout the Progressive era. It is important to note that businessmen's action at this level went more often than not hand in hand with activities designed to deal with problems growing out of competition or market regulation. The coal industry—which I will explore at some length—provides the clearest illustration: the working out of an interstate wage policy and the regularization of labor relations in 1898 was pivotal to ensuring stability in bituminous coal mining and rescuing the industry from disaster. Moreover, one need only look at the sprouting of employers' associations arising to deal specifically with the labor problem—whether at a general level, or at the level of industrial sectors, or even at the level of specific issues—and at the fact that their members held membership in trade associations at the same time. That the attempt to attain rationalization and stability in the sphere of labor and industrial relations did not result in the same amount of federal legislative measures, as was the case with regulation of competition, should not obscure the reality of the constant political activity it generated. By exploring this field of business activity this book intends to study a source of political and social conflict that was central to the process of rationalization and to the changes in power relations that occurred during the Progressive era. I hope that certain aspects of the labor movement's politics that have not received their due attention by historians will be uncovered, thus enabling us to evaluate labor's awareness of the changes that were taking place as a result of the rapid and widespread industrialization. Finally, although this investigation is not a study of progressivism as such, it will contribute to a clarification of some of the interpretative problems that still surround the Progressive movement—particularly concerning its relationship with business and with labor.

The expression *labor problem*, so often encountered in the political and business literature of the Progressive period, was far from being a mere rhetorical formula that had entered the political jargon of the time; it actually reflected one of the harshest realities of American society. Its magnitude and its importance must be assessed and analyzed to gain a more accurate historical understanding of the social climate existing at that time and of the imperatives that the American political and industrial establishment faced.

For most U.S. industrialists the labor problem meant that the path toward economic growth and expansion was by no means smooth; they had to reckon with the reality of the American laboring classes—their demands, their material needs, and their growing awareness of the necessity for organized action. This reality never manifested itself as dramatically as during the five or six years that followed the long depression of 1893-1896 when the American economy entered one of its most vigorous cycles of productive expansion. The labor problem is best expressed in the wave of strikes that, beginning in 1897, hit American industry with increasing force, reaching its highest level in 1903—a level that surpassed even the two famous years of industrial warfare, 1886 and 1894. It is important to analyze this cycle of industrial warfare briefly to assess the economic and political import of the labor problem in those years.[9]

From a total of 1,026 strikes in 1896 (the last year of the depression), the figure rose yearly until in 1901 it reached 2,924, the highest number of strikes per year in U.S. history. By 1903, the number had reached 3,495. A corresponding increase occurred in the yearly totals of strikers involved and of workers affected by the strikes. From a total of 183,813 workers involved and 241,170 workers affected by strikes in 1896, the figures climb to 308,267 strikers and 417,072 workers affected in 1899, reaching a high mark in 1903 with 531,682 strikers and 656,055 workers.[10] To these figures must be added the strikes lasting less than a single day, which were not included in the Bureau of Labor's statistics and which, according to the U.S. Industrial Commission, were "very numerous."[11]

Another important indication of the magnitude of the post-1896 wave of industrial struggles is provided by the number of establishments affected by the strikes. There were 5,462 establishments involved in strikes in 1896; the figure more than doubled in 1899 and jumped to 20,248 in 1903. Equally substantial is the increase in the number of days the establishments affected by the strikes had to remain closed: from 94,351 in 1896 to 239,885 in 1903.[12]

These quantitative data are sufficient to help us delineate the intensity of the industrial conflict of those years and its disruptive effects on the economy. An even more accurate picture emerges, however, by looking at some of the results that ensued from those struggles. A leading feature of these strikes is the remarkable degree of success they enjoyed. In 1896 success or partial success was achieved in 3,913 of the 5,462 cases. By 1903 the number of establishments in which strikes had been successful or partly successful for that year had climbed to 12,660,[13] though the proportion to the number of failures had narrowed considerably with respect to the previous years (showing that 1903, besides being the year of most intense and widespread labor struggles, also saw the beginning of a massive employers' counterattack). Again the strikes lasting less than a single day must be taken into consideration; "a large majority of [them]," according to the U.S. Industrial Commission, "result[ed] in favor of the workmen."[14]

A closer look at the character of those strikes—the demands and objectives for which the workers were striking—shows that the overwhelming majority of them were of an offensive character: strikes fought for increases of wages, reduction of hours, recognition of unions and/or union rules, and in sympathy with other striking workers. For the period 1897 to 1903 strikes fought around this type of demand represented more than three-fourths of the total.[15] Their breakdown was as follows: for increase of wages, 33.92%, and for increase of wages combined with various causes, 11.02%; for reduction of hours, 4.42%, and for reduction of hours combined with various causes, 6.65%; for recognition of unions and union rules , 20.01%, and for recognition of unions and union rules combined with various causes, 5.61%; in sympathy with strikes and employees locked out (elsewhere), 1.65%.[16]

The militant character of strikes fought for such objectives as recognition of unions and union rules, as well as in sympathy with other striking workers, is obvious. That of strikes fought for an increase of wages and related causes—the largest single category—stems from the workers' awareness of the onset of a period of economic prosperity and their determination to share in the economic betterment set off by the new cycle of productive expansion. Similarly strikes fought for reduction of hours indicate the workers' unwillingness to let economic expansion and prosperity be pushed over their backs. In 1903 at the height of industrial conflict, the *New York Times* in an editorial lamented the "tendency to diminished productiveness" of the American worker, which, according to the influencial newspaper, was evidenced by the "two fundamental principles very prominently put forward in recent labor disputes—to increase wages and to restrict output."[17]

Undoubtedly a most important result of the wave of industrial conflict under consideration—for both its political and institutional implications—was the rapid advance in the unionization of workers. It is here that the degree of success of those waves of strikes becomes even more evident. From 1897 to 1903 unionization increased about 400 percent, rising from a total of 447,000 union members to almost two million.[18]

It was the most dramatic jump in union membership of the whole Progressive period, equaled only during the World War I years of economic mobilization.

If for some observers the "strike epidemic"—as *The Outlook* characterized it—was regarded as "a sign of prosperity,"[19] for industrialists and politicians, such as Senator Marcus Hanna, it was a clear indication that "this question of labor and capital [had] approached a crisis."[20] In both cases, the waves of strikes—their mounting recurrence, their widespread character, and the militancy they expressed—had made the labor problem the leading national issue for American industrialists and politicians, and it demanded urgent solutions. A National Civic Federation conference on conciliation concluded in 1901 that "the very foundations of prosperity" rest upon "the relations existing between the employer and employee classes. . . . Here it seems everything in the industrial world begins and ends."[21]

That some solution was needed was a belief shared by all businessmen. What the solution should be became a major source of contention and division in the business community. To a large extent, this was a reflection of deeper divisions existing between various sectors of that community that had been brought about by the rapid and unbalanced development of American industry during the last decades of the nineteenth century. This growth had resulted in divisions between the more advanced (technologically and organizationally) sectors and the less advanced ones; between financial and industrial sectors; and between controlled sectors and highly competitive ones.[22] Hence, the various solutions to the labor problem that emerged throughout the Progressive era were often as diverse as the conditions of the various industrial sectors and their operational imperatives allowed them to be. This point needs to be stressed to clarify an assumption that historians have often uncritically held: that small businessmen were opposed—on the ground of ideological belief—to trade unionism whereas the big ones were at least ideologically open toward the idea and willing to experiment with it. An analysis of the coal industry—where the labor problem reached dramatic proportions—will show that the situation was much more complex; and that industry is by no means the only example.

It is in this context that collective bargaining (or the trade agreement, as it was often called) emerged as a solution to the labor problem and quickly gained preeminence over other solutions, to such an extent that the seven years of economic expansion that followed the 1893-1897 depression can be regarded as a golden age of the trade agreement.[23] Those years, in fact, saw the establishment of trade agreement systems at both the national and district levels in a multitude of industries and trades: coal mining, iron molding, machine, shipping, printing, and pottery.[24] In some of these cases the adoption of the trade agreement resulted from a deliberate choice on the part of the employers involved. In others it was largely forced by the mounting pressure of workers' militancy; in still others it grew as a result of intense and widespread publicity campaigns carried on, for instance, by national organizations such as the National Civic Federation. And finally, in other cases, the adoption of the trade agreement and labor relations policies based on it became an indispensable move to rescue the industry from collapse. This was the case in bituminous coal mining.

NOTES

1. Cf. Robert Ozanne, *A Century of Labor-Management Relations at McCormick & International Harvester* (Madison, Wis., 1967); Hugh G. J. Aitken, *Taylorism at Watertown Arsenal* (Cambridge, Mass., 1960); Stephen Scheinberg, "The Development of Corporation Labor Policy, 1900-1940" (Ph.D. diss. , University of Wisconsin, 1967).

2. Robert Wiebe, *Businessmen and Reform* (Chicago, 1968).

3. James Weinstein, *The Corporate Ideal in the Liberal State, 1900-1918* (Boston, 1968).

4. Gabriel Kolko, *The Triumph of Conservatism* (Chicago, 1963), 9.

5. Ibid., 4.

6. Ibid., esp. 3, 301-05.

7. Ibid., 201

8. Ibid., 3.

9. In the study of strikes there is often a tendency to isolate and focus the attention on major strikes—major from the standpoint of, for instance, the size of the strike and the seriousness of the conflict generated or the immediate impact it had on certain trade union organizations or industry, and so on. While the study of such "major" strikes is important, and in fact it will be pursued in the course of this investigation, one must caution against its tendency of becoming episodic, and hence of minimizing the importance for labor history of waves or cycles of strikes that cut across industrial sectors and have a common matrix in the particular economic conjuncture in which they occur (depressions, upswings,

conversions, reconversions). A recent example of such an "episodic" treatment of strikes is provided by Jeremy Brecher's *Strike!* (San Francisco, 1972), where the author jumps from the Pullman strike (1894) to the 1919 general strike, thus leaving out the entire strike activity of the Progressive era, with all its crucial economic, social, and political implications. For a fuller discussion of the point raised here and of some of its methodological implications, see Mario Tronti, "Workers and Capital," *Telos* 14 (Winter 1972): 25-62; and, by the same author, *Operai e Capitale* (Turin, 1971).

10. U.S. Bureau of Labor, *Twenty-first Annual Report of the Commissioner of Labor, 1906: Strikes and Lockouts* (Washington, D.C., 1907), 15 (hereafter cited as *Strikes and Lockouts.*)

11. U.S. Industrial Commission, *Final Report* (Washington, D.C., 1900-1902), 19: 868 (hereafter cited as *USIC Report*).

12. *Strikes and Lockouts,* 15.

13. Ibid., 490.

14. *USIC Report,* 868.

15. *Strikes and Lockouts,* 56-57.

16. Ibid.

17. *New York Times,* August 12, 1903, 8.

18. Cf. Leo Wolman, *Ebb and Flow in Trade Unionism* (New York, 1936), 16.

19. *The Outlook,* May 21, 1900, 93.

20. Marcus Hanna, "Industrial Conciliation and Arbitration," *Annals of the American Academy of Political and Social Science* 20 (July 1902): 23.

21. *Industrial Conciliation: Report of the Conference Held Under the Auspices of the National Civic Federation, Dec. 16 and 17, 1901* (New York, 1902), 204.

22. These divisions are summarized in Alfred D. Chandler, Jr., "The Beginning of 'Big Business' in American Industry," *Business History Review* 33 (Spring 1959): 1-31; cf. also Robert T. Averitt, *The Dual Economy* (New York, 1968); and for a more detailed treatment, see Alfred D. Chandler, Jr., *Strategy and Structure* (Cambridge, Mass., 1962).

23. During the first part of this study the expressions *trade agreement* and *collective bargaining* will be used interchangeably.

24. Cf. George Barnett, "National and District Systems of Collective Bargaining in the United States," *Quarterly Journal of Economics* 26 (1912): 425-443.

PART 1

The golden age
of the trade agreement,
1898-1905

1

THE INTERSTATE MOVEMENT IN BITUMINOUS COAL MINING

Few labor events have had as great an impact on the growth of collective bargaining in America as the 1897 bituminous coal miners' strike and the settlement that ensued. It occurred in an industrial sector that was a basic source of power for most industries at a time when the first signs of economic recovery were appearing, and it involved a large number of workers spread over the mining towns and industrial centers of four states. Furthermore, it occurred in an industry where social conflict and violence were common and widespread, largely because of the peculiar conditions under which miners and coal operators had to operate.

Seldom, in fact, has industry been so tied to natural conditions as bituminous coal mining. The immediate effect of these conditions was that the industry became one of the most competitive in the United States. The relative ease with which coal deposits could be reached and turned into productive enterprises facilitated enormously the entrance of new capitalists into the industry. As a Pittsburgh coal operator put it, "Anybody can go into the coal business in the Pittsburgh district because you only have to dig a hole in the ground and you can make the approaches and bring up the coal."[1] In a period of great economic instability such as the Gilded Age, when empire building was accompanied by continuous business failures, the bituminous coal trade, with its easy access, attracted large numbers of small- and middle-sized capitalists. The availability of labor supplies also contributed to making entrance into the trade relatively easy.

The coal operator further explained that these factors had "brought a-
bout too many mines: . . . when there was not anything to do in other
lines of industry, men [both capitalists and laborers] have flocked in there
who should have been at something else."[2] As a consequence, bituminous
coal mining became an extremely cluttered industry, whose major effect
was overproduction. In fact, throughout the Gilded Age (and to a lesser
extent during the Progressive era) overproduction was the leading characteristic of the industry; in times of deep depression—as in the 1893-1897
years—overproduction was as high as 50 percent in certain districts.[3]

The effects that overproduction had on coal prices were disastrous,
making the bituminous coal market a theater of fierce trade struggles. This
was particularly true in the area known as "the competitive fields," which
included Illinois, Indiana, Ohio, and western Pennsylvania, and which—together with West Virginia—produced more than 70 percent of all bituminous coal mined in the country.[4]

Other natural factors added to the character of competitiveness of the
industry. One was the location of the mines and their distance from the so-
called market centers—Toledo, Cleveland, Chicago, and Detroit. This had a
direct effect on the transportation component of the price of coal produced in the various mining districts. Another important factor was the
quality of coal, that is, its physical traits—whether it was of a thick-seam
or a thin-seam type. The quality had a direct bearing on the cost of mining;
the former type was easier to mine than the latter type. It also affected
the method by which miners were paid. In some districts miners were
paid on a "screen-basis" calculated on the portion of mined coal that
passed over a screen; in other districts they were paid on a "run-of-mine
basis," which meant all the coal they mined, including fine coal and im-
purities. This geological factor was important also in determining whether
it was feasible and profitable to introduce machinery, thus replacing pick
mining with machine mining. Where the coal vein was thick enough—as in
some districts of south and central Illinois, Ohio, and western Pennsylvania —machines had become increasingly widespread, beginning in the late
1880s.[5] According to some estimates machine mining yielded a profit
that was 8 to 18 percent higher than pick mining, thus giving some coal
operators a decisive market advantage over those who could not use machines.[6]

There was another cost component that gave the coal operators a certain space to maneuver in: the labor cost, or the wages paid to the miners.

Labor constituted the highest part of the overall cost of mining, taking up from 66 to 80 percent of the total.[7] Therefore, because of the centrality that these costs occupied, because of the largely unorganized state of miners, and because of the oversupply of that type of labor, miners' wages became the key element that the coal operators manipulated to determine their prices and gain advantageous positions on the market. Thus, mining wages became the crucial ground around which all the fierce market battles that gave the bituminous industry its character of anarchy and chaos revolved. Whatever advantageous position some operators had reached was merely temporary. Soon other operators would cut wages, thus forcing their competitors to follow a similar action. After a cycle of this type of warfare, the competitive positions of the various coal operators would be the same as at the start, except that wage scales and coal prices had plunged to a new low. This was the dynamics that characterized the bituminous coal industry. The disastrous results of these policies were evident not only to the miners, who experienced the consequences in their squalid and miserable conditions of life, but also to the coal operators. This appears evident from the statement released in 1885 by a group of coal operators and some miners' representatives from the competitive fields in an attempt to establish some joint machinery at the interstate level that would bring stability to the trade: "The constant reductions of wages that have lately taken place have afforded no relief to capital, and, indeed, have but tended to increase its embarrassments. Any reduction in labor in any coal field usually necessitates and generates a corresponding reduction in every other competitive field. If the price of labor in the U.S. was uniformly raised to the standard of three years ago the employers of labor would occupy toward each other the same relative position in point of competition as at present."[8] To these men, some solution had to be sought if the whole industry was to be rescued from total disruption. As they pointed out in their statement, "The intelligence and progress of the age demand this. Our material interests demand it. The internal peace of our country demands it. Respect for the dignity of American labor demands it. *The security of capital demands it.*"[9]

This joint effort—occurring at a time of industrial progress and extraordinary prosperity—led to the establishment of interstate conciliation machinery in the competitive fields whereby wage rates in the different mining districts were made uniform by taking into account the various differentials that affected the cost of mining. In addition to providing for

a wage scale, the agreement also established the Joint Board of Arbitration and Conciliation to adjust disputes.

This yearly experience of interstate agreements went on for a few years,
through ups and downs, until in 1889 it collapsed when the Illinois and
Indiana operators decided to withdraw.[10] The main reason for this failure can be traced to the lack of an adequate miners' organization through
which to compel the coal operators of the various districts; in fact, if it is
true that the wage differentials established in the agreement took into account factors such as the quality of the coal, the method of mining, and
the distance from key market points, it is also true that the agreement did
not take into consideration any of those exploitative methods of working
conditions that individual operators would enforce in their mines to gain
some competitive advantage over other operators.[11] The operators could
maneuver, in other words, by lowering the cost of mining—for instance,
by using false methods of weighing, by using screens with larger holes, and
by the notorious company stores.

The historical importance of this early experiment with interstate conciliation machinery lies in the widespread recognition on the part of the
coal operators of the crucial importance that wages took on as the element
upon which uniformity of competition and the stability and progress of
the industry depended, especially in times of economic upswings. The experiment also demonstrated that in the absence of an employers' organization of an interstate character, having the powers to ensure the compliance
of individual employers to the rules of the trade, it was unrealistic to expect that coal operators would abide by the agreement and maintain the
competitive positions assigned to them. It was becoming increasingly clear
that if the interstate movement were to succeed and if the competitive
equalization of all mining districts were to be achieved, the answer lay
with the miners and their ability to build up sufficient organizational
power to compel any district or any operator to abide by the conditions
agreed upon.

The formation of the United Mine Workers of America in 1890 was a
first major step toward that goal. Its membership was extremely low considering the total number of miners engaged in the industry and actually
experienced a steady decline during the first seven years of its life (from
about 20,000 members in 1890 to fewer than 10,000 in 1897). However,
the union had in effect created a central organization to coordinate the
efforts of the miners in the various districts and lay down organizational

rules and strategies. Most importantly, it had created a national body that could keep in close touch with the dynamics and state of the industry (trends in production, in the mining labor market, in mine legislation, working conditions in the various districts and in the overall state of the economy).[12]

The fruits of this new national organizational base became evident in 1894 at the height of the depression and in a period of fierce cutthroat competition that had sent coal prices and wages to an all-time low. The national convention of the UMW called a series of national suspensions of work to relieve the market and thus bring up coal prices, which would ultimately result in wage increases. The suspension did not succeed in its objectives mainly because of the importation into the competitive fields of anthracite and bituminous coal from West Virginia nonunionized districts that forced the miners to accept a compromise providing for a scale of prices to be effective from June 1894 to May 1895. Nevertheless, the historical significance of this suspension lay in the widespread response that the call found among the miners. On the specified day nearly 125,000 miners suspended work. From a series of two-week suspensions, as the convention had planned, the action erupted into a general strike that lasted eight weeks. By the end of the eight-week period, 180,000 miners had joined the strike.[13] The general strike of 1894 had therefore succeeded in mobilizing the overwhelming majority of the miners. It had served as a test to measure their determination and ability to act in compact and to take prolonged action on a national scale. The accusations directed by various delegates against President John McBride at the sixth annual convention for having called the strike off prematurely provide a further indication of the sentiment existing among the miners to fight more strenuously.

This show of strength and willingness to unite in action would be tested again three years later. With a membership of merely 9,731 and foreseeing a revival of the economy, the national convention of the UMW would call another general strike, which would prove decisive for the future of their union as well as of the bituminous industry.

By 1897 conditions in the bituminous fields and in the trade as a whole had reached their lowest level ever. Coal prices had gradually declined since 1891, a fall ranging from 11 percent in Illinois, to 28 percent in West Virginia, and to a dramatic 53 percent in Georgia.[14] There were innumerable cases of operators who ran their mines at a loss rather than close them down (an alternative that would have led them, they believed, to an even greater loss).

The number of miners in excess of the required production had consequently increased remarkably. In its investigation of mining conditions in the Pittsburgh district, the Pennsylvania legislative committee found in 1897 that "there are at least two miners engaged in the mining districts for every one man's work."[15] The *Black Diamond*, the official organ of the coal operators, outlined the conditions of the industry and the perspectives it saw for the miners: "Evidence is accumulating each week that there must be either a decrease in the number of mines operated in the West, or miners must accept lower wages. The operators who have their capital invested in productive property are not likely to go out of business, and allow their mines to remain idle. On the other hand, miners have the choice of adopting some other calling to make a living or accepting less pay for their work."[16]

"Adopting some other calling"—as the paper suggested—was not an easy solution in communities where mining was the only work available. The level of poverty many miners had reached, coupled to the fact that many miners were tied to their companies by accumulated debts, made even the prospect of moving a difficult one.[17] Nor would forcing the miners to "accept less pay for their work" be a viable solution. The accounts of miners' families bordering on starvation were innumerable and were getting widespread publicity by the national media. The *Black Diamond* itself acknowledged that the price of coal was "not sufficient to pay a living price for the labor employed in its production," adding that under those conditions it was natural that "out of sheer misery . . . revolt in the shape of a strike comes."[18]

Direct confrontation in the form of a general suspension of work seemed to be the only alternative—an alternative that even the coal operators themselves came gradually to accept. The day before the strike began, in fact, the *Black Diamond* expressed very clearly this change of attitude among many coal operators: "Many operators would cheerfully welcome a general strike, as it would clean up stocks, and might have the effect of establishing a sensible and practical differential in the four principal mining states of the Middle West, thus enabling all miners to make fair living wages."[19]

No doubt, the general attitude explains why—considering the large number of workers and of employers involved—the bituminous coal miners, strike of 1897 was one of the most peaceful and orderly ones of the entire period. It reflected not only the miners' determination to use their own collective power to share in the economic betterment that was setting in but also their determination to take a prime role in the regulation of their industry. The peaceful conduct of the strike also reflected the coal operators' acknowledgment that this new age of prosperity demanded a stabilization of the chaotic conditions that had prevailed in their industry and that this could be achieved only by recognizing the positive role the union would play.[20]

In January 1898 a historic interstate joint conference was held in Chicago among representatives of the miners' union and of coal operators from the competitive fields. It established scale rates based on differentials for the various mining districts that took into account all factors affecting the cost of mining and weighing. Moreover, it established the eight-hour working day and provided for a basic wage increase of ten cents per ton.[21]

The convention decided that henceforth this remarkable "industrial parliament" consisting of several hundred delegates between miners and operators would meet every year in late January and early February to work out a new agreement that would go into effect the following April 1. After the convened delegates elected a temporary chairman to welcome the delegates and open the conference, the proceedings would begin with the selection of permanent officers—a chairman, a secretary, and an assistant secretary—and the setting up of working committees: a committee on credentials, a committee on rules and order of business, both made up of two operators and two miners from each of the four states; and a scale committee made up of four miners and four operators from each state, which would play the central role in the negotiations. The rules of the Interstate Conference provided that each state would be entitled to an equal number of votes—four for the operators and four for the miners—and that any decision that was declared carried had to receive the unanimous vote of both the operators and the miners from all the states.[22] The annual conference was only the first stage in the workings of the Interstate Joint Agreement. Following the conference the operators and miners of each state would meet and try to arrive at a scale of wages for each field within the state on the basis of the differentials agreed upon at the annual joint conference.

The acknowledgment of the crucial role the UMW would play in maintaining stable conditions in the industry was clearly expressed in article

VIII of the agreement: ". . . the United Mine Workers' organization, a party to the contract, do hereby further agree to *afford all possible protection to the trade* and to the other parties hereto against any unfair competition resulting from a failure to maintain scale rates."[23] Clearly such a commitment did not merely entail the organizational power that the miners' union could use against violators of the agreement—operators and miners alike; it also entailed the power it would exert in equalizing that element of production—wages—upon which the delicate mechanism of the bituminous market depended. Thus, despite the apparent complexity that characterized the work of the annual joint conferences, the focal point of the machinery was the scale committee, in which the real work of the conference was ultimately transacted.[24] This committee was made up of four miners and four operators chosen by the scale committee from elected during the early sessions of the conference. After receiving the guidelines from the two parties, the committee would meet in an attempt to arrive at a wage scale, which it would submit to the entire conference for approval. Failure to reach an agreement on the proposed wage scale would result in the setting up of a subscale committee, which was made up of four miners and four operators chosen by the scale committee from among its members. Ultimately it was upon these eight persons that the success of the joint conference would depend. The sessions of this committee—which were secret—would often go on for days and even weeks because of the complexity of their work.[25] It was not just a matter of determining what a fair or living wage for the miners had to be; rather, all the conditions and factors of the coal trade had to be taken into account so that the wage scale arrived at was believed to be in the best interest of the industry. The principle upon which the determination of the wage scale rested was clearly expressed by John Mitchell to the U.S. Industrial Commission:

[It is] a fundamental principle of our interstate movement that the scale of prices is based not upon the earning capacity of the miners alone, but *principally upon the opportunity of each district to produce coal at a price which shall enable it to be sold in fair competition with every other district*; that is to say, no attempt was made to make wages uniform or earning capacity of the men equal between the different districts, or within the districts themselves, the principal object being to so regulate the scale of mining as to make the cost of production practically the same in one district as in another, regardless of whether or not the earnings of the miners are equal.[26]

This is why the response of the coal operators to the joint interstate agreement was enthusiastic—especially after its first year of successful operation. Many of them were quite frank in recognizing that the reason for its success rested largely on the union and on its beneficial effect on the industry. As Walter J. Mullins, a coal operator from Ohio, pointed out in his testimony to the U.S. Industrial Commission in 1899, "With an organization that is managed by conservative and able men, as has been the case with the miners' organization for some years past, *we have been able to form a fair basis of prices*. It has made our industry more stable, and has given a certain security to our operations that we could not have had if we were troubled by local disturbances, as was the case before the union was formed and made as solid as it is now."[27] The establishment of the annual joint agreement would now make it possible for "the mine owner and the operator to figure intelligently on his yearly contracts with some guarantee that prices will be maintained throughout the season of his contract."[28]

Herman Justi, commissioner of the Illinois Coal Operators' Association and a man who was thoroughly familiar with all aspects of the bituminous industry, emphasized the crucial importance that the adoption of wage scales had in regulating the competitive conditions in the market. As he put it, "the fact that all the coal operators in those four states paid substantially the same scale of wages and were operating under the same conditions of mining made it possible for every operator to know approximately what the product of every mine cost every other operator."[29] Moreover, the recognition of the miners' union had made the adoption of wage scales possible and had therefore played a crucial role in "bringing stability to the trade."[30] Indeed some operators regretted that the union was not strong enough to extend its powers over all mining districts of the country. a western Pennsylvanian operator said that "the one fault I have to find with the labor organization is that they are not able to regulate matters so that the entire thing will be uniform."[31] And the *Black Diamond* assured the UMW that the coal operators would "pledge their hearty support" to the union's expressed intention to launch organizing drives in the weakly organized states.[32]

The industrial relations structure in bituminous coal mining that emerged from the Interstate Joint Conference of 1898 rested on the recognition of the vital role the union played in bringing about stability to the trade. Far from antagonizing the union, the coal operators saw that it was in their interest to promote its growth and strengthen its hold over the miners.

In a more concrete way, the operators' attitude was demonstrated by their prompt concession of the checkoff, entitling them to withhold the union membership fee from the miners' pay, thus ensuring the union the revenues that were necessary to build and strengthen its organizational apparatus. Even more important, the checkoff system was a de facto recognition of the closed shop—a concession that has never been easily granted by employers, especially in that period of labor history. Moreover, the prompt agreement by the coal operators to the eight-hour day—as the newly elected president of the UMW, John Mitchell, explained—had the effect of employing more miners and therefore increasing the number of paid-up members in the union.[33]

Through the interstate joint agreement, moreover, a remarkable degree of rationalization and order had been brought to what had been one of the most chaotic and battle-stricken industries of the country. This resulted not only from the adjustment of miners' wages to the fluctuating conditions of the bituminous coal market but also from the power that the union would exert in rationalizing the mining labor market. A student of that industry commented, "the joint conference of the central field has become the central market for mine labor."[34]

An even more important source of order and stability for the industry resulted from the role that the union leadership would play in ensuring that any outbreak of conflict would be readily checked, both through the machinery for the adjustment of disputes and through the educational influence exerted upon the miners. Herman Justi, the Illinois coal commissioner, calculated that out of two hundred complaints brought to the Interstate Disputes Commission during the first year of the agreement's life, about 80 percent had been decided against the miners. The reason, Justi maintained, was "that the miners were not so thoroughly familiar with the agreement, and they had so many local organizations that local demands would be made, such as they had made prior to the interstate movement; the presumption on their part was that what they had done before they could continue to do even after this movement had been inaugurated."[35] Justi also explained how "the interstate joint movement has had a tendency to impress on the men the sacredness of the contract, thus making the task of the miners' officials less difficult in the carrying out of the agreements into which they entered on behalf of the men."[36]

The peaceful conduct of the strike and the high degree of cooperation exhibited by the coal operators in working out the interstate settlement should not minimize the actual organizational strength that the miners amassed through their collective action. Behind the facade of peaceful work suspensions and cooperative negotiations, there was a show of strength that many coal operators could not help but acknowledge. An Illinois operator commented some years later, "[We] were whipped to a standstill. Impoverished by our insane price-cutting and the long period of hard times, threatened with a total loss of all our markets on the very eve of returning good times, we simply had to take our medicine. . . . We were compelled . . . to submit to any terms the miners' union saw fit to impose."[37]

The strike saw in fact an exemplary mobilization of the workers' movement, with national trade unions not only contributing financially but also sending organizers into the mining districts to help organize the strikers.[38] The importance of the miners' struggle was also readily acknowledged by radicals. Eugene Debs devoted his time and energies to touring mining towns in Indiana and addressing large gatherings of strikers.[39] Miners who later joined the revolutionary Industrial Workers of the World pointed to the 1897 miners' strike as a glorious chapter in workers' history. W. W. Cox, a miner and an IWW organizer, was one of these; for him 1897 was "a year that almost every coal miner points to with pride . . . because never before were the coal miners so united, so completely fixed in their minds as to a given purpose."[40]

The miners' show of their collective power, the union's commitment to ensure stability to the industry, the operators' acknowledgment of the beneficial role of the union to their trade, and the immediate results that the enforcement of the interstate agreement had on the bituminous industry made the 1898 interstate agreement, in the words of J. E. George, "an excellent example of collective bargaining."[41] A Harvard University labor economist who had followed closely the events in the bituminous industry, George saw in the interstate joint conference of 1898 "the most remarkable gathering of employers and their workmen ever in this country."[42] And John Commons, a young economist who was amassing material to construct his theory of collective bargaining, after attending for a week the sessions of the national joint conference, considered it an unprece-

dented example of "constitutional government in industry."[43] Clearly
the experience of the interstate joint agreement had done a lot to convince many people that the trade agreement pointed the way toward a
peaceful solution to the labor problem.

NOTES

1. U.S. Industrial Commission, *Final Report* (Washington, D.C., 1900-
1902), 12:87 (hereafter referred to as *USIC Report*. Cf. also John Brophy,
A Miner's Life (Madison, 1964), 38.

2. *USIC Report,* 12:87.

3. Ibid., 78.

4. *Eighteenth Annual Report of the US Geological Survey:Part V, Coal*
(Washington, D.C., 1896), 19, 31.

5. In 1891 6.6 percent of the entire bituminous production was machine mined. By 1896 the ratio had gone up to 14.17 percent, and by 1902
it was 26.09 percent; cf. Andrew Roy, *A History of the Coal Miners of the
United States* (Columbus, 1907), 152, and Isador Lubin, *Miners' Wages
and the Cost of Coal* (New York, 1924), 23.

6. *USIC Report,* 12:87; cf. also Lubin, *Miners' Wages,* 102ff.

7. Arthur E. Suffern, *The Coal Miners' Struggle for Industrial Status*
(New York, 1926), 13-14.

8. Chris Evans, *A History of the United Mine Workers of America,
1860-1900* (Indianapolis, 1900), 1:149.

9. Ibid. (emphasis added).

10. Arthur E. Suffern, *Conciliation and Arbitration in the Coal Industry of America* (New York, 1915), 32-33.

11. Suffern, *Miners' Struggle,* 41.

12. Roy, *History of the Coal Miners,* 262-87, 350; Suffern, *Conciliation
and Arbitration,* 33-37.

13. "The Movement Among Coal-Mine Workers," Bureau of Labor Sta-
tistics, *Bulletin 51* (1904): 390; Evans, *History of the UMWA,* 2:350-57;
Roy, *History of the Coal Miners,* 325-35; *United Mine Workers' Journal*
(May 10, 1894): 1-2.

14. John E. George, "The Coal Miners' Strike of 1897," *The Quarterly Journal of Economics* 12 (January 1898): 192.

15. Quoted in ibid., 194.

16. *Black Diamond* (March 27, 1897).

17. Brophy, in his autobiographical *A Miners' Life,* 26ff., 51, has described vividly this kind of hardship, as well as the difficulty miners had
finding jobs in other industries.

18. *Black Diamond* (August 28, 1897): 1; cf. also Roy, *History of Coal Miners,* 350; George, "Coal Miners' Strike," 190.

19. *Black Diamond* (July 3, 1897): 1.

20. *The Outlook* 56 (July 31, 1897): 780, hailed the strike and the willingness shown to arrive at uniform wage scales "a new phase of the labor question"; not just "the solidarity of labor and the solidarity of Capital, but . . . a new phenomenon . . . their alliance."

21. Cf. John E. George, "The Settlement in the Coal-Mining Industry," *Quarterly Journal of Economics* 12 (July 1898): 447-60; Suffern, *Conciliation and Arbitration,* 153-55.

22. Suffern, *Conciliation and Arbitration,* 191-94.

23. "Movement Among Coal-Mine Workers," 393 (emphasis added).

24. Ibid., 399.

25. *USIC Report,* 12:698.

26. Ibid.; for an analysis of how the interstate agreement worked at the state level, cf. Ethelbert Stewart, "Equalizing Competitive Conditions," in John Commons, ed., *Trade Unionism and Labor Problems* (New York, reprinted 1967), 525-33; Suffern, *Conciliation and Arbitration*, 179-220.

27. *USIC Report,* 12:166.

28. Ibid., 173.

29. Ibid., 677-78.

30. Ibid., 682.

31. Ibid., 75.

32. *Black Diamond* (January 29, 1898): 1.

33. *USIC Report,* 12:47.

34. Suffern, *Conciliation and Arbitration,* 142.

35. *USIC Report,* 12:680.

36. Ibid., 678.

37. U.S. Commissioner of Labor, *Eleventh Special Report* (Washington, D.C., 1904), 392.

38. George, "Coal Miners Strike of 1897," *op. cit.,* 203; *UMWJ,* (July 29, 1897).

39. Ray Ginger, *Eugene Victor Debs, A Biography* (New York, 1966), pp. 212-213.

40. *Industrial Union Leaflet No. 12,* "An Address to Coal Miners" (n.d.), p. 1.

41. John E. George, "Settlement in the Coal-Mining Industry", *op. cit.,* p. 458.

42. Ibid., p. 460.

43. John Commons, *Myself* (Madison, 1964), p. 72. Also John Commons et. al, *History of Labor in the United States* (New York, 1918), vol. III, p. XV.

2

THE STRUGGLE FOR THE TRADE AGREEMENT IN THE ANTHRACITE COAL INDUSTRY

While the establishment of the Interstate Joint Conference was yielding its fruits in terms of stability of labor relations and trade conditions, a major labor crisis was brewing in the anthracite mining industry; by 1902 it burst into one of the most dramatic confrontations between labor and capital. Significantly the explosion of the labor problem in the anthracite industry during the years 1900 to 1902 did not come about because of the lack of a trade agreement framework but rather because of the attempts made to introduce the agreement as a basis of uniform labor relations.

After the success achieved in the bituminous industry, nothing seemed more natural than to extend the trade agreement to anthracite mining, where more than 140,000 workers were employed. On the surface all factors seemed to favor such a process: the geographical proximity and the affinity of operations between the two fuel industries, the overwhelmingly favorable response the UMW had met in the public eye, the bituminous coal operators' satisfaction with the operation of the Interstate Joint Conference. Yet, at a closer look, some crucial differences loomed, making the anthracite industry a theater of fierce confrontation and threatening to undermine many of the premises on which the protrade agreement forces had built. An analysis of these differences, as they gradually moved to the forefront, will underscore the extent to which the extension of the trade agreement, far from being merely a matter of prolabor campaigning, involved coming to terms with the concrete economic and political conditions characterizing a given industry. The anthracite coal strike of 1902, more than any other labor event, dramatized this reality, considering the time and circumstances in which it happened and the social and political forces it called into play.

The geographical configuration of the anthracite industry contrasted sharply with that of the bituminous industry. Bituminous coal deposits were spread over a large number of states, extending from the Midwest to the southern sections of the country; anthracite mining was extremely concentrated territorially. Its coal deposits were all located in the northeastern region of Pennsylvania, where five counties produced 96 percent of the country's total output in an area not larger than 484 square miles.[1] The effect that this factor had on the development of the industry—its pattern of ownership, control, and its labor relations policies—was crucial. By placing the industry under the jurisdiction of a single state, it made relations between government and the industry uniform, thus expediting the solution of problems emerging in that sphere of business activity. But it also acted as an enormous stimulus in favoring the entrance of railroad companies into the anthracite mining business. This was particularly true during the railroad construction boom of the post-Civil War years—a period also marked by such a rapid increase in the demand for anthracite coal that it opened new prospects in the coal-carrying business. This process was also facilitated by a series of legislative enactments by Pennsylvania that made it possible for the railroad companies not only to acquire vast areas of coal lands but also to carry out mining operations. Railroad companies made extensive use of these lands policies. The Philadelphia and Reading Railroad (a company that played a leading role in the anthracite industry), for instance, acquired between 1870 and 1875 no less than 100,000 acres of land—virtually all the available coal lands in the Schuylkill district—and then obtained a charter allowing it to go into mining operations through a subsidiary company, the Philadelphia and Reading Coal and Iron Company.[2]

This integration of anthracite mining operations with the railroad industry became increasingly a dominant feature of the anthracite industry. It was not the only characteristic. A parallel development was the attempts by the major railroad corporations and coal mine owners to control the anthracite trade by the two classic practices of eliminating competition and fixing prices. The precarious state of the anthracite market, especially during the depression periods of the 1870s and 1880s, was a major stimulus for this tendency.[3] Of no less importance, however, was the rise of labor unions in the anthracite fields as a force to be reckoned with. The Workingman's Benevolent Association was the most noted of these anthracite miners' unions—an organization that soon exhibited a high degree of discipline and cohesion among its more than 35,000 members and a promptness of action. In its six years of life—before it was crushed by the Philadelphia and Reading Coal and Iron Company in 1875—the WBA was able to exert a remarkable degree of control on mining operations and on the trade by obtaining a sliding scale contract and enforcing annual suspensions of work to prevent market prices of coal from falling too low.[4]

Starting in the early 1870s and up through the 1890s, industry-wide combinations among the leading coal carriers and mining companies were periodically organized as attempts to control the trade. Though not always successful in their purposes, these combinations had the effect of strengthening the community of interest among the dominant railroad coal companies and of gradually eliminating the independent coal operators who had little means to oppose the freight rates policies enforced by the coal carriers. The integrated character of coal mining and the coal-carrying operations made this process possible. As subsidiaries of the railroad companies, the coal companies were in a position to sustain low profit margins, or even losses—the latter being amply compensated for by the exorbitant profits the railroad would make on hauling the coal to tidewater points.[5] This state of affairs was succinctly explained by J. Brook, an independent operator, to the Industrial Commission: "the advantage on the part of the owners of a railroad is that we [the independent operators] simply get a profit at the mine, if there is any, while if the railroads do not make anything there they do on carting it, for the price for carrying anthracite coal is about 10 mills per mile, while the average rate for bituminous coal is in the neighborhood of 2½ mills. That is one of the leading troubles in the anthracite region." According to Brook, this was the underlying reason forcing most of the independent operators out of the anthracite business. Through the control the railroad companies exerted over coal prices and freight rates, Brook predicted, they would ultimately "close up every independent operator in this way."[6]

The years following the great depression of 1893 to 1897 saw a new and major attempt at further consolidating the control of the industry.

Spearheaded by the Morgan interests, it involved the reorganization of the insolvent Philadelphia and Reading Railroad Company through the medium of a holding company, the Reading Company, which owned and controlled both the coal-carrying and the coal-mining operations of the new enterprise. Then the Reading went on and acquired the controlling interests of the Central Railroad of New Jersey, another leading coal carrier and owner of coal land. As a result of this combination, nearly one-third of the total shipment of coal and about 63 percent of all unmined coal in Pennsylvania came under the control of the Reading Company.[7]

Similar steps were taken by another major railroad corporation, the Erie Railroad, which starting in 1898 sought and gained the control of several coal carriers and mining operations.[8] In addition, the five largest railroad companies acquired jointly the controlling interests of the Lehigh Valley Railroad and created a system of interlocking directorates to ensure more efficient concerted actions.[9] On the eve of the great anthracite strike of 1902, virtually the entire anthracite industry had come under the control of a handful of railroad corporations.[10] They were thus in a position to set the price of coal from month to month, determine the volume of production, and allot tonnage quotas among themselves. Moreover, any potential threat that might have come from the independent operators was dispelled by binding the latter to the combination through the so-called 65 percent contracts: over a seven-year period, the independent operators would turn their entire coal output to the railroad companies and get 65 percent of the selling price of coal at tidewater points.[11]

As this massive process of consolidation was underway, a wave of labor militancy was sweeping the entire anthracite regions, spurred by the astounding successes of the UMW in the bituminous fields. Soon after the victory of 1898, the UMW, under the leadership of its new president John Mitchell, saw the organization of the anthracite fields as one of its most immediate goals.[12] Though aware of the difficulties involved, UMW officials were quite confident that the unionization of the anthracite mine workers would follow suit. This optimism, however, would soon clash with a harsh reality. Unlike the bituminous coal fields—where even before the establishment of the Interstate Joint Conference miners had been able to maintain a minimum of organization and exert a certain influence on the trade—no trace of organization had been left among the anthracite mine workers ever since the "Long Strike" of 1875, when the Working-

man's Benevolent Association was crushed by the railroad combination.
Since then the consolidation of ownership and control of the industry had
been paralleled by the extension of absolute power over the mine workers.
Concerted action in controlling the anthracite trade had also meant concerted action on the part of the coal interests in developing common policies and practices with which to deal with their labor force.

One such area of employers' cooperation had been the enforcement of
what today would be called a "manpower policy." It consisted in making
massive use of the increasingly available supplies of immigrant labor power,
mainly from southern and eastern European countries, to effect a gradual
shift in the composition of the mining labor force. The objective of this
policy was twofold: to procure ample supplies of cheap labor, since anthracite mining operations required unskilled laborers working alongside
skilled miners, and to effect a diversification of the labor force along ethnic lines to weaken the strength of the miners of English-speaking stock
who had formed the backbone of the unions and had displayed a high
level of militance and organizational skill.[13] To a large extent, this policy
achieved its goals. From a total of 1,925 eastern and southern European
immigrant workers brought into the anthracite region by the end of the
1870s, this figure climbed during the following two decades to a total of
89,000—well above one-third of the total labor force of the anthracite
industry.[14] This massive process of creating an assortment of workers of
different nationalities yielded its fruits: miners' struggles, although re-
curring regularly, generally remained circumscribed and seldom over-
flowed into the anthracite region as a whole. Moreover, and most importantly, these struggles did not find any organizational outlet because of
the harsh control that the coal companies were able to enforce in the
mines as well as in the social lives of the mine workers, but also because
of the antagonism that grew between the new immigrants and the English-
speaking miners.

It would be an oversimplification, however, to explain this antagonism
merely in terms of ethnic behavioral differences, as most contemporary
accounts and analyses have done.[15] More often than not, this antagonism
was rooted in the peculiar character of the work process of anthracite
mining and in the occupational structure prevailing in the industry. For
instance, the division between skilled and unskilled followed ethnic lines
very much, with English-speaking workers occupied as skilled miners,
generally working on a contract basis, and the new immigrants working

as common laborers alongside the miners.[16] This practice made the common laborer as dependent on the miner with whom he worked as he was on the coal company that had hired him. Many of the grievances grew out of this type of work relationship and were therefore directed against the skilled miners. In the northern coal region of the Wyoming and Lackawanna valleys, for instance, where contract miners paid directly to the common laborers the equivalent of one-third of the coal mined, a widespread grievance was that laborers (the great majority of them "Slavs") were getting too little money considering the heavy work they had to perform vis-à-vis the skilled miners. They also complained that the English-speaking miners deliberately kept them in a position of laborers, despite their right to move to the position of miners after serving their two years of apprenticeship—as the state mining laws provided. That these grievances against the skilled miners were widespread is evidenced by the fact that by 1902, laborers in the northern region were seriously considering forming a separate organization to fight these issues.[17]

The antagonism and the divisions existing among the anthracite mine workers were not the only source of organizational weakness. Another order of difficulties peculiar to the anthracite industry stood in the way of forging a base of unity among mine workers. The greater diversity of geological conditions characterizing anthracite coal deposits (as compared to bituminous), coupled with the virtually absolute control that the coal companies had exerted over the mine workers, had resulted over the years in a remarkable variety of working conditions and managerial practices and policies. This was most noticeable in the area of wage policies. As a contemporary student of anthracite mining observed, "In different regions [anthracite miners] are paid on a different scale; and in the same colliery will be found miners working on contract at so much per car, others by the week; rockmen working by the yard, the price varying according to the kind of passage driven and whether it is timbered or not; inside laborers getting one price, outside laborers another, while breaker boys receive still another rate."[18] Such a variety of wage policies and methods of payment was a major source of weakness for the mine workers for it made even more acute the divisions existing among them, seriously undermining the possibility of their uniting in action over wage demands. At the same time these policies yielded substantial economic benefits for the coal companies; by 1900 the level of wages in anthracite mining was considerably below that of bituminous mining.[19]

So firm had been the control of the coal companies over the labor relations of the industry that the mine workers' agitation in the summer of
1900 for an industry-wide strike came to them as a major surprise. The
organizing drives that the UMW had launched in the preceding year in
the anthracite regions had not been greatly successful in terms of new
membership figures. But they had had a major impact in spreading the significance of the bituminous miners' struggle among anthracite mine workers, as well as generalizing across the entire anthracite region the workers'
grievances and demands. This became clear at the convention of the delegates of the three anthracite districts held in Hazleton, Pennsylvania, in
August, where a list of grievances was drawn up, dealing in detail with all
the injustices that the anthracite mine workers felt were embodied in the
coal companies' labor policies.[20] This convention clearly signaled the beginning of mobilization of the anthracite mine workers. During the following month, all attempts to prevent a strike on the part of the UMW national officials were of no avail, so strong was the determination of the anthracite mine workers to have a head-on confrontation with the coal companies.

When the strike call was officially issued on September 17, the response
of the mine workers was beyond all expectations. Out of a total of 142,500
mine workers in the anthracite region, between 80,000 and 100,000 responded to the strike call on the first day. Two weeks later, nearly all the
anthracite mine workers had joined.[21] An age of organizational paralysis
had come to an end.

Fears that the strike would spread into the bituminous regions, and thus
culminate in a general miners' strike, brought about the most enormous
political pressures. Senator Marcus Hanna, who immediately stepped into
the situation, exerting pressures on both the UMW officials and the coal
and railroad combinations, clearly realized the threat that a potential
general agitation of all mine workers would have been for a Republican
success in the presidential elections due to take place that fall.[22] His pressures yielded their results. In what became essentially a political settlement,
the coal companies agreed to grant a 10 percent advance effective until
April 1, 1901. By October 29 work in the anthracite fields had resumed.[23]

The historical importance of the strike lies in the fact that the anthracite mine workers had proved capable of overcoming their isolation and
the divisions existing among themselves, clearly expressing a determination
to organize around their grievances and strengthen their position against
the coal companies. It is from this standpoint that the strike of 1900 was
a major victory for the anthracite mine workers, and not so much on ac-

count of demands actually won. In fact, all of their grievances concerning working conditions and methods of payment around which they had agitated were not even considered by the coal companies. The 10 percent advance, more than a compromise, was the valve that defused a very explosive situation. It was the easiest solution for both the coal companies and the UMW officials: it enabled the coal companies to stave off the most massive tide of militance that had ever occurred in the region by leaving untouched all the aspects and conditions of mine work, thus firmly retaining control of labor relations and it allowed the UMW officials—who all along had assumed a cautious posture—to bring the strike to a relatively early settlement, thus preventing a protracted confrontation, which they felt could have seriously undermined the growth of the union and turned public opinion against it.

Above all the strike had shown how determined the coal and railroad combination was to keep the UMW out of its affairs—a posture that would soon prove to be an insurmountable obstacle for the extension of collective bargaining to the anthracite mining industry. In an industry whose main characteristics were the remarkable diversity of mining conditions and the extreme lack of cohesion among its work force, the union appeared as the only homogenizing element; it was the organization that could turn all the various and diverse grievances of mine workers into a unified program of action. And even more significantly, by becoming the spokesman for all those grievances, the union would pose a direct challenge to the entire mechanism of social control that the coal companies wielded in the anthracite coal communities.

The railroad directors' fears that the establishment of the UMW union in the anthracite fields would inevitably erode their powers were more than founded, especially when they looked at the experience of the UMW in the bituminous industry. There the mine workers' organization had ensured the stability of the trade, but not without its taking on the function of comanaging the wage structure of the industry upon which the delicate mechanism of "competitive equality" depended. Clearly the railroad directors were determined not to see this happening in their industry where miners' wages did not play at all the same regulatory function; coal prices were directly fixed by the owners and hence disengaged from the wage structure obtaining in the anthracite fields.

As the April 1, 1902, deadline approached and John Mitchell, aided by third parties such as Senator Hanna and National Civic Federation officials, embarked on a series of diplomatic maneuvers aimed at laying the groundwork for a more permanent and comprehensive agreement, the intransigence of the coal and railroad combination toward the UMW became increasingly evident. The reasons adduced by the railroad presidents against any interference by the UMW in anthracite mining were many, ranging from technical to purely emotional and ideological ones. The reason most commonly presented was that the UMW was primarily a labor organization of the bituminous industry, and therefore its leaders were unfamiliar with conditions existing in anthracite mining. The union's attempt to extend its influence over the anthracite fields was viewed as arbitrary, stemming from a desire "to control the entire fuel supply" of the country.[24] Trade and working conditions existing in bitunimous mining were not necessarily the same in anthracite mining. Therefore it was impractical to try to make wages uniform in the various anthracite districts by adjusting them in joint annual conferences. To accede to this plan would mean, according to G. F. Baer, president of the Philadelphia and Reading Railway "[to] unsettle all the labor conditions of the various anthracite districts each year." And his company, Baer went on to emphasize, would "not favor the plan of having its relations with the miners disturbed every year."[25] Moreover, no wage adjustment was necessary, because, Lackawanna Railroad president, W. H. Truesdale, proudly explained, the miners "are prosperous and contented" with their present wage conditions.[26]

Some of the more technical reasons were presented by Baer, who maintained that the nature of the anthracite business was such that no advance in wages could be contemplated by the operators, and that therefore conditions had to continue as they were. Baer explained that of all the anthracite production, 40 percent was destined to manufacturing and 60 percent to household and heating use. The first share of production had to be sold in the market "below the cost of mining" because of the competition it faced from bituminous coal. Any wage advance based on that production was therefore unthinkable if that coal had to be marketed at all. Any wage advance would have to be drawn from the other 60 percent of production. But this alternative also was unthinkable, Baer stated; it would affect ordinary people and the public at large who used anthracite for household purposes: "Were we to increase the price of coal," Baer maintained, "then the cry would be that the coal barons are oppressing the poor."[27]

And finally there was the problem of the operators' social and economic control over the miners' labor power—a problem that had been heightened by the steady rise of militancy in the anthracite fields, especially after the show of strength exhibited by the anthracite mine workers in the strike of 1900. E. B. Thomas, representative of the Erie Railroad Company and the Lehigh Valley Company, stated, "So far the apparent effect [of the UMW] has been that at no time during the last twenty years has a greater spirit of unrest and agitation prevailed among anthracite miners than has existed during the past years." This, according to Thomas, had already produced serious consequences in the production of anthracite coal, which, for his company, had declined by 600,000 tons from April 1 to October 1, 1901.[28] President Baer, even more frank, went right to the heart of the question: the UMW's attempt to extend its jurisdiction over the anthracite region and force uniform scales of wages would have the effect of producing "divided allegiance" among the workers. For Baer— soon to become famous for his "divine rights of management" theory— this was contrary to sound business principle because "there cannot be two masters in the management of business." Total control over the miners and strict enforcement of work discipline were the exclusive prerogatives of management. There was no guarantee that the UMW officials could enforce work regulations. But management could "through its power to discharge."[29]

These views were made explicit by the railroad directors in their response to John Mitchell's invitation to a joint conference held in Scranton, Pennsylvania, on March 12. Their position was reaffirmed in the course of a meeting held at the end of March between four railroad presidents and a delegation of UMW officials and arranged by the Conciliation Committee of the National Civic Federation.[30] Coupled with a success in delaying strike action by a month, this meeting was the only concrete result the National Civic Federation could produce after months of intense efforts at getting the two parties to reach some kind of a compromise.[31]

Early in May a call ordering a temporary suspension of work to begin on May 12 was issued by a UMW strike committee. Two days later a convention of all three anthracite districts was held in Hazleton, Pennsylvania, in which the delegates voted to turn the temporary suspension into a fullfledged strike.[32] The great anthracite strike of 1902 had begun.

Both for its magnitude and for the political crisis it embodied, the anthracite coal strike of 1902 has been covered by most standard American labor histories. One monograph in particular, authored by Robert Cornell, has provided a most detailed account of the day-to-day development of the strike, the public response it generated, and the series of maneuvers and countermaneuvers pursued by third parties, culminating in President Roosevelt's personal intervention and the appointment of an arbitration commission empowered to hand down a binding award. What concerns us here is determining what effect the strike had in forcing a solution to the labor problem in the anthracite coal industry and to what extent the provisions contained in the award represented a success or a setback in the fight to extend collective bargaining to that industrial sector.

Few strikes had had a greater impact on public opinion, forcing the American people to take sides for or against the miners or the coal interest. As the strike dragged on from week to week, through the summer months and then through the fall, it laid bare to the public eye—much more than the steel strike of the previous year had done—the efforts of a giant industrial combination to crush a labor organization and establish undisputed control over its work force and its labor relations. More importantly, as far as public opinion was concerned, the strike progressively revealed the method the coal combination was intent on pursuing: driving the miners and their families to starvation, thus forcing them to a total surrender.

To a large extent, getting the attention of the American public was part of the strategy of what former coal miner and author Andrew Roy described as "the best managed of any strike that ever occurred in the United States."[33] President Mitchell was in fact able to make excellent use of some of the most talented prolabor reformers—people like Walter Weyl, Henry D. Lloyd, John Commons, Isaac Hourwich, and Clarence Darrow, who helped with the necessary statistical, legal, and public relations work. Moreover, keeping 150,000 miners and their families compact and disciplined for a period of over five months was not an easy task. Here again Mitchell and his UMW lieutenants gave another remarkable example of good leadership. To be sure, much groundwork had been done during the preceding few years by John Fahy, president of the Schuylkill district and central figure in the organizing of anthracite coal miners. Fahy deserves much of the credit for the remarkable accord exhibited during the strike by miners of different ethnic origins. He had pursued a policy of placing capable ethnic leaders in high office in the UMW organization. The Lithuanian Adam Ryscavage in the Wyoming district, the Slav Andrew Matti in the Lehigh District, the German-Pole

Anthony Schlosser, and Paul Pulaski, considered "the chief Slavic labor organizer," were some of the people who provided the crucial leadership in the mining communities and established liaison with the national officers.[34]

When in early October President Roosevelt saw the necessity to intervene personally in the strike, he was not motivated simply by the desire to avert an economic and social crisis of vast proportions. The political atmosphere the strike had produced had become a matter of major apprehension—and not only for the president. Outcries that the government step in and take over the mines—an alternative that Roosevelt himself considered—were growing.[35] A popular weekly, the *Independent*, reflected clearly this general state of mind in one of its comments:

Thousands of men who have heretofore regarded the doctrines and projects of State socialism with indifference or hostility are now ready to ask for National or State ownership of these mines, or are thoughtfully considering this question without prejudice. The mine-owners, blind to the proofs of popular revolt against them, intoxicated with the power derived from profitable combination, have unwittingly done more in five months to promote in the United States that State socialism which they abhor than could without this help have been accomplished in a decade by all the avowed advocates and teachers of it.[36]

People who were closer to the scene of the strike expressed their concern for the growth of antibusiness sentiment and radicalization occurring among the miners and their supporters. For Easley, secretary of the NCF, the strike was increasing the influence of "the radical element, composed of the socialists, populists, and blatherskites generally [who] are fighting capital at every turn and trying hard to create class prejudice."[37] Mitchell, too, was disturbed by the "great and growing independent political sentiment in the coalfields" and by the inroads the Socialists were making.[38] This political dynamic that the strike had set in motion had to be stopped—and the sooner, the better.[39] Not to see this dimension in the presidential intervention would be to miss the significance of the forces that had been unleashed by this confrontation.

It is also important to point out that, although Roosevelt stepped into the dispute "as an independent force representing a neutral view and the public interest,"[40] the move that broke the stalemate—the president's threat that he would launch an inquiry into the connection between the railroad and the coal companies—was clearly directed against the railroad interests.[41] Under these circumstances, the appointment of a commission empowered to arbitrate the dispute and hand down a binding award had demonstrated that on the terrain of open confrontation, the mine workers and their families had succeeded in forcing on the powerful railroad interest a new course of action of serious political impact. "This is, as regards the [coal] capitalists, compulsory arbitration forced on them by the President, by a short cut," commented Henry D. Lloyd, a man who had a thorough knowledge of the railroad combination's power and its practices.[42] Behind the apparent show of enthusiasm of a compulsory arbitration fan, Lloyd's statement reflected the awareness that the powerful coal interest had been brought in line by the determined struggle of the miners. The appointment of a strike commission meant also that the cause of the anthracite mine workers was being brought before the highest tribunal for the first time, thus forcing it out of the confines into which the railroads had restricted it for decades. This was the extent of the anthracite mine workers' victory.

That the award handed down by the strike commission was designed to return the anthracite industry to its previous condition rather than to solve the underlying issue that had led the mine workers to strike, becomes evident after a careful analysis of its provisions. The only concrete concessions the mine workers won were a reduction of work hours from ten to nine for time workers (the miners' demand was for eight hours) and a wage advance of 10 percent for contract miners (the miners had asked for 20 percent).[43]

This "horizontal increase" of wages—as it was called by experts—allowed the railroad and coal companies to leave untouched the wage structure of the industry; therefore, methods of wage payments, differentials, and wage rates according to occupation remained firmly in the hands of the coal companies. Moreover, the decision by the strike commission to adopt the sliding scale had the effect of freezing the wage structure as it existed and undermined any possible future attempt by the miners to make wage demands the object of disputes.

The sliding scale—a practice the Lehigh and Schuylkill mine workers had rejected in 1900 on the ground that it "had always reduced, never advanced, their pay"—was presented by the commission as a "profit-sharing device."[44] It provided for an automatic increase in wages proportional to increases in the price of coal at tidewater points "if in the future the price of coal should become what might be called abnormally high."[45]

The wage structure was not the only area of labor relations left by the strike coal commission under the total control of the coal companies. Virtually all other aspects of coal mining—working conditions, methods of weighing, and occupational structure—were left untouched. This hands-off approach that the strike commission took was made explicit by the commissioner of labor, Carroll Wright, himself a member of the commission: "The anthracite commission did not undertake to deal with the character of the work performed, this being left to adjustment in each colliery in accordance with the prevailing conditions."[46]

The coal companies' control over the labor relations, which the strike commission sanctioned in its award, was further strengthened by the decision on the all-important demand presented by the anthracite miners' representatives: the recognition of the United Mine Workers of America as a bargaining agent for the anthracite mine workers and the establishment of a trade agreement. The commission skirted away from such a decision, stating categorically that this issue was not "within the scope of the jurisdiction conferred upon it."[47] In doing so, however, it adopted essentially the argument that the railroad directors had sustained all along: that the UMW was "an organization controlled by men engaged in the bituminous industry." To reinforce this point, the commission stressed that Mitchell had appeared before the commission "as the representative of the anthracite coal mine workers, and not in his official character as president of the United Mine Workers of America." The commission also took the opportunity to question some of the organizational features of the UMW, accusing it of irresponsibility: the fact that the UMW's constitution "permit[ted] boys of immature age [legal minors] and judgement to participate in deciding the policies and actions of a labor union" and that "a strike may be undertaken by a majority vote of the members of a district convention called for the purpose of considering a strike" and voting "by voice or show of hands."[48]

The commission then enunciated a series of principles in the areas of labor and industrial relations—an extremely significant fact in view of the widespread public attention focused on its pronouncements. It endorsed the principle of trade unionism as a basic right of the American worker, stating that "experience shows that the more fully recognition is given to a trades union, the more businesslike and responsible it becomes. Through dealing with businessman in business matters, its more intelligent, conservative, and responsible members come to the front and gain general control and direction of its affairs." The principle that later became known as "business unionism" had been officially enunciated by one of the highest industrial tribunals. Moreover, the union would be the best guarantee against "the extremist get[ting] a ready hearing for incendiary appeals to prejudice or passion, when a grievance, real or fancied, of a general nature, presents itself for consideration."[49] However, it seems that in the case of anthracite mining the strike commission had found a way to achieve that goal without the recognition of a trade union that, like the UMW, had given ample proof of its responsibility, conservatism, and businesslike methods.

More significantly, the commission condemned the practice of the closed shop and established the principle of the open shop: "The nonunion man," the commission stated, "assumes the whole responsibility which results from his being such, but his right and privilege of being a nonunion man are sanctioned in law and morals. The rights and privileges of nonunion men are as sacred to them as the rights and privileges of unionists."[50]

After such an elaborate presentation of its industrial relations philosophy, the commission added that "an independent and autonomous organization of the anthracite mine workers of Pennsylvania, however affiliated, . . . would deserve the recommendation of this Commission"—a reasoning that was totally in line with the railroad directors' views. But on the condition that "the objectionable features above alluded to [voting rights of legal minors, simple majority vote to call a strike, closed shop] should be absent.[51] Clearly the UMW and the anthracite mine workers had been put on trial.

When one considers some of the circumstances surrounding the anthracite coal strike of 1902—for instance, that it happened at the height of public endorsement of the principle of the trade agreement and that it occurred in an industry where the trade agreement had produced undisputed beneficial effects—one cannot help but notice the contradictory and ambiguous character of such an event. One the one hand, the strike had given a major thrust to the movement for collective bargaining. The overwhelmingly favorable public opinion that the miners' cause had attracted, the exemplary conduct of the UMW, and President Roosevelt's posture toward the obstinacy of the railroad directors undoubtedly strengthened the case for collective bargaining. On the other hand, the strike and the award handed down by the strike commission had raised a whole series of fundamental issues that in future months and years the movement for collective bargaining would encounter in various forms and degrees and that would pose serious difficulties for its extension. The open shop, which the strike commission had elevated as a basic principle of industrial relations, would become the rallying cry of antilabor forces throughout the Progressive period. The failure to recognize a union such as the UMW, which since the establishment of the Interstate Joint Conference as well as through its management of the strike, had given ample evidence of conservatism and respect for the "sanctity of the contract," was raising the question of how submissive a labor organization should be short of becoming a company union.

Another fundamental issue the strike raised was the feasibility of the trade agreement as the basis for industrial relations in an industry characterized by a high degree of control of ownership and integration of economic operations. The experience of the anthracite industry and of the railroad-coal combination had revealed to what extent the restructuring of an industry in terms of ownership and control presupposed total corporate control over its labor force and its labor relations, thus making the principle of collective bargaining untenable, if not obsolete.

Finally, the strike and its settlement had brought up in a most dramatic way the thorny question of compulsory arbitration: an issue that throughout the Progressive period would be the subject of heated debate. That the anthracite commission and its award had been a bitter lesson for U.S. labor leaders would be borne out by their impassioned attacks against any compulsory scheme for arbitration or investigation. But what the strike had undoubtedly done was highlight the emergence of a number of crusaders for the trade agreement, whatever their motives: men like Republican Senator Hanna, NCF Secretary Ralph Easley, and most of all John Mitchell, who in industrial and Progressive circles emerged clearly as the champion of the trade agreement.

NOTES

1. Peter Roberts, *The Anthracite Coal Industry* (New York, 1901), 5.

2. Eliot Jones, *The Anthracite Coal Combination in the United States* (Cambridge, Mass., 1914), 24-31; Francis Walker, "The Development of the Anthracite Combination," *Annals of the American Academy of Political and Social Science* 111 (January 1924): 236-37.

3. Roberts, *Anthracite Coal Industry,* 65ff.

4. George Virtue, "The Anthracite Mine Laborers," *Bulletin of the Department of Labor,* no. 13 (1897): 733-35; cf. also David Montgomery, *Beyond Equality* (New York, 1967), 159-62; Arthur E. Suffern, *Conciliation and Arbitration in the Coal Industry of America* (New York, 1915), 203-13.

5. Virtue, "Anthracite Mine Laborers," 757; U.S. Industrial Commission, *Final Report* (Washington, D.C., 1900-1902), 19:458 (hereafter cited as *USIC Report*).

6. *USIC Report,* 12:154, 156.

7. Jones, *Anthracite Coal Combination,* 62.

8. Ibid., 61.

9. Walker, "The Development," 241; Jones, *Anthracite Coal Combination,* 68.

10. *USIC Report,* 9:598.

11. Walker, "The Development," 240-41; *USIC Report,* 12:152. In 1898 a group of independent operators had posed a threat to the railroad-coal combination by projecting an independent railroad to tidewater, which would end their dependence on the freight rates policies of the large railroads. Though this attempt was immediately checked by the Morgan interests and ended in failure, it was feared by the latter that similar attempts would be initiated again.

12. *Proceedings of the Eleventh Annual Convention of the United Mine Workers of America* (Indianapolis, 1900), 17, 28, 48-49.

13. Virtue, "The Anthracite Mine Laborers," 749; Roberts, *Anthracite Coal Industry,* 103-04; Terence V. Powderly, *Thirty Years of Labor* (Columbus, 1889), 428-29. Powderly, former president of the Knights of Labor, a native of the anthracite region, and later U.S. commissioner of immigration, described the situation thus: "The immigration from Poland began to make itself felt in 1872. . . . The tide from Hungary began to set in in 1877. The railroad strike of that year created a desire on the part of the railroad operators to secure the services of cheap, docile men, who would tamely submit to restrictions and imposition. Hungary was flooded with advertisements which set forth the great advantages to be gained by emigration to America."

14. Suffern, *Conciliation and Arbitration,* 232.

15. Cf. especially, Frank J. Warne, *The Slav Invasion and the Mine Workers* (Philadelphia, 1904), 65-83; U.S. Bureau of Labor Statistics, "Collective Bargaining in the Anthracite Coal Industry," *Bulletin,* no. 191 (March 1916): 94ff; Suffern, *Conciliation and Arbitration,* 239, 240.

16. Peter Roberts, "The Anthracite Coal Situation," *Yale Review* 11 (1902-03): 34; Elsie Glueck, *John Mitchell, Miner* (New York, 1929), 68-70.

17. Roberts, "The Anthracite Coal Situation," 34.

18. Virtue, "Anthracite Mine Laborers," 753.

19. F. G. Fraser, "Anthracite Coal Miners' Wages," *Annals of the American Academy of Political and Social Science* 16 (1900): 153-55.

20. Robert J. Cornell, *The Anthracite Strike of 1902* (Washington, D.C., 1957), 41-43.

21. Ibid., 46-47; John Mitchell, *Organized Labor* (Philadelphia, 1903), 366.

22. Carroll D. Wright, "Report to the President on the Anthracite Coal Strike," *Bulletin of the Department of Labor Statistics,* no. 43 (November 1902): esp. 1204 (hereafter cited as *Wright's Report*).

23. Cornell, *Anthracite Strike of 1902,* 58.

24. *Wright's Report,* appendix E, 1211.

25. G. F. Baer to John Mitchell, February 18, 1902, in ibid., appendix C, 1176, 1177.

26. W. H. Truesdale to John Mitchell, February 18, 1902, in ibid., appendix C, 1179.

27. Ibid., 1209.

28. E. B. Thomas to John Mitchell, February 20, 1902, in ibid., 1180.

29. Baer to Mitchell in ibid., 1177.

30. Cornell, *Anthracite Strike of 1902,* 82-84.

31. Marguerite Green, *The National Civic Federation and the American Labor Movement* (Washington, D.C., 1956), 43-50.

32. Cornell, *Anthracite Strike of 1902,* 93.

33. Andrew Roy, *A History of the Coal Miners of the United States* (Columbus, 1907), 440.

34. Victor R. Greene, *The Slavic Community on Strike* (Notre Dame and Gordon, 1968), 145-48, 183, 201.

35. Cornell, ibid., 219, 220.

36. *The Independent* 54 (October 16, 1902): 2483.

37. Easley to Perkins, August 23, 1902, box 4, National Civic Federation Papers, New York Public Library.

38. Mitchell to Hanna, September 8, 1902, box 35, Mitchell Papers, Catholic University of America, Washington, D.C. For a report on socialist inroads made during the strike, cf. William Mailly, "The Anthracite Coal Strike," *International Socialist Review* (August 1902): 79-85.

39. Some years later, recalling the anthracite crisis, Roosevelt wrote, "I was anxious to save the great coal operators and all of the class of big propertied men, of which they were members, from the dreadful punishment which their own folly would have brought on them if I had not acted." Quoted in Richard Hofstadter, *The American Political Tradition and the Men Who Made It* (New York, 1948), 223.

40. Richard Hofstadter, *The Age of Reform* (New York, 1955), 236.

41. Cornell, *Anthracite Strike of 1902,* 213-19.

42. Quoted in Chester Destler, "On the Eve of the Anthracite Coal Strike Arbitration: Henry Demerest Lloyd at United Mine Workers Headquarters," *Labor History* 13 (Spring 1972): 286.

43. *Report of the Anthracite Coal Strike Commission,* in *Bulletin of the Department of Labor,* no. 46 (May 1903): 506 (hereafter cited as *ACSC Report*).

44. E. Dana Durand, "The Anthracite Coal Strike and Its Settlement," *Political Science Quarterly* 18 (September 1903): 386.

45. *ACSC Report,* 497, 498.

46. Quoted in Suffern, *Conciliation and Arbitration,* 260-61.

47. *ACSC Report,* 487.

48. Ibid., 486-91.

49. Ibid., 489.

50. Ibid., 490.

51. Ibid., 492.

3

JOHN MITCHELL: CHAMPION OF THE TRADE AGREEMENT

In the spring of 1900 John Mitchell wrote jokingly to Samuel Gompers that at the UMW headquarters they were "seriously contemplating the absorption of the American Federation of Labor."[1] We do not know how the AFL chief took the remark, but as the head of a union 117,000 members strong, Mitchell could afford this sense of humor. The UMW would in fact emerge out of that postdepression cycle of strikes as the largest labor organization of the entire federation.

If the mere numerical growth was in itself a remarkable accomplishment in the annals of U.S. labor, what was even more significant, historically, was the political impact that the UMW's growth had on the wider industrial scene. We have seen how there had been factors of a structural order either favoring or impairing its growth; but precise political choices had become necessary for the organization so that it could manage its growth and consolidate its gains. It was not simply a question of meeting the technical and economic requirements that the trade agreement framework demanded; the question was also how to utilize the struggles the organization had undertaken as the political articulation of a labor program that would respond to the industrial and political exigencies at a time when the labor problem transcended the confines of the single enterprise or sector and loomed as the most serious problem confronting American capital.

It is in this context that John Mitchell's leadership is of a crucial historical significance, not merely for the remarkable qualities of labor statesmanship that he displayed in leading his organization during that

delicate period of its life; Mitchell also understood—perhaps better than
any other labor leader of his time—the political terrain on which the
UMW and organized labor in general were moving. He therefore was able
to mobilize wider social forces and direct the growth of his organization
so that it came to embody a precise political program. Mitchell's organizational accomplishments were also backed by an intense work of elaboration and propagation of the philosophy of the trade agreement, making
him, even after he left the presidency of the UMW, labor's most outspoken exponent of that philosophy.

When at the 1898 annual convention of the UMW John Mitchell was
elected national vice-president, many miners were bewildered by the
sudden elevation of this young and relatively unknown union official
to such a prominent position. Mitchell's rise in the organization had in
fact been phenomenal.

Born in Braidwood in the coal region of northern Illinois in 1870,
Mitchell had known all the harsh experiences confronting miners' children
in those years.[2] In his case, these were compounded by the loss of both
of his parents during his early childhood—a loss that could scarcely be
compensated by the strict Presbyterian upbringing he received from his
stepmother and the heavy share of domestic labor he had to do to help
support the family. Like most other children in his community, Mitchell began working in the mines at the age of twelve, and inexorably
his lot became one with that of the thousands of miners who in those
years were struggling to improve their squalid existence. While still a
teenager he joined the local chapter of the Knights of Labor, sharing
the excitement of those who saw in the dramatic rise of that organization the hope for a brighter future. And after the Knights' collapse and
the formation of the United Mine Workers of America in 1890, he, like
most of his fellow miners, joined the organization that had a bright future
in store for him.

Mitchell was fortunate to have grown up in a town that had produced
some of the most active and militant miners of the state; men like Dan
McLaughlin, who had been mayor of the town and an early advocate of
interstate agreements in bituminous mining, and in whose house young
Mitchell lived for a while; and like William Ryan, one of the most able
organizers in Illinois and later a leading national officer of the UMW. In
the nearby town of Spring Valley, where Mitchell settled for most of the

1890s, he met another person who would exert a strong influence on his life: Father Power, a priest dedicated to assisting the miners in their struggle for a better existence. The priest introduced Mitchell to the current reform literature and exerted a strong influence in shaping the young miner's social consciousness. This friendship also taught Mitchell the important role that the local clergy could play in assisting miners in their organizational efforts—a teaching that Mitchell would put very effectively into practice during the anthracite coal strike of 1902.

These influences must have given Mitchell a strong sense of purpose, for he soon started to study law on his own and increasingly took an interest in local public affairs. While still in his early twenties he managed to get elected to the board of education of Spring Valley, and in 1894 he began his active participation in union affairs under the direct influence of Ryan, who at that time was leading an organizing drive in Illinois. By 1896 Mitchell had gotten his first appointment in the organization as secretary-treasurer of his Illinois subdistrict, acting also as legislative representative of the miners in Springfield.[3] The following year he had climbed one step higher, being elected to the board of the Illinois district.[4] But 1897 was also the year of the establishment of the Interstate Joint Conference, and it was in this strike that Mitchell distinguished himself for his organizing ability, gaining the admiration of UMW President Michael Ratchford.[5]

Mitchell's efforts had been limited to southern Illinois; and it was from this region of the bituminous fields that the greatest threat to a successful settlement of the strike came. His task was basically to bring in line the southern Illinois miners who refused to accept the national scale agreed upon by the national board.[6] This had been a crucial job, however, because the failure of any one of the four states to accept the terms of the interstate agreement would have undermined the whole interstate wage mechanism. The event had been demanding enough to bring out many of Mitchell's qualities as a national organizer: his ability to convince miners, to discipline them if necessary, and to build up a consensus among them. Mitchell was able to capitalize on this success and gain the necessary support for his election to the vice-presidency at the 1898 national convention.

Soon after this election the *UMW Journal*—no doubt reflecting the feeling of many mine workers—commented on this "promising young man" and on his "limited . . . experience in the broad field of mining affairs" as compared to other prominent leaders in the organization.[7] The

correctness of this comment found a prompt verification at the historic
Interstate Joint Conference, which immediately followed the UMW national convention. Here Mitchell's role in the long and painstaking work
of ironing out the complex technicalities of the interstate agreement was
conspicuously minor, reflecting his inexperience at this level of operation. His main efforts were instead directed—as in Illinois a few months
earlier—toward persuading the more recalcitrant delegates and advising
moderation among miners and operators alike whenever an impasse was
reached.[8]

It is to this kind of work that the young vice-president was called upon
in the months following the conference. The establishment of the interstate agreement had been only the first step; the follow-up work was
equally crucial and exacting, especially during the first year when the
mechanism was being put to a test. It was essential to ensure the stable
operation of the agreement by promptly circumventing any outbreak of
local disputes. As Illinois Operators' Commissioner Herman Justi had put
it, the mine workers had to be educated and disciplined to the value of
the interstate agreement and its terms.[9]

It was again from southern Illinois that the most serious threat to the
agreement came; operators from Pana and Virden refused to live up to
the agreed wage scales and sought to upset the equality of competition.
The ensuing social conflict, which eventually led to the noted Virden
massacre, embodied in itself all the social and political tensions the UMW
would increasingly encounter in the following years: operators' insubordination, miners' militance, the importance of black strikebreakers, armed
confrontation.[10] The intense exchange of correspondence between Mitchell—dispatched to the scene of the struggle—and President Ratchford
throughout that period reveals the complexity of the situation and the
enormous difficulty of enacting a strategy that would bring the conflict
under control and restore the effectiveness of interstate agreement.[11]
Mitchell's success in this mission shows the kind of terrain on which he
was at his best: striking a compromise under even the most adverse conditions but also exerting on the miners the kind of discipline and self-
control necessary to mold the organization into a unified whole.

The passage from the vice-presidency to the presidency was neither
automatic nor an established tradition in the UMW. What had become
traditional, instead, was for senior officials and national leaders to go on
to political positions. This time it was Ratchford's turn. In the spring of
1899—according to Illinois district president and Mitchell's close friend,

William Ryan—Ratchford had informed Mitchell that he might soon leave the presidency for an appointment to the industrial commission being created by President McKinley and that there were strong chances that he, Mitchell, might climb to the head of the union.[12] It is doubtful that Mitchell could have amassed the necessary support on his own to defeat some of the stronger and better known contenders. But as soon as the appointment to the Industrial Commission materialized, Ratchford threw his weight in Mitchell's direction. Pursuing a course of action not provided for by the UMW constitution, Ratchford retained the office of president and installed Mitchell as acting president until a new president was elected by the national convention the following January. According to one authoritative source, "Ratchford most likely remained in office in order to preside over the 1899 convention and aid Mitchell in his bid for election as President."[13]

Exactly to what extent Mitchell appeared as the ideal successor in Ratchford's eyes is only a matter of conjecture. It seems legitimate to assert, however, that Ratchford had considered Mitchell the man most qualified to lead the organization in the new direction it had embarked on. Mitchell did not have the thorough experience and knowledge of the coal business that Ohio district president Tom Lewis had nor did he have the impassioned rhetoric and impressive style of western Pennsylvania's Patrick Dolan.[14] What he could offer was coolness of judgment, rational behavior even in the most tension-filled situations, and an ability to persuade and strike a compromise. These were the qualities most needed by the UMW now that the organization was making its historical move from the realm of open confrontation and struggle to one where the rules of the game were dictated by legality and contractual relations. The trade agreement and its rules necessitated a certain kind of ethic that both rank and filers and leaders had—in their own ways—to internalize. Mitchell, more than any other national leader, seemed to embody this ethic and seemed to display an unusual potential for articulating it and making it work within the organization. Moreover, unlike some of the other contenders, Mitchell had not been embroiled in union factional fights, and his political record was spotless.

During the turbulent sessions of the 1899 UMW national convention, Mitchell was able to exploit well these assets and, with the help of Ratchford, to get the necessary support ensuring his election over his opponent Tom Lewis. Ratchford had not just left Mitchell the presidential seat, he had also left him a political line to follow.[15]

Mine workers were a substantial political force at the local and state level from the very beginning. This was particularly true in coal-mining states where the intricate system of state mining laws brought miners' leaders in continuous interaction with the state government, state legislatures, and politicians in general.

In some of these states, where the mine workers represented the largest single group of the labor force, their vote was often determining for the victory or the defeat of a political candidate. "Reward your friends and punish your enemies" had been a reality in coal-mining counties and states long before Samuel Gompers elevated it to the official labor policy of the AFL. Ohio was one of these states. There, a recent example had been offered at the 1898 senatorial election when Michael Ratchford had mobilized his own Ohio UMW district to push Marcus Hanna to victory.[16] Hanna qualified quite well as a friend of labor, at least in his home state of Ohio. He had been one of the first businessmen to extend recognition to unions—a position he never modified under even the most adverse economic circumstances. In the eyes of many miners, this had made Hanna a progressive employer, especially when compared with the rabidly antiunion stance of many coal operators.

To say that Hanna was also a prominent and influential businessman would be an understatement. The economic resources that Hanna commanded—both for their vastness and their diversity—brought him into contact with many sectors of organized labor and with the leading financial interests in the country, thus providing the basis for the central political role he would play in the arena of labor-capital relations. Hanna's base of operation was centralized in M. A. Hanna & Co., a partnership that always retained the character of a family business. In the words of his biographer, Herbert Croly, this firm "constituted the nucleus of a widely ramified system of corporate and firm properties, individual properties, and personal and corporate alliances."[17] In addition to the many coal mines that Hanna owned in several bituminous districts of Ohio— and which made him a prominent coal operator—were a number of iron ore mines and a leading lake transportation fleet that he operated. This fleet, operated through the Cleveland Iron Mining Co., allowed the Hannas to extend their influence over the whole Lake Superior region. Moreover, Hanna's influence over the powerful Pennsylvania Railroad Company was a direct one because this was the line connecting the Lake Superior docks to the furnaces of western Pennsylvania. Hanna's firm had not gone into steel manufacturing, but its influence on that industrial sector was equally substantial; several members of his partnership held directorate positions in a number of steel-producing companies.

In this context, the miners' organization occupied a central role to the extent that much of Hanna & Co.'s trade operations hinged on the production, shipping, and sale of coal. Stable relations with the UMW were therefore a prerequisite for ensuring the stability of trade conditions—a policy that the Ohio senator had already made quite operative with Daniel Keefe's longshoremen union. That the UMW would become a major area of intervention for Senator Hanna would become increasingly evident as the organization grew in numbers and influence; Hanna would exert an ongoing influence on it—if not to impose a political line, certainly to prevent it from taking any wrong steps. This was part of the legacy that Ratchford had left to Mitchell.

The test for Mitchell came just a few months after he delivered his first presidential address at the eleventh mine workers' convention—a speech punctuated by antibusiness rhetoric, which called for an active involvement in grass-roots politics. In 1900 Hanna was not just the businessman from Ohio concerned with the stable operation of his economic interests. He was also the chairman of the National Committee of the Republican party, committed to mobilizing all his political resources and influences to ensure the reelection of his friend William McKinley and thus to extend economic prosperity for at least another four years. With a membership of 117,000 and an indirect influence on hundreds of thousands of unorganized mine workers, the UMW figured high on Hanna's list of political forces to be mobilized. But more than the mere voting power the UMW could command, Hanna's main concern was that the miners' organization would play a role of social control so as to prevent any outbreak of labor unrest that might endanger a Republican success in the presidential election. Thus, as early as March of that year the National Committee of the Republican party informed Mitchell of their desire to have all labor disputes in the mining regions settled before the opening of the campaign.[18] But throughout the summer of that year a major labor crisis was brewing in the anthracite mine regions, which eventually resulted in the industry-wide strike. Hanna's unofficial mediating role between the Morgan interests and Mitchell was crucial in bringing the strike to an early end, thus preventing a major labor-capital confrontation. The essentially political character of that settlement clearly

emerged from an interview that Commissioner of Labor Carroll Wright
had later with some of the railroad directors. George Baer put it this way
on that occasion:

Shortly after this strike was inaugurated, Senator Hanna met a number
of gentlemen and insisted that if the strike was not settled it would extend to Ohio, Indiana, and Illinois, and the election of Mr. McKinley
and Mr. Roosevelt would be endangered. He insisted that he was authorized to settle the strike, through Mr. Mitchell, if the operators would
agree to a 10 percent advance in wages. After a great deal of pressure
had been brought to bear upon the presidents of the coal companies and
positive assurance was given that the situation was really dangerous, Mr.
McKinley sending to me personally a gentleman to assure me that Ohio
and Indiana were in danger unless some adjustment was made, we agreed
to put up a notice.[19]

The settlement had been nothing less than a postponement of a greater
confrontation to come, but it had given Mitchell the opportunity to prove
himself in the knotty art of forging alliances and maneuvering above the
heads of the mine workers. That he passed this test became clear from the
public eulogies that Hanna would pour out and from the close working
relationship that developed between the two men. Mitchell proved to have
understood clearly the complex terrain on which his organization was
moving in its attempt to extend the trade agreement to all sectors of coal
mining: the open confrontation where the power of the mine workers
provided the basis for action and the behind-the-scene maneuvers, where
the demands advanced by the mine workers had to be translated into
their broader political implications.

On the occasion of the steel strike of 1901, Mitchell learned how
tricky this latter terrain could be. This event is significant because it also
shows how far he was willing to push in that direction even at the cost
of undermining the aspirations of some sectors of labor.[20] Here Mitchell—
along with Gompers and Frank Sargent of the Brotherhood of Locomotive Firemen—was called upon to play a central mediating role between
the Morgan interests and T. J. Shaffer's Amalgamated Association of Iron,
Steel and Tin Workers. They were acting not only as members of a special
National Civic Federation conciliation committee but also as prominent
leaders of organized labor. There is no doubt that had Shaffer's expectations of total support from organized labor been realized, the strike would

have resulted in the fiercest labor-capital confrontation of those years. Whatever Mitchell's and Gomper's judgment on the strategic value of such a confrontation, the fact remains that, especially as far as Mitchell was concerned, strong sentiment had come from many quarters of the UMW in favor of coming out in support of the Amalgamated. This was particularly true among the mine workers of western Pennsylvania where most of the struck steel mills were located. Under such pressures from his own organization, Mitchell had given Shaffer his word that the miners would come out in support of the strike should U.S. Steel executives reject a proposal to which Morgan had in principle assented—a promise on which Shaffer counted quite a lot.[21] Mitchell's subsequent hands-off attitude may have not been the underlying cause of the failure of the strike and the historic defeat of the Amalgamated, but it reveals the order of priorities in his strategy. At closer viewing, it appears in fact that the UMW president seized upon this opportunity to capitalize as much as possible on his conservative conduct and from his role as a leader who put the sanctity of the contract above any other matter.

Mitchell was thinking more of the future of his own organization and the deadlines that awaited it (in extending the trade agreement to the anthracite industry) than of the lot of the steel workers for whom he had been called to intercede and rally support. Mitchell later admitted to Gompers that at the time of the steel strike he was trying to secure a conference with the presidents of the coal-carrying railroads, and since the same interests controlled the steel and anthracite industries, "a good impression made in one struggle [would] transfer to the other arena."[22] That Mitchell was being encouraged to move in that direction by some of his NCF associates appears evident in a letter that NCF's secretary Ralph Easley wrote Mitchell during those hectic days: "I have told people here how you have talked at the conference. . . . Carry out the policy you spoke of or see if you can, and we will get you in such a position in the steel strike settlement that you can get anything you want for your organization."[23]

Early in September, when it became apparent that the strike was going to end in total defeat for the Amalgamated, Mitchell began to draw a balance sheet of his involvement in the strike. In a letter to his friend W. Wilson, he wrote: "Our connection with the negotiations has done much to strengthen our organization and I believe that the influence of the steel corporation can be used to help us should we need it. At least

Mr. Schwab [president of U.S. Steel] said to me in confidence that any
time I wished to discuss labor matters with him he would receive me and
give careful consideration to all I said. He also said for myself personally,
he desired to have the privilege of talking to me on any labor troubles
that might arise."[24]

It did not take long for Mitchell to see how ephemeral those promises
were and what the character of his gains had been. When the time of the
confrontation with the coal-carrying railroads approached in the spring of
1902, not only did Mitchell fail to get the Morgan people to keep their
word, but even Hanna and all the NCF resources were not enough to
move the railroad directors. Mitchell shifted his action to another arena—
public opinion. It was here that he was able to gather widespread support
from both the labor movement and the public at large, which proved to
be a determining factor in the outcome of the confrontation. By depict-
ing the anthracite miners' struggle as the most progressive strike in the
most unprogressive industry, Mitchell was able to translate that confrontation into a language to which Progressive America was most sensitive
and thus to mobilize the aid of many Progressive forces, both individuals
and organizations.

If Hanna had failed through his political and business influences to prevent the confrontation, during the course of the strike, he succeeded in
exerting on Mitchell and the UMW the kind of pressures that show to what
extent he enjoyed a free hand in intervening in the affairs of the mine
workers' organization. When the senator found out that a special national
convention was about to be called by the miners to consider the possibility of bituminous workers' coming out in support of the anthracite workers, Hanna's intervention to avert a national miners' strike was immediate.
In a letter to Mitchell—which stands out for its dramatic tone—Hanna
expressed his "*alarm*" concerning "the talk about a sympathetic strike."
He then hit Mitchell where the latter was most sensitive: "I know public
sentiment is fast tending toward the side of the men in this trouble and
you *must* not permit *any act* to change it. Therefore, any drastic means
which would demoralize the business of the country and make the inno-
cent suffer would turn public opinion against your organization."[25] In a
subsequent letter, Hanna asked Mitchell to stall off the special convention so that the senator would have time to mobilize support among the
bituminous workers against a national strike. He also requested from
Mitchell the names of men who were most qualified to do such work.[26]

It was now up to Mitchell to translate these pressures into organizational strategy within the UMW. He gave Hanna a free hand to do his work of persuasion among rank and filers. The *Chicago Record Herald* later confirmed that Hanna sent agents to all bituminous districts to persuade miners against breaking their contracts.[27] In his report on the strike, Easley describes how all the labor representatives on the NCF's committee were mobilized to do a similar work, "contending with the anthracite miners that 'it would be better a thousand times to lose their strike than to break those contracts.' "[28]

Mitchell succeeded in delaying the special convention until mid-July,[29] and then, at this convention through an impassioned defense of the "sanctity of contracts," he was able to gather support for an alternate course of action: the establishment of a special relief fund to support the anthracite struggle.[30] Mitchell's ability to contain the widespread sentiment among miners in favor of a national strike stands as one of his greatest accomplishments in channeling the struggle of the mine workers into a course that was compatible with the political pressures exerted on his organization. This action would echo Lincoln Steffens's remark of a month later: "The hardest fight of a conservative labor leader is always within the union, and Mitchell's finest work has been done there."[31]

The fact that the UMW received from the Anthracite Strike Commission what amounted to a probationary sentence—it had to prove itself capable of acting responsibly before being considered a party to an agreement with the coal-carrying railroads—did not in any way undermine Mitchell's repute; on the contrary, the UMW president emerged from the strike as the most prestigious labor figure of his day.

There were continuous talks and rumors that he might soon move to a top-level political position—perhaps the governorship of Illinois, the vice-presidency of the United States, or even the presidency of the AFL.[32] He also became the labor leader most featured in the Progressive press. The formula always seemed to be the same; Mitchell's profile of his accomplishments as labor leader and statesman were coupled with his philosophy of the trade agreement and its corollary—the sanctity of the contract, the conservative, educational influence of the trade agreement on the rank and file, and its stabilizing effect on trade conditions.[33]

In one of those eulogies written by the famous muckraker Lincoln Steffens, Mitchell was contrasted to the "old-fashioned labor leaders" and was presented as the embodiment of a new type of labor statesman. "Mitchell has a policy," remarked Steffens, "which the employers understand much better than their employees. . . . He has the personal respect of both . . . the miners and Wall Street."[34] Steffens had been able to capture not only the outward appearance of Mitchell's policy but also its substance. The great accomplishment of Mitchell's policy had in fact stemmed from his ability to adapt the growth of his organization to the industrial and political exigencies required by the economic expansion of those years and by the administration that attended to it. If the trade agreement involved both a relation of power between capital and labor, as well as the recognition of trade exigencies, it was the latter element that prevailed in Mitchell's philosophy. In his articulation of the principle of competitive equality, Mitchell had outlined the basic policy of the interstate agreement: that wage levels would be so adjusted as to regulate competition in the trade and thus further the growth of the industry. A few years later, Mitchell acknowledged what risk the UMW leadership was taking in "imposing terms on the miners that are 'compatible with the interest of the coal industry.' "[35] Referring to the rebellious feelings among the rank and file against the UMW leadership, Mitchell confided his concern to a friend: "This has been by far the worst year in the history of our organization. Every settlement we have made has been against the wishes of a vast majority of our delegates. We have literally been compelled to shove our agreements down the throats of our delegates."[36] And again, two years later, when safeguarding the interest of the coal trade meant that the bituminous miners had to endure a cut in their wages, Mitchell barely succeeded in staving off the wave of dissatisfaction and criticism rising among the miners.[37]

But to safeguard the stability and improvement of business conditions meant also to favor the administration that was in power. Hence, Mitchell's relations with the Republican administration acquire a peculiar historical significance. At a time when pure and simple unionism and the trade agreement meant—in the words of Hanna—not to "inject politics into labor,"[38] Mitchell established a permanent, and at times intense, entente whose implications often went beyond the confines of the coal mining industry. To a large extent this entente was mediated by Hanna, who acted as a sort of labor minister during the McKinley and early Roosevelt administrations and who often reaped large, personal benefits from this arrangement. Other times Mitchell's favors were more overtly political in nature—for instance, when he kept the senator informed of political movements in the coal regions that posed a threat to Hanna's friends. In the case of Republican Congressman William Connell from Scranton, Pennsylvania, who was receiving strong opposition for his re-nomination in 1902, for Mitchell this meant running counter to the efforts being made by labor forces "to nominate a labor candidate"—even though Connell was noted, as Mitchell himself admitted, for his "opposition to our amendment to the territorial mining laws."[39]

After Hanna's death, Mitchell's working relationship with President Roosevelt became a personal and direct one. To a large extent, this had been facilitated by Mitchell's conduct during the anthracite labor crisis of 1902 when Roosevelt had been impressed by the conservative and rational behavior of the UMW chief. Mitchell would occasionally be consulted by the president regarding proposed labor legislation. He would recommend to Roosevelt candidates for the office—as in the case of Charles Neill who in 1906 replaced Carroll Wright as commissioner of labor.[40] And in 1906, when negotiations for the renewal of the interstate agreement had reached an impasse, the president promptly responded to Mitchell's confidential request, using his personal influence in a behind-the-scene fashion in order to resolve the difficulty.[41] Mitchell's proadministration and pro-Republican posture would also become conspicuously evident in 1906 when the AFL executive council issued its indictment against the Republican administration—the so-called labor bill of grievances—and Mitchell declined to attach his name to it on the ground that he had not seen the document.[42]

But if in the pursuit of "Mitchell's policy"—as Steffens called it—and in the furtherance of the trade agreement Mitchell had made use of his personal relations and of the UMW platform, he had also made ample use of an extraunion platform—the National Civic Federation. His involvement in that organization, both as a prominent labor member and later as the chairman of the trade agreement department, reveals the extent to which the articulation of a trade agreement policy reached far beyond the confines of the coal industry.

NOTES

1. Quoted in Philip S. Foner, *The Policies and Practices of the A. F. of L., 1900-1909* (New York, 1964), 345.

2. The standard biography of Mitchell is Elsie Gluck's *John Mitchell, Miner* (New York, 1929), a work that throws much light on the personal life of the miners' leader but that shows little awareness of the labor context of the period. A more thorough analysis of Mitchell's career is Joseph Gowaskie's "John Mitchell: A Study in Leadership" (Ph.D. diss., Catholic University of America, Washington, D.C., 1968), based on an excellent use of Mitchell's papers.

3. Gluck, *John Mitchell*, 25.

4. Ibid., 26.

5. Cf. *UMW Journal* 7 (October 1897): 1; cf. also David J. McDonald and Edward A. Lynch, *Coal and Unionism* (Indianapolis, 1939), 45.

6. Gluck, *John Mitchell*, 29-39; Gowaski, "John Mitchell," 11.

7. *UMW Journal* 7 (January 1898): 4.

8. Cf. *Proceedings of the First Annual Joint Conference of the Coal Miners and Operators of Illinois, Indiana, Ohio, and Pennsylvania, January 17, 1898* (Columbus, n.d., The Lawrence Press); cf. also Gowaski, "John Mitchell," 14.

9. U.S. Industrial Commission, *Final Report* (Washington, D.C., 1900-1902), 12:680.

10. For a thorough analysis of this conflict, see Victor Hicken, "The Virden and Pana Wars," *Journal of the Illinois State Historical Society* 51 (Spring 1959): 263-78.

11. This correspondence is found in box 81 of the Mitchell Papers, Catholic University of America Archives.

12. Gluck, *John Mitchell*, 45.

13. Gowaskie, "John Mitchell," 26; Gluck, *John Mitchell*, 50.

14. Profiles of these two miners' leaders are given by Andrew Roy, *A History of the Coal Miners of the United States* (Columbus, Ohio, 1903), 381-83; Gluck, *John Mitchell*, 40-42.

15. For a critical discussion of Mitchell's election to the presidency, cf. the Socialist Labor party pamphlet *Arm and Hammer* 2 (July 1899), copy in box 14, Mitchell Papers, Catholic University of America.

16. Gluck, *John Mitchell*, 38.

17. Herbert Croly, *Marcus Alonzo Hanna, His Life and Work* (New York, 1912), 63. The information contained in this chapter is taken from chaps. 7 and 8 of this work.

18. Mitchell to W. D. Ryan, March 29, 1900, box 2, Mitchell Papers.

19. "Report of Interview of Commissioner of Labor with Messrs. George F. Baer, R. M. Olyphant, E. B. Thomas, and David Willcox," in Carroll D. Wright, "Report to the President on the Anthracite Coal Strike," *Bulletin of the Department of Labor Statistics*, no. 43 (November 1902): appendix E, 1204.

20. The events surrounding the strike are well known and have been analyzed by several historians. Cf. especially, David Brody, *Steelworkers in America: The Nonunion Era* (Cambridge, Mass., 1960); John Garraty, "U.S. Steel Versus Labor: The Early Years," *Labor History* 1 (Winter 1960): 3-38; Foner, *Policies and Practices,* 78-86.

21. Marguerite Green, *The National Civic Federation and the American Labor Movement* (Washington, D.C., 1956), 28-31; Mitchell to Easley, August 31, 1901, box 2, NCF Papers, New York Public Library.

22. Mitchell to Gompers, June 13, 1903, box 183, Mitchell Papers.

23. Ralph Easley to Mitchell, n.d. (probably end of August 1901), box 10, Mitchell Papers.

24. Mitchell to W. Wilson, September 6, 1901, box 21, Mitchell Papers.

25. Hanna to Mitchell, May 20, 1902, box 35, Mitchell Papers.

26. Ibid., May 29, 1902, box 35, Mitchell Papers.

27. *Chicago Record Herald,* July 21, 1902.

28. Quoted in Cornell, *Anthracite Coal Strike of 1902,* 103.

29. Mitchell expressed his tactics to the senator: "Under our constitution I am compelled to call a National convention upon the application of five Districts. Five Districts have already petitioned me to convene the convention, although I have kept these requests from the public and even from my own colleagues, with the hope that something might occur which would bring about a settlement." Mitchell to Hanna, May 22, 1902, box 35, Mitchell Papers.

30. Cornell, *The Anthracite Strike of 1902,* 116-17; Gowaski, "John Mitchell," 177-79.

31. Lincoln Steffens, "A Labor Leader of Today: John Mitchell and What He Stands for," *McClure's* 19 (August 1902): 356.

32. John Mulholland to Mitchell, November 8, 1902, box 33; Mitchell to "My dear wife," March 10, 1903, box 183: Mitchell Papers.

33. Cf., among others, Elizabeth Morris, "John Mitchell, the Leaders and the Man," *The Independent* (December 25, 1902); F. J. Warne, "John Mitchell, the Labor Leader and the Man," *Review of Reviews* (November 1902); Walter Weyl, "The Man the Miners Trust," *The Outlook* (March 1906); L. Steffens, "Labor Leader of Today." Mitchell took a very active part in publicizing the philosophy of the trade agreement by making an able use of the press network and any other public opinion channel he could mobilize. In this he was greatly aided by the personal and ongoing collaboration of Walter Weyl—who became a leading publicist of the period.

34. Steffens, "Labor Leader of Today," 355.

35. Mitchell to H.N. Taylor, April 2, 1902, box 1, Mitchell Papers.

36. Ibid.

37. Gowaskie, "John Mitchell," 194-99.

38. Stephen Scheinberg, "Theodore Roosevelt and the A.F. of L.'s Entry into Politics," *Labor History* 3 (Spring 1962): 132.

39. Mitchell to Hanna, July 30, 1902, box 35, Mitchell Papers.

40. Mitchell to Roosevelt, December 10, 1903, box 8, Mitchell Papers.

41. Ibid., February 22, 1906; Roosevelt to Mitchell, February 24, 1906: box 8, Mitchell Papers.

42. Gompers to Mitchell, telegram, March 20, 1906; Mitchell to Gompers, telegram, March 21, 1906: box 48, Mitchell Papers; *American Federationist* 13 (September 1906): 690.

4

THE NATIONAL CIVIC FEDERATION'S TRADE AGREEMENT CAMPAIGNS

The increasing attention the National Civic Federation is receiving from historians of the Progressive era stems from a clear acknowledgment of the central role this organization played in the reform movement of its period.[1] While there is substantial consensus on the composition of this organization, on the financial and political support on which it rested, and on the wide social forces it mobilized, a certain amount of ambiguity exists in regard to its short- and long-range objectives, the nature of the relationship existing between its labor members and its business members, and most importantly, the specific industrial and political needs it fulfilled.

The fact that the leading industrial and financial interests and the trade union establishment would join together in an organization purporting to benefit both employers and workers during one of the highest points of class warfare in the United States raises a number of complex questions. Faced with such a situation, it is not difficult to fall into moralistic interpretations by, for instance, explaining the behavior of the central historical actors on the basis of some abstract standard of ethical conduct (for example by claiming that the NCF labor members betrayed the trade union movement) or by pursuing a personalistic interpretation whereby events are explained in terms of the particular human qualities of the leading historical figures.

By focusing on the specific function the NCF fulfilled in the context of the dramatic emergence of the labor problem and by analyzing the

centrality of the trade agreement campaigns in the work of the federation, this chapter aims at clarifying some of the ambiguities raised above
and at the same time bringing one step forward our inquiry into the
trade agreement movement. If in fact the trade agreement was the
essence of trade unionism—as John Mitchell put it—and its advocacy
was part of the process of trade union advancement, with the NCF the
trade agreement acquired the character of a movement.[2] This was so
both for the diverse social forces the NCF was able to mobilize behind
its program and also for the impact its work had on the nation's industrial and political order.

When the National Civic Federation was launched in 1900, its program
appeared a most ambitious one by any standard; its founders envisioned
it as becoming a sort of "people's congress," a forum gathering "the best
brains of the nation" and dealing "freely [with] the great problems of
the day which were being handled only by the politicians in Congress and
in the state legislatures."[3] Its immediate program provided for a series of
national conferences on many subjects of industrial and public policy.
Soon, however, its leaders found themselves compelled to direct all their
resources and activities toward the most critical issue of the day—the relations between capital and labor. This was not an academic choice or one
associated with the leadership of the organization in this early period;
rather it was made necessary by the mounting conflict existing between
labor and capital, which demanded the study and articulation of solutions
that would have at the same time an immediate effect and a lasting character.

That this choice was most timely is borne out by the remarkable success the NCF began to enjoy as soon as it entered this field of endeavor.
At its first national conference in 1901, which was devoted to the topic
of industrial conciliation, the degree of success toward which the NCF
was headed had become apparent by the enthusiastic response of its
participants and the widespread attention the conference received nationally. Using a somewhat inflated vocabulary, S. W. Campbell, secretary of the Western Association of Shoe Jobbers and Manufacturers,
expressed a feeling typical of that of many other participants. For him
the conference had "laid the foundation for a connection between Capital and Labor, the like of which has never before been reached in the
history of the world."[4] In the course of this conference the importance
of the trade agreement was beginning to emerge as the model of indus-

trial relations best suited to prevent strikes and to minimize industrial disruption.[5] In large part, this was possible by the contribution made by the labor leaders who joined the ranks of the NCF and undertook in the ensuing months and years a central role within the organization. The labor leaders—for instance, John Mitchell, Daniel Keefe, president of the International Longshoremen's Association, J. W. Sullivan of the Typographical Union, W. D. Mahon, president of the Amalgamated Association of Street Railway Employees of America, Martin Fox, president of the Iron Molders Union, and of course Samuel Gompers—represented sectors where trade agreements had already been in operation. For the leaders of the NCF it was a matter, therefore, of utilizing to the utmost these trade agreement experiences, of studying their various aspects, and thus elaborating a model of industrial relations which would be valid for other sectors of American industry. Labor economist John Commons, who in this early period worked full time for the conciliation committee of the NCF, believed that the trade agreement would provide the mechanism for the "self-government of industry."[6]

These educational activities on the value and significance of the trade agreement for American industrial conditions intensified in the course of the following four years. During this period no fewer than three national conferences were devoted to the topic of the trade agreement, and in 1904 the NCF set up a permanent Trade Agreement Department. It was no coincidence that the two men who cochaired this department, John Mitchell and Francis Robbins (the largest employer of bituminous coal workers), represented an industrial sector where the trade agreement had yielded its most substantial fruits.[7]

Throughout these years the NCF became the official reference point for employers who wanted to base the industrial relations of their businesses on the trade agreement and wanted to be provided with both information and technical advice on how to set one up. The request for such services came not only from businessmen but also from government agencies. In 1901, for example, Warren Reed, chairman of the Massachussetts Board of Arbitration and Conciliation, asked for advice on the "formulation of some plan to deal with the labor problem," which he wanted to embody in his annual report to the Massachusetts legislature.[8] An important addition to this work of education was the publication, starting in 1903, of the *Monthly Review,* which soon had a wide circulation in industrial circles and among the professional public at large. The

Review became the most important national publication devoted to the discussion of the trade agreement and of a whole range of subjects and data related to it.

By the end of 1904 the editors of the *Review* could look with a certain pride at the industrial scene and at the fact that "more than fifty trade agreements [were] already [in existence] in the great national indus- tries."[9] The pride of the NCF leaders was more than justified; a large number of these agreements had been concluded directly by the NCF members or through the federation's offices. Among these were the agreement between the National Founders Association and the Iron Mold- ers Union, the interstate joint agreement in bituminous coal mining, the agreement between the Erie Dock Managers and the Longshoremen, the United States Steel-Metal Workers agreement, the Lithographers agree- ment, the agreement between the Newspaper Publishers' Association and the Typographical union and the Pressmen's union, the agreement be- tween the Brewers' Association and the Brewers' Union, the agreement between the Theatrical Managers and the Musicians' Protective Union, the agreement between the New York Metal Trades Association and the Boilmakers, the agreement between the New York Truckowners and the Contractors' Protective Association and the Teamsters' Union, and the New York Clothing Trades agreement: these were some of the most important agreements, showing the magnitude of the NCF involvement and its centrality in this field of endeavor.[10] This success, however, should be put in proper perspective; virtually all these agreements con- cerned unions and enterprises whose representatives were members, or even officers, of the federation. Moreover, in several cases these agree- ments were renewals of ones that had been in existence before the establishment of the NCF.

Concomitant with the work of publicizing and elaborating a trade agreement policy was another aspect of activity that immediately en- gaged the efforts and the resources of the NCF: the intervention of the federation in industrial disputes as a private mediation and conciliation body. It is essential to bring out this two-pronged approach the NCF took toward the labor problem, first, because it allows us to assess better the extent and the character of its successes in the industrial relations field and, second, because it makes it possible to place into a proper historical perspective the elements of continuity and discontinuity in the federa- tion's activities throughout the following years. The former aspect of this work—the promotion of the trade agreement—remained a long-range goal of the NCF; it never ceased to be the organization's official policy in the field of industrial relations, even after the labor struggles marking the years around the turn of the century began to subside. In 1908, in fact, the federation appointed John Mitchell as a full-time officer heading the Trade Agreement Department, and a few years later an attempt was made to revamp this aspect of the federation's work.[11] As late as 1919, the NCF produced and gave widespread publicity to "An Ideal Collective Contract" as part of its campaign to counter the antiunion efforts characterizing the postwar period.[12]

The intervention of the NFC in industrial disputes was a task that had a more immediate character. Here its main objective was to bring to an end as rapidly as possible any outbreak of industrial conflict, either upon the request of the parties to the dispute or by directly taking the initiative. Whether their intervention in a dispute resulted in the setting up of a trade agreement between the two parties was a matter of secondary importance. In this capacity the NCF embarked on an intense mediation and conciliation work involving some of the most important industrial dispute of those years. The machinists' national strike of 1900, affecting no fewer than 45,000 workers throughout the country and several dozen employers associated with the National Metal Trades Association, the U.S. Steel strike of 1901 and the 1902 anthracite coal strike are a few instances of the tasks that immediately confronted the NCF and show the magnitude of the work it engaged in.[13]

The enlistment of Hanna in the ranks of the NCF in 1901 gave this aspect of the federation's work a major impetus. It was not merely the prestige that Hanna gave the NCF in industrial and financial circles—a prestige that was a major asset in making the work of mediation effective; Hanna was also bringing to the federation a long and seasoned experience in labor-capital alliances and an influence extending to all political, business, and labor levels. His presence as president of the federation until his death in 1904 served to cement the coalition of forces that the NCF in effect represented.[14]

The establishment of the Industrial Department in December 1901, comprising some of the major employers and union presidents associated with the federation and designed "to obviate and prevent strikes and lockouts, [and] to aid in renewing industrial relations where a rupture has occurred," gave the NCF an organizational vehicle that surpassed any existing government agency both for its volume of work and for its effectiveness.[15] In effect, the NCF was filling an institutional vacuum generated by the extremely rapid development of the American produc-tive apparatus—the gap between the potential of conflict brought about by the growth of new productive forces and the existing institutional mechanisms designed to mediate such conflict.[16]

One only need look at the limitations of the existing agencies of mediation and arbitration. With the exception of the railroad transpor-tation sector, where the Erdman Act provided the machinery for the arbitration of interstate disputes, all other agencies—namely the various state boards of conciliation and mediation—had jurisdiction only in their respective states.[17] This situation made them virtually powerless to deal with disputes involving corporations whose operations extended to several states. This limitation had become increasingly evident with the rapid pro-cess of merger and corporate consolidation that had linked up business operations in many locations to the directives of the central offices. In his testimony to the U.S. Commission on Industrial Relations, John Lundrigan—former commissioner of the New York State Board of Media-tion and Arbitration—described in detail the difficulties his office en-countered in disputes of this character.[18] Moreover, state board media-tors complained about the inadequate resources at their disposal and about the lack of information necessary to keep them in closer touch with the industrial situation. The officers of the New York State Bureau of Mediation and Arbitration, for instance, felt that "the work of the Bureau [was] greatly hampered by . . . the inability to learn promptly of the existence of a strike or lockout, or what is perhaps of more im-portance, a threatened strike or lockout."[19] As late as 1910, at the National Convention of State Arbitration Boards held in Washington, D.C. (the first convention of this kind), state mediators took cognizance of the inadequacy of the existing machinery of mediation and arbitration. Faced "with the latter-day growth of industrial effort through the consoli-dation and amalgamation of productive agencies represented by employ-ing interests as well as the employees' unions and associations"—one report stated—and "with the fact that industry has eliminated State lines in every sense of the word," the convention admitted the failure of state boards to deal effectively with the problem of industrial disruption. The only solu-tion, it was felt, was for unions and employers to set up their own local boards of conciliation and arbitration "through the vehicle of the trade agreement."[20] This recognition of the boards' limitations was also expressed in the support that their officers generally gave the NCF work and in the assistance they often requested from the federation—at least during these years.

By contrast, the performance of the NCF was impressive. Relying on the enormous resources at its disposal, the NCF was in a position to intervene promptly in a dispute and exert its influence before the disruption spread; it could also mobilize the necessary means to prevent interruption of production. Geographical distances did not constitute any major obstacle for the NCF. One case often cited by both advocates and enemies of the federation involved a threatened strike in Iberia, Louisiana, between the International Longshoremen's Association—with headquarters in Detroit—and a transcontinental railway—with offices in San Francisco. Within six-hours' notice, the NCF men, acting from their New York office, were able to postpone the strike and to get the two parties to agree on an investigation of the matter.[21] By 1905 the NCF could look with pride to its accomplishments in the area of industrial disputes. It had been involved in about five hundred cases and could claim success in mediation and prevention of strikes and lockouts in about three-fourths of them.[22]

In one of his rare public speeches, delivered at the 1901 NCF Conference on Industrial Mediation and Conciliation, Hanna placed the labor problem in the context of the economic and political juncture of the country with the starkest clarity. "The great productive capacity of this country," Hanna told his audience, "has forced upon us the aggregation of capital and the creation of great material wealth seeking opportunity for investment. This rapidly increasing wealth must find investment, and to make the investment in industrials [sic] secure we must have industrial peace." And just as "the trusts have come to stay," he continued, so it is with "organized labor": both "are but forward steps in the great industrial evolution that is taking place."[23] Hanna's pronouncement would in effect become the programmatic line of the NCF for the ensuing years. The establishment of the Industrial Department, which grew out of that conference and was chaired by Hanna himself, the exceptional organizational skills of Ralph Easley, and the precious collaboration of top labor leaders would quickly turn that program into a well-enacted political strategy.

If there was one important element distinguishing Hanna and Easley from many other capitalist spokesmen of their day, it was their acknowledgment of the objective power the workers' movement was consolidating within the American productive apparatus—even if this power was not directly reflected in the formal political framework of the country. The gains won by labor during that current cycle of strikes, both in terms of union growth and of working and wage conditions, provided concrete corroboration.

It was essential that this power—part of the process of industrial evolution—be channeled into an "evolutionary" course and not a "revolutionary" one, as Easley and his associates continually reiterated. Above all, it was essential to avoid the Homesteads and the Pullmans—not only because they were costly economically but also, and more importantly, because they were politically dangerous. In order to accomplish this, there was no better way, no more progressive way, than to extend to trade unions social and institutional recognition, thus ensuring that their development would follow a path compatible with the productive expansion of those years. For Hanna this was both a practical and a political exigency. That organized labor deserves the trust of the employing class, he told the same audience, "is demonstrated by the fact that where the concerns and interests of labor are entrusted to able and honest leadership, it is much easier for those who represent the employers to come into close contact with the laborer, and, by dealing with fewer persons, to accomplish results quicker and better."[24] Politically the extension of institutional recognition to the trade unions seemed the best avenue to inject a much needed stability in the relationship between capital and labor, thus defusing the potential threat flowing from the confrontation of those two social forces. As Hanna put it on another occasion, "my plan is to have organized union labor Americanized in the best sense, and thoroughly educated to an understanding of its responsibilities, and in this way to make it the ally of the capitalist, rather than a foe with which to grapple."[25]

It is not difficult to see how in this strategic perspective, the American Federation of Labor would constitute the essential terrain of intervention in order to make this program operative. Even if the AFL represented only a minority of the American labor force—as its enemies continually charged—in reality it had already emerged as the dominant force over the workers' movement, at least in the eyes of the American capitalist class. The prompt adherence of some of the top AFL leaders (such as Gompers and Mitchell) to the NCF industrial program, moreover, made such a project concrete and realizable. Even before the establishment of the Industrial Department and before Hanna took official charge of the NCF industrial work, the outline of this political operation had become evident. During the intense activity of mediation during the U.S. Steel strike of 1901, Easley in fact made clear to Hanna the direction in which the NCF should move with respect to the AFL leaders. "If this trouble gets settled," Easley wrote, "I want to get the labor end of our Committee with you some place where you can read a riot act to them and make them understand what they have to do to keep the friendship of yourself and friends. They will take anything from you because they believe in you."[26] Besides revealing the frame of mind in which Easley operated, this note is even more significant when one considers that it was the labor leaders who put pressures on Hanna so that he would get involved in the NCF work.[27]

A program of this kind could hardly have been accomplished without the active cooperation of the labor establishment. As Gompers explained to the members of a committee of the New York Central Federated Union, "the National Civic Federation, *without a well-organized, thoroughly alert trade union movement, would be absolutely futile,* and perhaps its very existence unnecessary."[28] The labor leaders had in fact brought to the NCF the experience associated with a number of well-established trade agreement systems, and they took an active role in the day-to-day operations of the organization, guarding it against the repeated attacks coming from various labor quarters.

How can one explain the labor leaders' active association with the leading spokesmen of the American capitalist class at a time when class warfare in the United States had reached such a high level? For Gompers and Mitchell, the labor program of the NCF, far from hindering the growth of the trade union movement, offered the possibility of pursuing goals that were common to the NCF and the AFL. As Gompers put it, "with the growth in our movement, the greater intelligence our membership manifests, the higher and deeper the interests of our fellow-workers in the success of the cause of labor, in the same degree will the National Civic Federation be helpful to us in attaining the purpose for which we are organized, and to attain them with the least possible friction or contest.[29]

One of these common goals was the need to strengthen the AFL hegemony in the face of a growing workers' movement and to consolidate its position of power vis-à-vis other social groups. In this sense, the social recognition of the labor movement—which the NCF advocated—

coincided fully with the theory of trade unionism held by Mitchell and Gompers; however, this demanded a continuous action aimed at holding in check not only the social and economic groups that directly opposed this process but also the working class as a whole.

An important illustration of this communality of objectives was the action that both the NCF and the labor leaders undertook against sympathetic strikes. These strikes were a major source of concern for the NCF leaders, both because they posed a serious threat to the legality of the trade agreement, which the NCF and organized labor were seeking to establish, and also because they were a form of workers' warfare that in many cases escaped the control and planning of labor leaders. Although there are no available statistics on sympathetic strikes for the period under review, we do know that between 1898 and 1903 strikes not ordered by labor unions averaged one-fourth of the total strikes;[30] one can safely infer that a large portion of this number were sympathetic strikes.

Apart from the more or less regular recurrence of these strikes and their disruptive effects on industrial production, sympathetic strikes were viewed by the NCF and the labor leaders as a potential political danger. As an expression of working class solidarity, sympathetic strikes generated an atmosphere most conducive to the growth of rank-and-file militancy—a militancy that in most cases manifested itself as outright defiance of top-level union leadership and strategy. Thus the NCF, backed by its labor members, conducted vigorous campaigns in its press and in its public conference decrying this kind of strike. Some of the most delicate and exacting maneuvers carried out by the NCF and its labor members during this early period were aimed at preventing sympathetic strikes, which could have had disastrous effects on their policies as well as on the nation's economy. This was evident with two of the most significant labor-capital confrontations of this period—the U.S. Steel strike of 1901 and the anthracite coal strike of 1902. In the Steel case, the NCF failed to bring about an agreement that would be satisfactory to the Amalgamated workers, as Easley himself admitted.[31] It had, however, succeeded, largely because of the efforts of Mitchell and Gompers, in preventing other sectors of organized labor from joining the steel workers in a sympathetic strike.

In the case of the anthracite coal miners' strike, the NCF leaders were forced to realize how subtle the dividing line separating a sympathetic strike from a general strike could be. When the strike was well into its third month, Easley expressed to Gompers great apprehension when he

learned "that a scheme was on foot to have the Executive Committee
of the American Federation of Labor—representing organized labor of
this country—call on Mr. Morgan—as the recognized head of organized
capital, to learn his attitude toward their cause." Unless Morgan took a
position against the attitude of the anthracite operators, Easley continued,
"a convention [would] be called of the representatives of all the crafts
engaged in his various interests, the purpose being to bring about a general strike."[32]

Despite the fact that the NCF's efforts at getting a trade agreement
established in anthracite coal mining had failed, the NCF leaders could
claim the strike a victory in another sense: the "riot act" approach had
worked admirably, and what could have been the major general confrontation between capital and labor up to that time had been averted. Hanna
proclaimed publicly that "the test had come and the men have won the
confidence of the people of this country."[33]

Another objective the labor leaders felt they could pursue in common
with the NCF concerned the ideological campaigns the federation undertook against the socialist threat, as well as against the antilabor movement
led by the National Association of Manufacturers and other employers'
associations. But if the NAM opposition was a frontal one and could be
easily identified for the radicalism of its antilabor public campaigns, the
socialist threat was much more difficult to deal with; to a large extent it
was rooted within the labor movement, which became its main vehicle
of action. Gompers, Mitchell, and other NCF labor members, who had
to face an ongoing socialist opposition at all levels of their labor movement, found in the NCF and in its antisocialist ideological campaigns a
most resourceful and authoritative ally. The NCF leaders saw the organization as the vanguard of a national movement, whose main task would
be to block the inroads of socialism in American society. As early as
1901, in fact, Easley expressed to Hanna his concern about the "danger
of revolution and anarchy" the country was facing and proposed to make
the most effective use of the NCF as a "movement" against those forces.[34]
Hanna shared thoroughly this concern. For him, too, the "menace" of the
day was "the spread of a spirit of socialism, one of those things which
is only half understood and is more or less used to inflame the popular
mind against all individual initiative and personal energy, which has
been the very essence of American progress." Hanna seemed to be confident that the American labor movement would succeed in remaining

immune from such a threat. "Many of the ills that have crept into labor organization are importations from older countries," he maintained, "and will not live here because they are not fitted to our conditions." Moreover, Hanna continued, "The American labor unions are becoming more and more conservative and careful in their management, and are not likely to be led away from the straight road by hot-headed members."[35]

Apart from these factors, which were prompted by the need to guard the growth of the AFL unions from internal and external attacks, the labor members all shared in varying degrees the belief that the industrial work and program of the NCF coincided in large measure with the objectives of the labor movement as they envisaged them. For instance, Mitchell's overzealous and highly ideological support of the NCF was tempered by a more cautious and realistic attitude exhibited by Gompers in this regard. To conclude that Gompers was "ensnared by the NCF leaders into a "program of collaborating with the employers" is to oversimplify a relationship that was much more complex.[36] A careful review of Gompers's long association with the NCF, based on the records of this organization, reveals that his participation in the federation's industrial program rested on his keen awareness of the social and economic power the AFL commanded among wide sectors of American society. In a very important sense, Gompers had joined the NCF on his own terms and on the assumption that concrete benefits would accrue from this association. The social recognition the NCF granted to the labor movement was an essential precondition for the institutionalization of labor's economic power, which was a basic tenet in Gompers's conception of "industrial self-government." In this context the trade agreement—something that had been invented neither by capitalists nor by politicians but had evolved from the workers' organized strength—made this perspective concrete and realizable. It also made the NCF and its trade agreement policy an important ally through which this goal could be partially pursued.

For Gompers the trade agreement—as an institution founded on the workers' economic power—and the NCF—as a nongovernmental body in which industrial decisions could be jointly made—fitted quite well with his "voluntarism" and with "his basic mistrust of politics and [his] determination to rely solely upon economic organization."[37] Gompers's active involvement in the NCF's trade agreement program, therefore, made his voluntarism not merely an ideological conception but a political praxis.

Although his concept of the trade agreement as the basis for the self-regulation of industry was articulated with greater lucidity during the last years of his life, it had been developed since his early association with the NCF and was reflected in the work he envisaged as growing out of that association. In this work there was already foreshadowed his distinction between "political government" and "industrial government," as well as the need to differentiate between "political law" and "industrial law." In later years this distinction would become increasingly clear-cut, and he would write, "Political law, where it touches industry, for the most part fumbles and retards. The first idea of the political law-maker is to forbid something; to forbid trusts, to forbid strikes, to forbid the very things that make for progress and development of civilization," for "political government scarcely knows what is going on." Gompers thus saw the necessity for industry to develop its own law, for this alone could regulate its functioning, promote its progress and efficiency, and bring about true industrial democracy. Contrary to "political law," "industrial law," Gompers added, "is designed to make things work." In this context collective bargaining (as the trade agreement was in later years called) was central for this self-regulating industrial order that Gompers envisaged. Through collective bargaining, in fact, industry would both legislate and enact industrial laws. "Industry goes on, making laws. Employers make laws and workers make laws. Both sitting together make laws." He continued, "the laws that are built as a result of organization are the laws that can be agreed to by those who must live under them. That is important. There may be much crudeness, but in the end it is the way of democracy at work." In this dualism between political government and industrial government and between political law and industrial law, Gompers seemed confident about its final result: "Industry is more powerful than politics, and it will find a way to be served."[38] But by the time Gompers was writing these words, collective bargaining was well into the darkest period of its history.

If the NCF constituted the platform through which some of the leading exponents of capital and of organized labor sought to pursue a common objective—the orderly growth and integration of the American trade union movement in the political economy of the country—the trade agreement became the institutional structure that permitted this political operation to be carried out. The trade agreement policy was therefore accompanied by an intense ideological activity aimed at strengthening in the minds of the public its value and its significance. The ideology that NCF spokesmen articulated for this purpose was the notion of the "harmony of interests." The relationship between strategy and its corresponding ideology designed to make the former more effective needs to be stressed so that the educational activity of an organization such as the NCF is viewed not in a vacuum but rather as responding to precise programmatic exigencies.

The notion of "harmony of interests" among social classes was a postulate with roots in classical liberal theory, but the leaders of the NCF applied it most effectively to the solution of the labor problem. Capital and labor must cease to view each other as enemies or as constituting inherently opposing forces. They had a common task to perform in the great process of American progress and prosperity. As Hanna stated in front of a congressional committee in 1902, "It would be a misfortune at this time in our history, in our condition, to divide this industrial question by raising the issue that one part of it is labor and the other part capital. Those interests are identical and mutual."[39] For Louis Brandeis—who was very active in the New England Civic Federation and a leading advocate of the cause of organized labor—employer and employee were partners; this realization on the part of both sides, Brandeis argued in the pages of the *NCF Review*, was a crucial guarantee to insure industrial peace, efficiency, and progress.[40] And Ralph Easley, the founder and the main influence behind the NCF, repeatedly took pride in pointing out that his organization was the only one that "would bring capital and labor into harmony."[41]

Of all the NCF labor members, John Mitchell was no doubt the most articulate propounder of that ideology. In the preface to his much publicized book, *Organized Labor,* Mitchell emphasized that there was "not even a necessary fundamental antagonism between the laborer and the capitalist . . . the interest of the one is the interest of the other, and the prosperity of the one is the prosperity of the other." Not without reason Mitchell dedicated the book "to a better understanding between those two great factors of production," "labor and capital."[42]

Resting on the postulate of the "harmony of interests" between capital and labor, the trade agreement could therefore be extolled by NCF spokesmen for the vital function it would play in bringing about indus-

trial peace in a conflict-ridden America. John Mitchell summarized this
point better than anyone else. He told an NCF audience, "The trade
agreement is the bridge between labor and capital. It restores, as far as
it is possible to do, the personal relationship, the mutual interest which
existed prior to the advent of the factory system. It is an acknowledgment of the interdependence of labor and capital, a recognition of the re-
ciprocity of interests of employer and employee."[43] For Daniel Keefe,
president of the International Longshoremen's Association and a central
labor figure within the NCF, the trade agreement was "the great and
ultimate factor in the solution of the industrial problem." He predicted
that the trade agreement "will in the near future establish an economic
unity of interests between the two great contending forces, that will
eventually become co-operative in its broadest sense, and the final
relations will be that of business partnership."[44]

As their advocates saw it, one of the leading features of the trade
agreement was that it enhanced the respectability of organized labor
by allowing it to enter into a contractual relationship with capital. The
existence of a contract, labor and business leaders would point out, was
clear evidence that both parties considered the other worthy of respect
and of being entrusted with the social responsibility that such a relation entailed. Hence the repeated emphasis by conservative labor leaders
on the "sanctity of the contract" and on the duty of workingmen to
honor it. When at the 1908 convention of the United Mine Workers of
America, Bill Haywood, who represented the Western Federation of
Miners, stood up and warned the miners that the contract was the
weapon the employer used to "bind miners up for a period" or "to
make it impossible" for miners "to do anything for themselves or anybody else," Mitchell refuted that position, stressing that "the contract
system in [their] organization was one of its fundamental principles."[45]

Through its contractual relationship with the employers, labor could
learn the virtues of business practices and principles, thus making its
partnership with capital more stable and effective, even during times of
unfavorable trade conditions. "The trade agreement in modern commer-
cialism," James Duncan, secretary of the Granite Cutters' International
Association of America, stated at the 1908 NCF conference on trade
agreements, "may well be termed the safety-valve to profitable and progressive manufacturing business."[46] And John Mitchell could point with
pride to the coal-mining dispute of 1904 when the miners had "voted to

accept a reduction in wages." "I think," Mitchell stated, "their action has done more to strengthen and encourage this trade agreement than any other one thing that has happened in our industrial affairs."[47]

Some attentive industrial relations theorists saw immediately the implications of the 1904 settlement between the miners and the coal operators for the future of American labor relations. F. Warne concluded an article for the *Annals* by stating that "trade unionism under the stimulus of the UMW of A has come to be a business operation on a large scale."[48] John Commons, a most perceptive student of labor relations, saw in the miners' willingness to accept the imperatives of the coal trades, even when that meant a cut in wages, "an unusual evidence of business sagacity." This was due in large measure to the nation's "business management as well as [to] the trade agreement system which made such an outcome possible."[49]

The kind of industrial and labor relations engendered by the trade agreement system made it possible for workers to be educated in the virtues of democratic organizations and decision-making processes. "The bitterest radicals," G. W. Traer, president of the Illinois Coal Operators Association, pointed out, "learn about the employers' difficulties, competitive and otherwise, to an extent which they could learn in no other way, and after several meetings frequently become conservative men."[50] This was as much true for the labor leadership. According to Brandeis, stable trade unionism allowed labor leaders to gain an invaluable experience, which "almost invariably makes the leaders reasonable and conservative."[51]

According to some NCF employers, even the workers' personality and outward appearance could be affected by such a process. For Francis Robbins, president of the Pittsburgh Coal Company and cochairman of the NCF's Trade Agreement Department, the trade agreement had had an "elevating effect upon the intelligence and character of the union leaders." Ever since the trade agreement had been introduced in the bituminous coal trade, "one is struck," he told an NFC audience, "by the change in the personality of the miners' delegates. Instead of seeing flannel shirts, hob-nail shoes, no vests, and often no coats, you [now] meet a body of men as well dressed as any body of men gathered from the middle class in any Eastern city. There had been a corresponding change in the intelligence, as shown in the faces of delegates and particularly perceptible in those who have argued scale questions [with the workers] . . . for the past fifteen years."[52]

Tight and constant leadership control over the rank and file was essential to the success of the trade agreement system. This was best evidenced by the attitude that NCF-associated labor leaders took toward the sympathetic strike. "Sympathetic strikes should never be countenanced or sanctioned by this organization," Daniel Keefe told the longshoremen at their 1904 annual convention. He went on to stress that "our honour and integrity as an organization is bound up in our contracts and agreements, and our very manhood [is] at stake; to violate those contracts by a sympathetic strike would be suicide and dishonor."[53] For many employers, the necessity of exerting a constant control over the rank and file was prompted by the functional requirements of production. After all, it was the labor leader who, through close contact with the employers, knew the conditions of the trade and thus was in a position to serve best the interests of the men. Moreover, "by dealing with fewer persons," as Hanna put it, "it becomes possible to accomplish results quicker and better."[54]

The exercise of restraint over rank-and-file militance was therefore a basic precondition for the attainment of stable trade relations and thus for the success of the trade agrement. Writing to John Commons in 1914, Easley asserted with satisfaction that "the national leaders of the trade unions . . . had seldom been defied by their local organizations." Had it been otherwise, Easley continued, "the trade agreement would not be worth defending."[55]

By utilizing an extraparliamentary and extragovernmental agency, the NCF had succeeded, during its first five years of activities, in carrying out one of the major political undertakings of the entire Progressive era. It had contained some of the most disruptive effects resulting from the dramatic emergence of the labor problem and had channeled the growth of the trade union movement along a course that best fulfilled the economic and political needs of an expanding industrial state; all this, with the least effect on the political apparatus of the country. In a very basic way, the trade agreement had provided the institutional framework to make this operation possible. As a form of contractual relation between employers and unions that had already come into existence in a number of trades and industries, the trade agreement was made to embody the essence of democratic legality for the field of industrial and labor relations and elevated to a universal policy for the pursuit of industrial peace. In the meantime, however, profound changes were underway in the industrial framework of the nation—changes that threatened the status quo of narrow craft unionism and hence, to a large extent, the very organizational basis on which the trade agreement was made to rest.

NOTES

1. The most detailed study of the NCF is Marguerite Green, *The National Civic Federation and the American Labor Movement, 1900-1925* (Washington, D.C., 1956); cf. also Gordon M. Jensen, "The National Civic Federation: American Business in an Age of Social Change and Social Reform, 1900-1910" (Ph.D. diss., Princeton University, 1956); Philip S. Foner, *The Policies and Practices of the American Federation of Labor, 1900-1909* (New York, 1964), 61-110; James Weinstein, *The Corporate Ideal in the Liberal State* (Boston, 1968); cf. also the debate between Foner and Weinstein in James Weinstein and David W. Eakins, *For a New America* (New York, 1970), 101-24.

2. John Mitchell to the editor of the *United Mine Workers Journal,* July 31, 1908, box 87A, Mitchell Papers, Catholic University of America.

3. Quoted in Greene, *National Civic Federation,* 9.

4. S. W. Campbell to Easley, December 21, 1902, box 2, NCF Papers, New York Public Library.

5. Cf. *Industrial Conciliation: Report of the Proceedings of the Conference Held Under the Auspices of the National Civic Federation, December 16 and 17, 1901* (New York, 1902). Most of the papers given at this conference were reproduced in *Annals of the American Academy of Political and Social Science* 30 (July 1902).

6. John Commons, *Myself* (Madison, 1964), 72, 82ff.

7. *American Machinist* (May 16, 1901): 535; "For Industrial Peace," *Monthly Review* (NCF, June 1903): 6-9, 15; "A National Conference on Trade Agreements," *Monthly Review* (July 1904): 11-16; Cf. also Green, *National Civic Federation,* 85-86.

8. Warren Reed to Easley, October 23, 1901, box 2; M.F. Bowen to Easley, September 29, 1903, box 81: NCF Papers.

9. *NCF Review* (January 1905): 13

10. Cf. ibid. (June 1903): 12, 17; "A National Conference on Trade Agreements" (July 1904): 12, 14-17; (August 1904): 15.

11. "Trade Agreements to Be Promoted," *NCF Review* (September 1908): 1; Easley to Gompers, March 6, 1911, box 79a, NCF Papers.

12. Clarence E. Bonnett, *Employers' Associations in the United States* (New York, 1922), 410.

13. Cf. Green, *National Civic Federation,* 20-33, 43-56.

14. Ralph Easley, "Senator Hanna and the Labor Problem," *Independent* (March 3, 1904): 483-87; Herbert Croly, *Marcus Alonzo Hanna* (New York, 1912), esp. chap. 25.

15. "By-Laws of the Industrial Department of the NCF," quoted in Green, *National Civic Federation,* 500 (appendix II).

16. This is a dimension of the NCF's work that has not been sufficiently brought out by the historians of the federation. Neither the quasi-conspiratorial approach taken by Foner, nor Weinstein's emphasis on the educational and consciousness-building role of the NCF, take into due account the structural need that this organization fulfilled in the specific context of the labor problem of those years.

17. George Barnett, *Mediation, Investigation and Arbitration in Industrial Disputes* (New York, 1916), provides a thorough study of the operations of the state boards of New York, Massachusetts, and Ohio.

18. *U.S. Commission on Industrial Relations, Final Report and Testimony* (Washington, D.C., 1916), 2: 1907-1919 (hereafter cited as CIR, *Final Report).*

19. *Fifteenth Annual Report of the Board of Mediation and Arbitration of the State of New York [1901]* (Albany, 1902), 12.

20. CIR, *Final Report,* 2:1955-61. Similar views were voiced by some state mediators at an NCF conference on arbitration, in 1911; cf. *Proceedings of the Eleventh Annual Meeting of the National Civic Federation, New York, January 12 to 14, 1911* (New York, n.d.), esp. 248-52.

21. *The National Civic Federation: Its Methods and Its Aims* (New York, 1905), 19-20.

22. Jensen, "National Civic Federation," 124-25.

23. Marcus A. Hanna, "Industrial Conciliation and Arbitration," *The Annals* 20 (July 1902): 23-24.

24. Ibid., 25.

25. Marcus Hanna, *Mark Hanna, His Book* (Boston, 1904), 32.

26. Easley to Hanna, July 17, 1901, box 2, NCF Papers.

27. Green, *National Civic Federation,* 40.

28. Gompers to the Committee of the New York Central Federated Union, April 28, 1905, in *NCF Review* (May 15, 1905).

29. Ibid.

30. United States Bureau of Labor, *Twenty-first Annual Report of the Commissioner of Labor, 1906: Strikes and Lockouts* (Washington, D.C., 1907), 32.

31. Easley to Shaffer, September 10, 1901, box 2, NCF Papers.

32. Easley to Gompers, August 25, 1902, box 3, NCF Papers.

33. *NCF Monthly Review* (April 1903): 2.

34. Easley to Hanna, September 12, 1901, box 2, NCF Papers.

35. Hanna, "Industrial Conciliation and Arbitration," 36, 39, 44.

36. Foner, *Policies and Practices,* 61.

37. William M. Dick, *Labour and Socialism in America: The Gompers Era* (London, 1972), 113.

38. Samuel Gompers, *From Politics to Industry* (Washington D.C., n.d.), also appeared as article in the *American Federationist* (May 1923): 3ff.

39. Quoted in Stephen Scheinberg, "The Development of Corporation Labor Policies, 1900-1940" (Ph.D. diss., University of Wisconsin, 1967), 17.

40. "The Employer and Trade Unionism," *NCF Monthly Review* (August 1904): 11.

41. "Our Enemies," *NCF Monthly Review* (October 15, 1904): 8.

42. John Mitchell, *Organized Labor* (Philadelphia, 1903), ix, xii.

43. *NCF Review* (November 15, 1909): 10.

44. Ibid. (October 15, 1904): 6.

45. *Proceedings of the Annual Convention of the United Mine Workers of America, Indianapolis, January 21-February 3, 1903* (Indianapolis, 1908), 285.

46. *Proceedings of the Annual Convention of the National Civic Federation, New York, December 14-15, 1908* (New York, 1909), 24.

47. *NCF Monthly Review* (July 1904): 12.

48. Frank J. Warne, "The Miners' Union: Its Business Management," *Annals of the American Academy of Political and Social Sciences* 25 (1905): 85.

49. John Commons, ed., *Trade Unionism and Labor Problems* (Boston, 1905), 35.

50. *NCF Convention Proceedings,* 37.

51. *NCF Monthly Review* (August 1904): 10.

52. *NCF Review* (April 1913): 13.

53. "Against Sympathetic Strikes and for the Adherence to Trade Agreements," *NCF Monthly Review* (October 15, 1904): 6.

54. Hanna, "Industrial Conciliation and Arbitration," 25.

55. Quoted in Green, *National Civic Federation,* 64.

PART 2

The crisis of
organization in the
American labor movement

5

INDUSTRIAL CHANGES AND THE STRUGGLE FOR CONTROL

The middle of the first decade of the twentieth century has been characterized as "the beginning of a new era" in the organization of American industry.[1] To be sure, the transformation of the American industrial apparatus was a process that had made great leaps forward throughout the latter part of the nineteenth century; but in the first years of the twentieth century this process reached an unprecedented level, encompassing virtually all aspects of business activity. Under the thrust of the rapid economic growth that followed the 1890s depression, American industrialists saw themselves compelled to seek new organizational strategies in order to maintain and strengthen their newly acquired position of prominence in foreign markets, as well as to stabilize market conditions at home.[2] Of all the changes occurring in the organization of the economy in those years, the concentration of capital and the creation of giant corporations have attracted the widest attention from both students of that period and contemporary observers. To a great extent, this interest is more than justifiable, especially when one considers the dramatic manner in which such concentration occurred and the serious repercussions it had on the political and social framework of the nation.[3]

This process, however, was accompanied by other changes in the organization of industry—changes designed to rationalize further production methods so as to increase productivity and thus improve the economic performance of enterprises. The ample availability of new technology, new factory production techniques, and unlimited labor

supplies—all elements that especially characterized the years around
the turn of the century—added a major impetus to this movement. But
while these resources were available, how to gain full access to them
was a problem that in varying degrees confronted employers of all
industrial sectors. It was not merely a matter of finding new organizational solutions enabling them to utilize such available resources to the
utmost; it was also imperative for employers to break any barrier restricting their freedom of maneuver and impairing the achievement of
higher levels of development.

The craft organizations represented one such barrier. Especially in
sectors where skilled workers occupied a central role in the process of
production, craft organizations held considerable power. Through the so-
called union rules, craft unions had been in a position to impose on employers conditions bearing on virtually all aspects of the organization of
production: the manner in which new machinery and new work techniques were introduced, the number of apprentices to be allowed to
work in a given shop, the method of wage determination, and control
over the classification of work.[4] The shop committee—the basic union
structure that made sure that these rules were enforced and respected—
was a reality that few employers could escape.

The immediate effect of these rules was a restriction of output. An
inquiry conducted by the U.S. commissioner of labor in the early years
of the century among a large cross-section of industrial sectors indicates
that the limitation of output resulting from the enforcement of work
rules ranged from 10 to as high as 30 percent.[5] That such restriction reflected a position of power that unions held at the shop-floor level is
shown by the complaint voiced by one employer: "The [shop] committee controls the amount of output from molders. I think our output is
limited about 30 per cent. . . . Five years ago men were hunting jobs
and were amenable to the orders of the foreman; now we are hunting
men and when the foremen complain of reduced output the men
simply walk out."[6] In machine shops, for instance, one of the ways
through which productive capacity was restricted by craft organizations was through the so-called one-man-one-machine rule. As the expression implies, this regulation prevented members of the International Association of Machinists, one of the largest and most powerful
unions, from working on more than one machine at a time.[7]

In a circular letter to IAM's organizers, sent out by the union headquarters, the results of this rule were summarized as follows: "We pre-

vented the introduction of the two-machine system in 137 shops, employing 9,500 men. It is safe to say that if this system had been introduced the force of men would be reduced one-eighth; hence, in this we have saved the positions of 1,188, whose daily wages would amount to $2,613.60 per day, or $818,056.80 per year."[8]

But saving jobs was not the only justification for the enforcement of this type of rule. Machinists, as well as other skilled workers, were also fighting the increase in the speed of work resulting from the introduction of more advanced machinery and of new methods of wage payment that usually accompanied it. In no other case did American manufacturers face as fierce opposition from craft organizations as in their attempt to introduce piecework in their shops.

For the employers, piecework was more than just a technique of wage payment; it was an employers' policy designed to deal with the labor problem at the shop level. It allowed employers to utilize to the utmost the productive capacity of the workers and the machinery by inducing them to work more and faster. It also gave employers a great flexibility in planning the amount of output on a weekly, or even on a daily, basis. Moreover, piecework in all its variations—such as the so-called premium plan or the bonus system—enabled employers to break the rigidity of the wage structure by linking wages to the desired productivity levels. They thus took the determination of wages away from the autonomous control of the craft organizations.[9] Piecework thus resulted in substantial cuts in labor costs and a corresponding increase in productivity, an increase that was further boosted by the widespread practice of cutting rates. Employers adopting the piecework system claimed generally that it resulted in a 15 to 25 percent greater output as compared to the day-wage system.[10] It is therefore understandable that employers were enthusiastic about these systems. "The present is an unusually favorable time for the adoption of the system," wrote the *American Machinist,* a leading business journal, in 1901.

Shops are crowded with work and a greater output is wanted, while additional good workmen are hard to get. Peace in the industrial world seems to be assured for some time to come, and the opportunity for educating the workman to see its advantages to them is correspondingly great. Actual trial has never yet failed to do this and to make the workmen its enthusiastic advocates. Now is the time to convert them to it on a large scale and to thus lay the foundations for continued harmony.[11]

The workers' conversion, however, would not be easy in coming. Especially in the highly competitive sectors, where the position of a manufacturer could be improved by a quick change in the organization and methods of work, the battle became fierce. The machine industry provides the best example. Here the struggle for and against productivity was further intensified by the threat that German manufacturers began to pose, beginning around 1902.[12] The machinists' response, more than a mere resistance, became an all-out attack against productivity-boosting methods. At the same time when the IAM was fighting nationally to enforce the nine-hour day, thus strengthening the idea of the day-wage basis of remuneration, the union also began a campaign to oppose the introduction of new systems of wage determination. In July 1901 the IAM adopted a new section in its constitution that prohibited its members from accepting piecework.[13] Two years later, after a referendum among its members, the section was revised and made even more restrictive; members were "not to accept piece-work, premium incentives, task or contract system, under the penalty of expulsion."[14] A union report for 1901 stated that in that year "piecework was prevented in 114 shops, affecting 2,800 men"; it admitted that it had, however, been introduced "in 49 shops, affecting 3,653 men."[15] The record for the following two years shows the magnitude and the intensification of this struggle; "thirty-seven lodges . . . [had] prevented the introduction of the piece-work system in shops employing 4,500 men."[16]

Besides viewing piecework as a threat to their power over working conditions, skilled workers considered it pure and simple theft. As a union officer put it, "A change in method of work in a shop whereby each workman will have to expend from 50 to 100 per cent more energy, which in turn will produce 50 per cent to 100 per cent more product for the same pay, fully meets his idea of robbery."[17] Even employers would often concede this point: "Piece prices are fixed only to be cut as soon as the employee develops the ability to increase production," a New England industrialist admitted; "It does not require any great length of time for a workman to realize that he will get about the same amount of money whether he works fast or slow."[18] Moreover, workers knew that once piecework was introduced in a shop, the chances for wage raises would virtually vanish. An officer of the Metal Polishers' Union put it this way: "There is no record of a case where men get an

increase on piece price; it is cut, cut, from year to year, and men must
work harder for the same money. Day wages are often increased; piece
prices seldom, or never."[19]

This struggle against higher productivity was carried out not only by
unionized workers but also by nonunion workers. The same New England
industrialist referred to above explained, "[Also] in open shops there is
limitation of output, both by concerted action and by individuals acting
for themselves solely. It is following out the laws of self-preservation
that we have the limitation of output."[20] In a very important sense, this
was a daily struggle at a shop-floor level of a particular type of labor
force that for decades had played a central role in the development of
industry and in the building up of the labor movement but now stood
in the way of a more rapid and dynamic expansion of American productive resources.

Finally, craft unions stood as a rigid barrier to a full utilization of the
labor market. The dramatic expansion and recomposition of the work
force—enhanced by the high rate of immigration and internal migration
of those years—made it imperative for employers to enjoy a free hand
so they could mold the expanding work force according to the technical
requirements of production.[21] Craft unions, however, undermined this
possibility. Through the enforcement of rules determining the number
of apprentices to be allowed in a shop, through the limitations imposed
on the number of helpers, and through the closed-shop policy where
they could enforce it, craft organizations exerted a control on the
supply of labor power that went beyond the confines of the factory
shop, extending into the labor market at large. In a very important
sense, they controlled not only the distribution of skilled labor power
but also the mechanisms for its reproduction.

A general manager of a Chicago molding plant expressed this state of
affairs very clearly: "This rule against non union men prevents employers
from using or getting at any surplus of labor that is adrift and interferes
with the natural law of supply and demand in labor. . . . Restriction is
20 per cent over that of five years ago, and as we cannot permit the
total output of our plant to decrease, the continuous employment of
more men becomes necessary."[22] Richard Moldenke, secretary of the
American Foundrymen's Association, warned his associates in 1903
of the dangers that unions posed to the foundry industry through their
control of the supply of skilled labor. This, he felt, prevented a fuller

utilization of their plants' capacity. "You may not be aware," he stated, "that many foundries are already running two shifts and could easily arrange for three if there were molders enough available."[23]

How to cope with the power that craft organizations held in the process of production was a problem that had confronted employers ever since workers had begun to organize. But if the problem was a common one, the answers were by no means uniform. Monopoly corporations, for instance, were able to command vast financial resources and political power. They were thus in a position to risk an all-out confrontation with the unions in an attempt to drive them out of their sectors. In the case of the anthracite coal industry, this strategy dated back to the 1870s when the industry came under the control of a handful of railroad companies. The steel industry provides another illustration of this strategy, which was begun by Carnegie with the Homestead strike and was carried to its completion by U.S. Steel in the early 1900s. The attack against the Amalgamated Association of Iron, Steel and Tin Workers went hand in hand with a whole series of corporate policies designed to undermine the power that steel workers held by virtue of their skills and thus to restructure the work force, making it totally subordinate to the new productive goals of the steel giant.[24]

Other large manufacturing corporations pursued similar courses of action, combining overt antiunion tactics with long-range managerial policies and production techniques designed to weaken gradually the position of skilled workers in the process of production. The National Cash Register Company—the leading manufacturer and exporter in its field—and the International Harvester Company—which held the monopoly on harvesting machinery production—provide two of the major illustrations for this period.[25]

Other corporate giants, such as General Electric, which operated in new manufacturing sectors where skilled workers were not so central to the organization of work, found themselves in a better position to make full use of the technical and labor resources available. Thus, GE instituted in some of its plants, with relative ease, a full-fledged apprenticeship program, which played a major part in the corporation's attempt to create its own internal labor market and thus assume full control over its labor relations.[26]

Manufacturers who lacked the resources to fight unions on their own but operated in highly competitive sectors were more vulnerable to the restrictions exerted by skilled workers and had to seek different means. Employers' associations rose to meet this need. These organizations, in fact, provided the vehicle by which employers could unite their resources and carry out a combined effort aimed at weakening the power of the craft organizations and eventually eradicating them from their sectors.[27] Employers' associations were not entirely new to the American industrial scene. The Stove Founders' National Defense Association, for example, had been organized in Cincinnati in 1886, and throughout the years had played a central role in working out labor relation policies among its members.[28] Following the turn of the century there was a major proliferation of these organizations, as well as a radical antilabor turn among the ones already in existence.

This development in capitalist organization and the role these associations played in the struggle to rationalize production have been largely overshadowed by the open-shop movement, which roughly dates from that period and was led by the National Association of Manufacturers. As important as this movement was in the struggle between capital and labor, it tended to give total prominence to the ideological and institutional face of that struggle—and in fact this is where labor and business historiography have generally placed their emphases.[29] In the NAM's campaigns aimed at eradicating trade unionism from American industry, labor unions were portrayed as "socialistic," essentially "un-American" organizations that posed a fundamental threat to "individual liberty" and to the freedom of contracts. At a more fundamental level, however, these campaigns responded to the need to break the barriers that craft unions had raised against a fuller development of American productive capacity. In his historic speech marking the beginning of the NAM's antilabor campaigns, the association's president, David M. Parry, went to the root of the problem: "Organized labor," he told his audience,

takes no account of the varying degrees of natural aptitude and powers of endurance displayed by individuals and seeks to place all men in each particular trade on the same dead level as respects his daily output and his daily wage. Thus a premium is placed upon indolence and incompetency and there is a restriction of human effort, reducing the aggregate production and increasing the cost of things produced. . . . It foists upon employers rules limiting the number of apprentices, some unions going so far as to say there shall be no apprentices.[30]

To the attacks that the NAM undertook at the propagandistic and legislative level, there corresponded the efforts by employers' associations to undermine the autonomy of unions at the level of production and to impose on their work force policies designed to transfer the determination of industrial relations fully into their hands. But more than merely complementary, these movements were different fronts of a concerted employers' attack against the power of skilled workers and their corresponding organizations. The dual membership that most manufacturers held in both types of employers' organizations, as well as the interlocking leadership existing among them, provides ample evidence for this assertion.[31]

Though operating in different industrial sectors and despite differences in organizational framework, most employers' associations worked out industrial relations policies that were strikingly similar in their objectives. Employers had to have free access to the labor market by controlling hiring and firing policies and by determining the number of apprentices to be trained in their shops; moreover, they had to gain undisputed control over all matters pertaining to amount of output, methods of work, and systems of wage payments.

Articles 1, 4, 5, and 6 of the declaration of principles adopted by the National Metal Trades Association—a leading national employers' association with a membership of over 300 firms employing more than 30,000 workers—are representative of the kind of relations employers sought to establish with their work force:[32]

Concerning Employees. 1. Since we, as employers, are responsible for the work turned out by our workmen, we must have full discretion to designate the men we consider competent to perform the work and to determine the conditions under which that work shall be prosecuted, the question of the competency of the men being determined solely by us. While disavowing any intention to interfere with the proper functions of labor organizations, we will not admit of any interference with the management of our business.

Apprentices, etc. 4. The number of apprentices, helpers and handymen to be employed will be determined solely by the employer.

Methods and Wages. 5. We will not permit employees to place any restriction on the management, methods or production of our shops, and will require a fair day's work for a fair day's pay.

Employees will be paid by the hourly rate, by premium system, piece-work or contract, as the employers may elect.

Freedom of employment. 6. It is the privilege of the employee to leave our employ whenever he sees fit, and it is the privilege of the employer to discharge any workman when he sees fit.[33]

The attempt to enforce these labor policies was by no means confined to the manufacturing sector. In the building construction industry, for instance, where a number of employers' associations came into existence after the turn of the century, craft unions were increasingly being confronted by labor policies designed to put an end to the long-established union rules.[34]

The implementation of these policies, however, could not occur without a fierce and protracted confrontation. In 1903 was a widespread mobilization of employers' associations; the NAM launched its antilabor program, and there was a major intensification of the struggle in the area of productivity. By 1904 this struggle had reached its highest peak: over one-third (38.92%) of the strikes fought in that year involved recognition of unions and union rules, affecting no fewer than 7,129 establishments.[35] And the number of lockouts resulting from that cause was the highest ever.[36]

This confrontation was made even sharper by the sudden deterioration of business conditions. Beginning in the second half of 1903 and continuing well into 1904, a short but severe recession hit the American economy.[37] For many employers this crisis provided the grounds for intensifying their attacks against labor organizations, whose ranks were being decimated by the high rate of unemployment. One report submitted to the board of directors of the International Harvester Company in August 1904 recommended, after surveying the current general business conditions, "it would seem that we are in a more favorable position today to have a fight with Labor, if necessary, than we have been for some time past or are likely to be in for a long time to come. The general situation as regards supply of labor is that the supply exceeds the demand and there are a great many men out of employment and ready for work. The labor unions in general are not financially strong; they have spent a large amount of their resources fighting strikes up to date. It is not believed that they want to have any serious fight." One month later, at the expiration of the union contracts, this strategy was successfully put into effect.[38]

The business crisis also gave employers the opportunity to effect changes in methods of production that had been fiercely opposed by craft organizations. W. P. David, vice-president of the National Machine Tool Builders' Association, told his associates at the height of the recession, "We must take advantage of the present depression to improve our plants, introducing new methods and making such changes as we may find necessary in the production of our machines."[39]

Many unions, even powerful ones, were soon forced on the defensive. In a circular letter sent out in September 1903 by the executive of the International Association of Machinists, machinists were advised to be extremely cautious in undertaking any strike action. The letter describes the climate surrounding the employers' attack:

The general trend of business throughout our jurisdiction is not the best at this time. In some sections of the country business is gradually easing off and large reductions in force are taking place. The various manufacturing associations are, in many instances, only too willing to force strikes upon us with a view to disrupting our local unions and depleting our treasuries. We must be exceptionally careful not to give these associations any undue advantage over us, and exercise the greatest care and diplomacy to avoid any unnecessary trouble at this time.[40]

In June of the following year, an executive memo sent out from IAM's headquarters asked the membership whether to suspend article XXII, section 2, of the union's constitution—the clause that forbade machinists to work under any form of wage payment other than on a day basis.[41]

The struggle became particularly fierce in the Chicago area, one of the main centers of American manufacturing. A labor paper reported in the summer of 1904, "Shops in Chicago, backed by all the capitalistic organizations which have been fighting unionism, are making the greatest efforts ever known in that city to break up our unions there, and they are willing to sacrifice a large sum of money in that effort."[42] According to the *International Metal Worker*, employers' organizations—particularly those in the metal trades—had intentionally concentrated their efforts in the Chicago area, hoping that once unions were defeated there, they would easily yield in other parts of the country.[43] Samuel Hays, in his labor column for the *International Socialist Review*, described the employers' attack as a "war of extermination . . . against the metal workers, such as the moulders, machinists, metal polishers

and brass workers etc." and predicted that it "[would] be continued
and made more general." "As far as I am able to learn from official
journals and discussions with national union representatives," Hays
added, "practically all organizations will be on the defensive in 1905."[44]

By the end of 1904, the employers' offensive had come to fruition.
The growth of unionization appeared effectively checked, and the following year, 1905, would actually show the first decrease since 1897.
The percentage of strikes lost was the highest since 1894, totaling almost
50 percent of all strikes for the year. Moreover, wage cuts had been
forced by employers in virtually all industrial sectors.[45]

But other effects, of a longer-range nature, had been put in motion
by this capitalist offensive. Through the stepped-up introduction of new
machinery and the reorganization of work processes, employers were
creating chaos among craft unions. In some instances, in fact, these
changes had the effect of making certain trades obsolete; in other cases,
new categories of workers, who could not be fitted into any of the
existing craft delineations, were coming into being at a fast rate. In still
other cases, craft demarcations that had been rigidly set up and jealous-
ly guarded by craft unions were being blurred under the effects of these
changes. A writer in the *Blacksmiths' Journal* summed up the effect
these changes were having for his trade and for the power relations
between unions and employers:

We have made tools, formers and machinery, and the boy and the helper
are using them in ever increasing numbers, with a more than corresponding decrease in blacksmiths . . . the apprentice system seems to be becoming obsolete, many corporations preferring to advance helpers to run the
forge and the furnace. . . . In many parts of the country where our unions
are established there are very few eligible members and it becomes somewhat burdensome to maintain a good working union and be strong enough
to make any demand and expect to get it, and then should any trouble
occur, the corporations can, would, and do get along for months, if necessary; with helpers, heaters, and helpersmiths. This is the weak point in
our armor where we could be easily defeated and our employers understand this.[46]

The immediate effect this process had for organized labor was internal
warfare among craft unions. Jurisdictional disputes—which had been part
of the labor movement since the establishment of the AFL—intensified
at an enormous rate in the years around and after the turn of the century,

plaguing the unions and engaging the AFL bureaucracy in endless wrangles.[47] The problem became so acute that at the 1902 AFL convention, Gompers had to devote a large part of his presidential report to this issue, warning his audience that the rapid escalation of jurisdictional disputes could soon throw the federation "in the midst of an internecine contest unparalleled in any era in the industrial war."[48] Gompers also expressed this concern in private. Writing to a union official in 1903 on the subject of "jurisdictional divisions and separations," he said, "I have had much experience, and it is the most heart rending, most destructive, most time-consuming of anything else in our work, bringing forth less results for extraordinary efforts than any thing that has yet come to my observation in the labor movement."[49]

What most worried both union officials and members alike was the effect that these diputes had in weakening their organizations in the face of the mounting employers attacks. John Frey of the Iron Molders described the situation: "Several groups whose joint labor is required to manufacture the finished product are members of different national unions, and this results not only in dividing their forces, but in making it possible for the manufacturer to play one organization against the other in the same plant, using one union or a group of unions to break the strike of another union."[50]

Increasingly, and from various AFL quarters, the root cause of this problem was being traced back to the rigid separations that craft organizations enforced in the workplace. As interunion quarrels spread and union defeats multiplied, it seemed inevitable that a growing number of union officials and members would question the very form of organization on which the trade union movement had traditionally rested. If there was one basic point on which the criticisms against the strict craft autonomy principle converged, it was that the structure and policies of craft organizations had to be changed and adjusted to the new industrial conditions and trends. "As long as the policy of strict trade autonomy is pursued," said John Frey in 1903 in a confidential letter to Gompers, "so long will contentions arise among different unions as to where one type of work stops and the other begins."[51]

What Frey and other top AFL leaders would express in private was being voiced publicly and openly in many quarters of the federation. The solutions put forward, however, were far from being unified and reflected instead the immediate problems that the various unions faced in the context of their respective trades. Delegates of the Commercial

Telegraphers Union, for instance, saw the main source of their weakness in the fact that contracts of various unions began and expired on different dates; the consequence was that "allied bodies are frequently forced to combat the best interests of each other, thereby defeating the main objects of unionism." They therefore issued in 1904 a resolution calling for "all organizations connected with the American Federation of Labor [to] cause agreements or such contracts to begin and expire upon a certain date."[52]

The machinists, who perhaps more than any other trade were confronted with an increasing number of handymen in their shops and with a growing proliferation of new job specializations, saw the necessity of loosening the strict requirements of their craft so as to include these new categories of workers. An IAM official put it this way in 1903: "In my opinion we cannot completely solve this problem until we have taken entire control of the machine shop, when we will be in a position to make an agreement covering the employment of all who work therein."[53]

Similarly John Frey felt that "the principle of one union in a trade" was the solution to the problem of multiunion jurisdiction and all its negative consequences.[54] Craft unions such as the machinists' and the iron molders' could certainly afford considering this type of solution since they were the largest and most powerful of all the metal trades. For smaller metal crafts a solution of this type would have meant abdicating their jurisdictional claims, and in many cases, ceasing to exist.

Another type of solution put forth was the amalgamation of two or more unions where the new work processes had considerably blurred craft demarcations. In 1904 this policy was pursued by the International Association of Machinists and the Allied Metal Mechanics.[55] Unions in related trades who saw the weakness deriving from rigid craft separations but who were unwilling to amalgamate advocated the formation of federations or alliances. It is in this context—characterized by increasing criticism against the craft autonomy principle but also by the lack of a unified organizational alternative—that industrial unionism emerged as the rallying cry among wide sectors of organized labor.

The growth of this sentiment was clearly reflected at the 1903 AFL convention where for the first time a resolution favoring industrial unionism was introduced. Although defeated, the resolution precipitated a long and heated debate, prompting a sharp reaction from the AFL leaders, Gompers in particular. His indictment of industrial unionism was quick to come. He told the audience that "the attempt to force the trade unions into what has been termed 'industrial organization' is perversive of the history of the labor movement, runs counter to the best conceptions of the toilers' interest now, and is sure to lead to the confusion which precedes dissolution and disruption." Trying to mobilize support against the spread of this sentiment, he added, "It is time for the AFL to solemnly call a halt. It is time for our fellow unionists entrusted with grave responsibilities to stem the tide of expansion madness lest either by their indifference or encouragement, their organizations will be drawn into the vortex that will engulf them to their possible dismemberment and destruction."[56]

Similar resolutions had been introduced and debated at the level of state federations as well as of national and international union conventions. It was the signal of a conflict destined to intensify and soon precipitate the AFL—and indeed the entire American labor movement—into one of the major organizational crises of its history, with crucial consequences for the development of industrial and labor relations.

NOTES

1. Alfred D. Chandler, Jr., "The Beginning of 'Big Business' in American Industry," *Business History Review* 33 (Spring 1959): 25.

2. From 1895 to 1905 U.S. exports of manufactured goods increased by 198 percent compared to increases of 75 percent for Germany, 40 percent for England, and 25 percent for France; Albert K. Steigerwalt, *The National Association of Manufacturers, 1895-1914* (Grand Rapids, 1964), 50; cf. also USIC *Report of Industrial Commission,* 19:551, and William H. Becker, "American Manufacturers and Foreign Market, 1870-1900," *Business History Review,* no. 4 (Winter 1973): 466-481.

3. Cf. especially Gabriel Kolko, *The Triumph of Conservatism* (Chicago, 1967).

4. For some contemporary analysis of union rules, cf. Solomon Blum, "Trade-Union Rules in the Building Trades," in Jacob H. Hollander and George E. Barnett, eds., *Studies in American Trade Unionism* (New York, 1907), 295-319, and, in the same volume, F. W. Hilbert, "Trade-Union Agreements in the Iron Moulders Union," 221-60; cf. also Walter E. Weyl and A. M. Sakolski, "Conditions of Entrance to the Principal Trades," in *Bulletin of the U.S. Bureau of Labor Statistics,* no. 67 (November 1906).

5. Eleventh Special Report of the Commissioner of Labor, *Regulation and Restriction of Output* (Washington, D.C., 1904) (hereafter referred to as *Eleventh Special Report*).

6. Ibid., 160.

7. *Machinists' Monthly Journal* 15 (1903): 619.

8. *Eleventh Special Report*, 143.

9. Discussions of these various systems were carried on on a regular basis in journals such as *American Machinist* and *Engineering Magazine;* cf. especially *American Machinist* 23 (1900): 418-20; 24 (1901): 121, 126, 1073, 1383. For a contemporary review and comparison of the various systems, cf. William H. Buckler, "The Minimum Wage in the Machinists' Union," in Hollander and Barnett, *Studies in American Trade Unionism*, 139-50.

10. *Eleventh Special Report*, 114; cf. also *Engineering Magazine* 18 (1901): 205.

11. *American Machinist* (September 26, 1901): 1063-64.

12. Ibid. (March 12, 1903, November 19, 1903): 1634.

13. *Machinists' Monthly Journal* 13 (1901): 650-52.

14. Ibid. 15 (1903): 619; cf. also *American Industries* (June 15, 1904):7.

15. *Eleventh Special Report*, 143.

16. Ibid.

17. Ibid.

18. Ibid., 153.

19. Ibid., 191.

20. Ibid., 153.

21. Cf. esp. the contemporary study by Isaac A. Hourwich, *Immigration and Labor: The Economic Aspects of European Immigration to the United States* (New York, 1912), and William M. Leiserson, *Adjusting Immigrant and Industry* (New York, 1924).

22. *Eleventh Special Report*, 164.

23. *American Machinist* (July 16, 1903): 1021.

24. Katherine Stone, "The Origin of Job Structure in the Steel Industry," *Radical America* 7 (November-December 1973): 19-64.

25. On the NCR cf. Daniel Nelson, "The New Factory System and the Unions: The National Cash Register Company Dispute of 1901," *Labor History* 15 (Spring 1974): 163-78; on the International Harvester cf. the excellent work by Robert Ozanne, *A Century of Labor-Management Relations at McCormick & International Harvester* (Madison, 1967), esp. chaps. 3 and 4.

26. M. W. Alexander, "Apprenticeship in the Metal Trades," in John Commons, ed., *Trade Unionism and Labor Problems*, 2d series (New York, 1967), 235ff.; *NCF Review* (January-February 1906): 12.

27. For some contemporary analyses, cf. F. W. Hilbert, "Employers' Associations in the United States," in Hollander and Barnett, *Studies in American Trade Unionism*, 183-218; Clarence Bonnett, *Employers' Associations in the United States* (New York, 1922), Ray S. Baker, "The

New Employers' Association Movement," *McClure Magazine* 21 (July 1904): 279-92.

28. Hilbert, "Trade-Union Agreements," 194.

29. Cf., for instance, Albion G. Taylor, *Labor Policies of the National Association of Manufacturers* (Urbana, 1928); Steigerwalt, *National Association of Manufacturers;* Bonnett, *Employer's Associations,* chap. 10; Marguerite Green, *The National Civic Federation and the American Labor Movement* (Washington, D.C., 1956), chap. 3; Robert Wiebe, *Businessmen and Reform* (Chicago, 1968); Philip S. Foner, *The Policies and Practices of the American Federation of Labor, 1900-1909* (New York, 1964), Chap. 2.

30. *Proceedings of the Eighth Annual Convention of the National Association of Manufacturers of the United States of America, New Orleans, May 1903* (New York, 1904), 19-20.

31. Cf. Taylor, *Labor Policies of the NAM.*

32. Hilbert, "Employers' Associations," 198.

33. Quoted in Bonnett, *Employers' Associations,* 101-02.

34. Cf. the declaration of principles adopted by the Building Contractors' Council of Chicago and its essential similarity with that of the National Metal Trades Association, quoted above; in *Eleventh Special Report,* 277-78.

35. *Twenty-first Annual Report of the Commissioner of Labor, 1906: Strikes and Lockouts* (Washington, D.C., 1907), 58, 59 (hereafter cited as *Strikes and Lockouts*).

36. Ibid., 71, 73.

37. Willard L. Thorp, *Business Annals* (New York, 1926), 139.

38. Ozanne, *Century of Labor-Management Relations,* 67-70.

39. *American Machinist* (November 19, 1903): 1633-34.

40. Circular reproduced in *American Industries* (November 2, 1903): 3-4.

41. Reproduced in ibid. (June 15, 1904): 7.

42. Quoted in ibid. (August 15, 1904): 2.

43. *International Metal Worker* (July 1904): 66.

44. *International Socialist Review* (November 1904): 310.

45. Leo Wolman, *Ebb and Flow in Trade Unionism* (New York, 1936): 33; *Strikes and Lockouts,* 490; *International Socialist Review* (September 1904): 182-85, for a summary description of all the sectors affected by wage cuts.

46. *Blacksmiths' Journal* (June 1901): 13.

47. For a contemporary analysis of this problem see Solomon Blum, *Jurisdictional Disputes Resulting from Structural Differences in American Trade Unions* (Berkeley, 1913).

48. *Report of the Proceedings of the 22nd Annual Convention of the American Federation of Labor* (Washington, D.C., 1902), 13.

49. Foner, *Policies and Practices,* 205.

50. Ibid., 204.

51. Ibid., 203.

52. Ibid.

53. Quoted in *U.S. Bureau of Labor Statistics Bulletin,* no. 67 (November 1906): 689.

54. Foner, *Policies and Practices,* 205.

55. *International Socialist Review* (November 1904): 309.

56. *AFL Proceedings, 1903,* 18-19.

6

THE CRISIS OF ORGANIZATION IN THE AFL'S METAL TRADES

Because of the centrality it occupied in the history of the AFL, industrial unionism has been a focus of historical analysis both in terms of the conflict it generated between the AFL leadership and some of the industrial unions (such as the Brewery Workers and the Western Federation of Miners)[1] and also as a ground of ideological warfare waged by socialist trade unionists within the federation.[2]

This issue is of crucial historical importance not only because it dramatizes the organizational crisis within the trade union movement in the Progressive years but also because it raises the vital question as to whether the trade agreement policy pursued by the AFL was compatible with an organizational transformation of trade unions along industrial lines. The sentiment against the craft autonomy principle and in favor of industrial unionism continued to plague the AFL leadership. There were in fact substantial sectors of workers who—either for ideological or for pragmatic reasons—were not willing to embark on such a radical course of action as the founders of the Industrial Workers of the World took in 1905 but who nevertheless felt that changes in the organizational structure and policies of their unions were urgently needed to cope effectively with the changes in production and with the employers' attacks. The creation of industrial departments—starting in 1907—served to a large extent the purpose of staving off the growing agitation for industrial unionism and represented the major move undertaken by the AFL leadership during this period to come to terms with that issue.

Because of the extremely dynamic character of the industrial sector in which they operated, metal trades unions were among the first labor organizations to be confronted with the problem of how to coordinate their forces to cope more effectively with changing industrial conditions. An early attempt at close cooperation among a half-dozen metal trades unions for defensive purposes dates back to the mid-1890s— through it was short-lived.[3] But with the productive expansion that marked the years around the turn of the century, a similar attempt was revived, taking the form of a movement to create a federation of all metal trades unions. The *Iron Moulders' Journal,* for instance, expressed this new interest among workers, pointing out that "since employers have taken a hand in organizing and the trade union stands no longer opposed to the individual employer but to the association of employers, the necessity for closer affiliation or alliance among trade groups is coming to be better appreciated."[4] A major contributing factor animating this movement was in fact the rise in 1899 of the National Metal Trades Association—a national employers' association that embraced a significant number of metal and machine manufacturers and was designed to render uniform employer-union relations in that industrial sector.

It was Gompers who sought to initiate action among the metal trades unions because he saw the implications that the NMTA's emergence might have on the future of labor relations in that industrial sector. Toward the end of 1900, he contacted a number of metal trades union officials, calling their attention to a new NMTA policy of adjusting wages and working conditions with the unions involved "on a national, rather than a local basis."[5] Gompers requested that a conference of the metal trades unions be held in December 1900 during the AFL convention to consider possible lines of action.

At the December meeting no definite plan of organization was carried out, but it was decided to extend an invitation to all the metal trades unions in view of a convention to be held in St. Louis in July 1901.[6] The metal trades representatives who convened in July appointed a committee of eight members to draft a plan of federation. E. J. Lynch of the Metal Polishers was elected president of the new organization, which was called the Federated Metal Trades of North America and which was to continue "until the permanent organization is effected next December."[7] During the AFL national convention in Scranton, the metal trades federation was officially launched—though its constitution and programmatic guidelines were not yet completed.[8]

It is difficult to ascertain to what extent Gompers and the AFL executive were prepared to experiment with the new federation. It seems plausible to assume, however, that they did not have any intention of permitting it to constitute a major departure in organizational policy, particularly at a time when the famous Scranton declaration—sanctioning the craft autonomy principle—was being proclaimed.

Throughout 1901 metal tradesmen's support for a federation had gained considerable momentum, and it seemed unlikely that its most ardent advocates would be satisfied with changes that were only formal in character. Early in 1901 the *Iron Moulders' Journal* informed its readers of the growing sentiment among metal tradesmen in favor of such federation, pointing out that "from several large centers the officers of the unions have received urgent appeals to promote the organization of a Metal Trades' Federation."[9] A few months later Max Hays reported in his labor column for the *International Socialist Review* that "the movement to federate the metal working craft is gaining considerable headway," and he estimated that more than "50,000 men [would] be combined in May 1."[10]

This sentiment took a decisively militant turn in May when the NMTA violated the famous Murray Hill agreement—a national agreement that covered hundreds of firms and that was believed to be a major advance in collective bargaining policy.[11] The strike that grew out of this dispute—one of the major national ones of that period—resulted in the defeat of the machinists and signaled the antiunion militant turn of the NMTA, as well as the intensification of the capital-labor struggle in the metal trades sector.[12]

The International Association of Machinists' executive, who had taken a leading role in the preparatory work of launching a metal trades federation, was soon confronted by a significant minority within the union who demanded, among other things, "some concrete plan of industrial unionism to provide broader protection against the National Metal Trades Association than the individual metal unions had been able to provide."[13]

The AFL executive and some metal trades national officials feared that the machinists' outburst of radicalism might overflow into other metal trades unions and transform the metal trades federation into a major organizational vehicle toward industrial unionism. These worries had a role in affecting the future development of the federation. At the Scranton conference of the metal trades unions, in fact, the Iron Moulders Union decided to withdraw from the federation, explaining that "they

were not ready to take such a step."[14] A few months earlier, the union's
paper, commenting on the steps being taken to form the new federation,
had expressed a cautious attitude, warning the unions involved of the
necessity "to observe trade-union principles."[15] Obviously the Iron
Moulders Union—no doubt the most well-established among the metal
trades unions and with an enviable record of stable employer-union
relationships—preferred not to run the risk of being drawn into a process that could have led the metal trades federation to becoming a hot-
bed of organizational agitation.

That fears over the potential development of the metal trades federation were by no means limited to the Iron Moulders Union but were
shared by the AFL executive as well becomes clear from the action that
this body took (or more precisely, did not take) to complete the projected formation of the federation. Acting on the instructions received
at the metal trades union conference held in Scranton, the executive
board of the Federated Metal Trades of North America met in Toledo
in April 1902 to finish writing the constitution and framing the bylaws.
The new organization plan provided for the creation of local metal trades
councils, enabling the federation to become operative not only at the
national level but, more importantly, at the local level.[16] But in order
to do so, the federation was to be empowered by the AFL executive to
release subsidiary charters to the proposed local councils. Such a request
was wired to the AFL executive secretary, Frank Morrison. When the
answer from AFL headquarters came, it called for a sharp halt—and
was signed by Gompers: "Before Federated Metal Trades of N.A. can
secure charter from the AF of L," the telegram read, "individual
Nationals now holding charters must surrender them. Matter too complicated and important for your conference to attempt to finally
determine at this session."[17]

Clearly a decentralization such as the local-councils idea implied,
occurring at a time of stepped-up employer-worker confrontations and
of growing criticism against the strict craft autonomy principle, constituted too great a risk for the AFL to agree to. The charter-granting
power that the executive board of the Federated Metal Trades of North
America requested was never given, and the organization was left with
no other alternative than to abide by the rather loose and general guidelines laid down at the St. Louis conference the year before. This gave
the federation only the semblance of an organization; in effect, it
became a forum in which the various metal trades unions met periodi-

cally to try to resolve common problems (most important of which were jurisdictional disputes). This fact became evident from the two metal trades unions conferences held during the following years—in Pittsburgh in 1903 and in Washington, D.C., in 1904—where all the work was taken up resolving jurisdictional claims and attacking the United Metal Workers International Union.[18]

Why the United Metal Workers International Union? Very little is known about this organization, except that it was (under a different name) the third largest workers' organization represented at the IWW founding convention and that its general secretary, C. Sherman, became the first (and only) IWW president.[19]

In a very important sense, the UMWIU was both the product and the victim of the dramatic industrial expansion marking the early years of the century. Despite its small size and its short life, its history therefore provides some important insights into the conditions of the metal trades sector where industrial changes had some of the most disruptive effects, making the problem of the form of labor organization a most acute and widespread one.

The UMWIU's attempt to pursue an industrial unionism policy within the AFL shows the extent to which the federation—and in particular the metal trades unions—were not able or willing to adjust their organizational structures to the changing industrial conditions; it also throws more light on the background of the historic IWW founding convention when industrial unionism was proclaimed as a revolutionary program for the entire American working class.

At the time of its establishment in August 1900, the UMWIU counted only about 1,000 members, but during the ensuing three years (until the spring of 1904) it experienced an astonishingly rapid growth. It extended its influence in various industrial centers of the Midwest, as well as in several eastern industrial districts, such as Boston, New York, and Baltimore. But its major strength continued to be in the Chicago area, and by January 1903 the union's paper reported that seven more locals had been formed in that city.[20] In March 1903 the leading Chicago business agent noted that "the movement is growing very rapidly and new members are being added at the rate of 700 per month."[21] He requested that new halls be procured to meet the needs of an expanding membership. By August 1903—the third anniversary of the organization—the

UMWIU estimated that its membership in good standing had reached the 14,000 mark.[22] This proved to be its high point in terms of union strength; beginning in the summer of 1904, the union began to experience a rapid decline.

The remarkable success in the union's growth resulted not only from the organizing ability of its officials but also from the wide spectrum of trades that the union covered in its organizing drives. From a description of ten of the fourteen Chicago locals that the *International Metal Worker* carried in 1903, it appears that the union included among its ranks a variety of metal workers, including coppersmiths, patternmakers, wire workers, and surgical instruments makers. The union also organized semi-skilled metal workers engaged in the production of miscellaneous hardware items, or in machine shops, as it appears from jurisdictional agreement entered into with the International Association of Machinists in September 1903.[23]

Such an organizational policy repeatedly led the UMWIU into jurisdictional quarrels with other metal trades unions within the AFL; but it reflected the union's commitment to the goal of industrial unionism and the role that it intended to take on in the metal trades sector. Although the officials of the UMWIU, most notably C. Sherman, tried at first to deemphasize their commitment to industrial unionism, several of the AFL metal trades unions soon became aware that the UMWIU's organizing policies ran counter to traditional craft union principles. According to a top official of the International Association of Allied Metal Mechanics— a union that felt acutely the threat from the UMWIU—the "proposed plan of organization" that the United Metal Workers laid out at its inception was such that once implemented, it "would practically revolutionize all the National and International Unions then organized who were engaged in the metal trades" and would result in "the disruption of our organization."[24]

It was not until the end of 1904 that the various metal trades unions within the AFL were able to combine their efforts and wage open warfare against the UMWIU, ultimately forcing the union to withdraw from the federation. In the meantime, however, the UMWIU grew in strength and scored major successes in the Chicago industrial scene, increasingly evidencing its orientation toward industrial unionism. From the pages of the *International Metal Workers,* as well as through personal contacts with the AFL leadership, C. Sherman waged an ongoing criticism against

the craft structure of the federation. Jurisdictional disputes, Sherman
kept on insisting, were the greatest evil of the AFL. These disputes
did not reflect authentic needs of the rank and file but, on the contrary,
grew from the unions officials' "greedy disposition of wanting to control."
It was these useless disputes, Sherman maintained, that had prevented the
AFL from "doubling its present strength" during the past twenty-one
years of its existence. He therefore recommended "that every worker in
the movement, whether he be representing National, International, or
local union, spend all the time he can spare and all the money at his command for the purpose of organizing the unorganized." The jurisdictional
question would "work out its own salvation" once the remaining 80 percent of unorganized workers were organized.[25]

Sherman's polemics against Gompers after the AFL president presented
his report on the problem of jurisdictional disputes at the 1902 annual
convention of the federation were similar in tone. In an exchange of correspondence, Sherman questioned seriously the real validity of that report.
He argued against Gompers that those interunion battles would continue
unless the official leadership of the federation came to terms with the root
cause of the evil. The time had come for the AFL-affiliated unions to realize that they must "abandon insistence on craft autonomy and adjust
union structure along the lines of industrial production, and not spend so
much time and money quarreling and fighting over jurisdictional lines."
Sherman went on advancing his theory that once the union movement
oriented itself toward industrial unionism and thus organized the unorganized, "the jurisdictional question will be worked out to the satisfaction of the whole."[26] A few months later, at the 1903 AFL convention,
when agitation for industrial unionism intensified, Sherman was among
the leading sponsors of what became the first resolution on industrial
unionism to be presented at an AFL annual convention.[27]

The UMWIU's commitment to industrial unionism was also reflected
in the organizational structure that the union set up in the Chicago area
for the purpose of coordinating its efforts in improving the wage and
working conditions of its members. The focus of this combined action
was the Metal Workers Council, which was composed of four delegates
from each of the ten local unions. All grievances, strikes, or lockouts,
even if they occurred in only one local, were believed to affect all the
Chicago United Metal Workers and were therefore handled by the council.
The council employed two business agents who worked full-time coordinating organizational activities and settling grievances.[28]

Through this able coordination of efforts, the UMWIU had succeeded in securing advantageous agreements from employers. An agreement worked out in July 1903 between the Chicago Metal Working Council and the Metal Manufacturers Association of Chicago provided for a 10 percent increase and the nine-hour working day, and it covered eighty firms.[29] This agreement, moreover, had been reached without strike action. The record of militancy displayed by the union was also quite enviable. In July 1903 the UMWIU monthly journal reported that in the first thirty months of the union's existence, the council had been involved in 110 strikes, 97 of which had been won, 5 had been compromised and 8 were lost.[30]

One such strike had been fought against what was no doubt the largest and most powerful machines and tools producer of Chicago, the Deering Harvester Company. Here the existing conditions prior to the strike—the ten-hour day and a ban on unions—were considered by the UMWIU "a menace to the trade union movement."[31] The struggle against the Deering management was initiated and led by the UMWIU through its main business agent, John Kirkpatrick, who for days succeeded in rallying the support of a great number of workers, despite immediate counteraction by management resulting in a plantwide, truly "industrial" strike when other unions joined and lent their support, such as the woodworkers, the blacksmiths, the machinists, the painters, as well as the Building Trades Council of that city.[32] As a result of this ably coordinated action, better wages and working hours were secured for the workers, and about 70 percent of them "were enrolled as members in the various organizations"; 2,700 of the workers affected were members of the UMWIU.[33] One historian of the Harvester corporation calls the strike "a major company capitulation" in which management was forced to modify its previously unbending stand against unionized labor.[34]

But behind this rapid growth and show of strength, new forces were building up against the UMWIU that would soon explode, decimating the ranks of the organization and forcing it on a new course of action. Foremost among these forces was the opposition that began to mount against the UMWIU from among AFL-affiliated metal trades unions on the ground that the metal workers organized by the UMWIU belonged to their trade jurisdictions. To be sure, Sherman himself admitted that his organization was "built on the broad lines" and not on rigid craft lines, though he was quick to point out that the workers they organized were not taken away from other unions but came from the ranks of the unorganized. It is on this basis that Sherman contended that the attacks against his union were unjustified and were instead motivated by "jealousy" rather than by real concern for the workers' movement.[35]

The mounting opposition against the UMWIU was clearly manifested at a conference held in Pittsburgh in January 1903 where various AFL-affiliated metal trades unions met to resolve common problems. They made attempts to compromise grievances growing out of jurisdictional issues, many directed against the UMWIU; but they proved unsuccessful. On the second day of the conference, in fact, the UMWIU delegation decided to withdraw because, as Sherman later explained, "there seemed to be no disposition of compromise, but a complete demand of the various organizations upon what would ultimately absorb the whole jurisdiction of the UMW."[36] Moreover, the UMWIU delegation feared that a move was being prepared by the other unions' delegations to vote on a motion revoking the UMWIU charter. Such fears proved founded, for soon after a resolution was in fact passed asking the AFL executive to revoke the UMWIU charter.[37]

No action was taken by the AFL executive; Gompers preferred to pursue the diplomatic route by putting pressures on the unions involved, particularly the UMWIU, to meet again in conference and try to resolve their differences.[38] In January 1904, the metal trades unions met again in Washington, D.C., and Gompers himself presided over the conference. A conciliatory mood seemed to pervade this meeting, no doubt because of Gompers's presence and the weight of his authority. The AFL president was able to get two of the metal trades unions—the Boilmakers and the Metal Polishers—to conclude jurisdictional agreements with the UMWIU. A tentative agreement was also worked out with the International Bridge and Structural Iron Workers, the ratification of which was left with the AFL executive. But no agreement could be reached between the UMWIU and two other unions—the Allied Metal Mechanics and the Amalgamated Sheet Metal Workers—and the issues were referred to the AFL executive to act upon in a mediatory capacity.[39]

Despite the diplomatic success Gompers scored at the Washington conference in trying to bring about conciliation among the metal trades unions, open warfare against the UMWIU had already begun, led by the International Bridge and Structural Iron Workers (IB&SIW)—a much bigger and more powerful craft union—who seemed determined to extend their jurisdiction over metal work performed in shops (shop work), thus threatening the very existence of the UMWIU.[40] By early 1904 the

IB&SIW had already raided several UMWIU-affiliated locals in the eastern states and had succeeded in getting no less than seven of them.[41] Throughout 1904 the IB&SIW continued to pursue this line of action, and it even focused its attacks on the Chicago area, where the UMWIU was stronger and better organized.[42]

The lot of the UMWIU worsened even more as a result of the 1903 economic panic and the ensuing recession. By the summer of 1904 the effects of the downswing were being felt, particularly in the Chicago area's machine and metal industry, where employers seemed to concentrate their antiunion attacks. To the unions involved, it was clear that these efforts amounted to "the destruction of organized labor." A wave of strikes hit the Chicago metal industry and began to spread to other districts. In July 1904 the *International Metal Worker* reported that most of the UMWIU members in Chicago machine shops were on strike and that there were strikes in other cities. According to the journal, the metal manufacturers had concentrated their force in Chicago "believing that if they can destroy the force of the machinists and the metal workers in Chicago, it will be an easy matter to dispose of them in other points." The paper stressed the historical significance of the struggle—"whatever way Chicago goes, the United States will sooner or later follow"—and warned workers that it would most likely go on for several months. This prediction proved accurate; by September the conflict seemed far from receding, and during the Chicago Labor Day demonstration there was widespread alarm in labor circles over the future of industrial conditions.[43] It was at this time that the UMWIU made its first official endorsement of industrial unionism from the pages of its paper, stressing the urgent need for labor to merge its strength by organizing along industrial lines and thus to counter the offensive from capital.[44]

The fate of the UMWIU took a desive turn at the 1904 annual convention of the AFL held in San Francisco when the AFL executive rendered a decision on metal trades jurisdictional disputes centering around the UMWIU that ordered the "several classes of [UMWIU] metal workers [to] be divided and given to [the other AFL metal] trades."[45] This move, in effect, meant disbanding the UMWIU. It appears that this effort was surrounded by much behind-the-scene maneuvering. The ratification of the agreement between the UMWIU and the IB&SIW reached at the 1904 Washington conference, which would have regularized the jurisdictional relations of the two unions, never materialized. While the AFL executive delayed this ratification for almost a year, the IB&SIW went on with its raiding activity, taking away a substantial number of members from the UMWIU and thus weakening it considerably.[46] In a very important sense, the AFL executive committee's decision had come as a postmortem decree to sanction legally what it had tacitly assented to.

Weakened by the harsh employers' offensive and by the metal trades unions' attacks, confused by the AFL executive's diplomacy, and humiliated by the decision taken at the AFL convention, the UMWIU took the only path that enabled it to survive as a workers' organization committed to a policy of industrial unionism. It withdrew from the AFL and made preparations to structure itself as an industrial union.[47] This reorganization process was soon completed, and by June 1905 the union, under a new name (the Industrial Metal Workers), had converged into the nascent Industrial Workers of the World, where it represented the third largest block of workers and C. Sherman played a leading role in the foundation of the new organization.[48]

By 1905, therefore, the movement to federate the metal trades within the AFL appeared effectively checked and on the wane. The events surrounding the UMWIU had dramatized the failure of a movement that at its inception foretold good possibilities to effect concrete organizational readjustments enabling the metal trades unions to be better equipped in coping with industrial changes and employers' tactics.

After the dismal experience of the metal trades federation and after similar attempts by the building trades had been systematically checked by the AFL executive, the formation of trades departments came to many as a surprise. Several labor historians concur in maintaining that the creation of these departments was a move designed to counter the growing criticism and agitation in favor of industrial unionism.[49] The indications pointing toward the validity of this conclusion are not lacking. Agitation within the AFL, even after the traumatic experience of the IWW launching, did not seem to subside. At the 1905 convention of the International Association of Machinists, for instance, a proposal to implement industrial unionism through the amalgamation of all the metal trades unions into one single organization, though defeated, generated much heated debate.[50] Similar resolutions were introduced and debated at AFL national conventions.[51] Jurisdictional disputes continued to plague the AFL leadership and dominate the proceedings of the federation's conventions. Some of these disputes, such as the one involving the Brewery Workers (an industrial union), provided added fuel to the controversy. Moreover, the rise of the

IWW meant, at least in an immediate sense, that the AFL leadership had to guard itself also from attacks coming from the outside, especially because of the early IWW policy of trying to attract AFL rank and filers.[52]

Even more significant about the creation of these departments was the ability and diplomatic skills Gompers displayed in effecting an organizational change that responded to precise operational exigencies of the federation and was also a way to silence his industrial unionist critics.

Looking at it from a purely organizational standpoint, the new policy made a great deal of sense and seemed in keeping with the decentralized trends occurring elsewhere, for instance, in business and corporate organization.[53] Through these departments, a number of labor activities would be decentralized, made self-supporting by the unions involved, and dealt with in a more effective manner. This was true particularly of organizing activities, lobbying in connection with legislation peculiar to given sectors, tighter control over local labor developments, and jurisdictional issues and disputes.[54]

The magnitude of this change in policy was such that it could not prevent implications from being drawn out from both conservative and radical camps of the AFL membership. Thus the AFL leadership introduced the change with a high degree of circumspection, on the one hand reassuring conservative forces that the departments were "not a new idea," that in fact they had been recommended twenty years earlier, and that they would have the effect of "secur[ing] more firmly . . . the autonomy of each trade and industrial division," and on the other hand refuting industrial-unionists' critics that the change was evidence of real "progress, advance and development"[55] "and not the effect of new-found forms of organization" that would only lead to "an arbitrary autocracy composed of a few individuals."[56]

If Gompers and the AFL leadership intended to sell the idea of the departments as a surrogate for concrete changes pointing toward industrial unionism, they cannot be said to have been unsuccessful—at least in the short run—as it appears from the response that this move received among industrial-unionism advocates. Max Hays, one of the most attentive labor observers in the socialist camp, felt that with the formation of the Building Trades Department "ground work [had] been prepared that will in all probability lead to a much-needed departure from old moorings."[57] One year later, soon after the formation of two more departments (the Metal Trades Department and the Railway Employees' Department), he commented that "another nail has been driven in the coffin of the old-fashioned idea of trade autonomy," and added, "The present movement in the AF of L differs somewhat from the ambitious program mapped out by the ill-starred Industrial Workers of the World in that the component organizations in the departments will have complete jurisdiction over their own affairs, an important essential, but there is no predicting what will develop when the membership begin to get accustomed to each other."[58]

Similarly, the secretary of the predominantly socialist Brewery Workers—despite the severe treatment that his union had received by the AFL leadership—felt that "by forming these departments the principle of consolidation and concentration of power is being recognized, which will finally lead to full realization of the necessity of industrial organization." Shortly after, the union's paper, the *Brauer-Zeitung,* returned to this topic, pointing out that "the subdivision of the AF of L with departments controlling all crafts in certain industries is all that any true industrial unionist can desire at present."[59]

The new policy, however, was not so convincing to those within the metal trades who expected concrete changes flowing from the department. The Metal Trades Department (MTD) embodied all the features of an organizational decentralization and appeared to radical metal trades elements as a bureaucratic bulwark whose main purpose was to contain militant joint action at the local level. The department did provide for the creation of local joint councils—something that years before the Federated Metal Trades had been prevented from doing—but their voting power in departmental conventions and affairs was drastically inferior to that held by national unions. The latter, moreover, held control over the finances, thus limiting greatly local councils' initiative, particularly concerning strike action. Sympathetic strikes, which in a sense were the essence of joint militant action, were doubly checked by the national unions, who would withhold financial support, and by the MTD executive, who outrightly condemned them.[60]

Heading the department was James O'Connell, who had been elected to that position with the help of Gompers and the AFL executive.[61] A faithful Gompers ally, O'Connell had headed the International Association of Machinists since 1893 and had been the key architect in the growth of the machinists' union into one of the strongest craft organizations within the AFL. He had also been one of the pillars of the AFL in the years when a heated controversy over the department's structure and policies A major figure in the dominant AFL enclave, O'Connell had been a staunch opponent of any trend or movement pointing toward industrial unionism, whether it was in the form of Debs's American Railway Union or in the form of the IWW. O'Connell was to call this role into play increasingly in his own union as agitation for industrial unionism began to mount after the turn of the century. He would play a similar role as president of the MTD, which became "O'Connell's stronghold."[62]

From the very beginning, the department had become a theater of ongoing conflict between the conservative forces, who wanted the department to abide rigidly by the rules laid down in its constitution, and the radical forces, who wanted the department to become a stepping-stone for the creation of an organization amalgamating all the metal trades unions, thus bringing about industrial unionism in their sector. This became evident during the first MTD convention in December 1909 when a heated controversy over the department's structure and policies dominated the proceedings.

Leading the insurgent forces was the Detroit Metal Trades Council, which introduced a series of amendments to the constitution aiming at increasing local autonomy in case of strike action; allowing the department more autonomy from the constrictions of the national and international unions' constitutions; changing the basis of representation at departmental conventions by allowing one delegate from each national or international union (rather than in proportion to their membership) and one delegate from each affiliated local council; making it compulsory that all affiliated unions involved in a single plant sign agreements expiring at the same time.[63]

All these proposed amendments were defeated, but the impact that the insurgents' action had on the department's leadership became apparent at the second convention. There, President O'Connell went on attacking the "many" metal trades councils who, as he put it, "have no hesitancy in asking the officers of the Metal Trades Department to do things in absolute violation not only of the Constitution of the Department, but of the national and international organizations affiliated therewith." He urged "conservative and businesslike leadership" on the ground that the department was not yet strong enough to engage in militant activity. O'Connell enlisted the aid of Gompers whose address to the delegates clearly reflected his fears that the agitation among metal tradesmen would take the department on the path to industrial unionism. In his speech, the AFL president launched a stinging attack against industrial unionism, associating it with the "experience of the Knights of Labor," and calling it "a pot pourri, an industrial stew of the working people." Such ideas, Gompers stressed, "would simply mean destruction" of the labor movement. "Trade autonomy . . . trade integrity . . . trade pride"—these were the essential ingredients for the progress of the trade union movement, and were at the basis of the newly created industrial departments. Gompers emphasized how the departments reflected the true scientific organization of the labor movement in response to the ongoing changes occurring in industry: "You will find there the men of labor scientifically organized, each in his own industrial regiment, each in his own industrial department, each performing a different function, and yet acting in common to bring about one great result in the interest of all."[64]

But the agitation inside the department, far from subsiding, actually intensified during the following years. At the third annual convention the Grand Rapids metal trades council set off a protracted debate based on the demand that the necessary steps be taken "to bring about the amalgamation of all metal workers . . . into one organization to be known as the International Metal Workers." A similar resolution was introduced by the delegates of the Metal Polishers' union. Delegate J. Wilson, president of the Pattern Makers' Union and a staunch craft unionist, pointed out that there was "a sentiment in favor of this matter" and informed the convention with some alarm that unauthorized circular letters had been sent out asking "for a convention to convene in the city of St. Louis, Missouri, for the purpose of discussing this amalgamation."[65]

Wilson's alarm seemed justified, for during the following year the insurgents began to take positive steps. Acting on their own, they set up district councils for the purpose of carrying out in a more effective way joint metal workers' activities at the local level. The first three councils were set up in the Toledo, Pittsburgh, and Rochester areas. By the end of 1912 they were reported as being "active bodies" and holding "district meetings." In his report to the fourth annual convention of the department, President O'Connell expressed his strong disapproval of this development and questioned its legality. He warned the delegates that unless these councils operated in strict compliance with the department's guidelines, they "[would] undoubtedly in time assume to dictate the policy of the Department itself, if not the affiliated organizations." O'Connell also clearly resented the fact that "at no time during the year [had he] been requested or been extended an invitation to attend these district meetings."[66]

These must have been trying times for O'Connell, who in 1911 had lost the presidency of the IMA to his socialist opponent William H.

Johnston. Born in Nova Scotia in 1874, Johnston had begun his career in the machinist trade at the age of fourteen, working as an apprentice in the Rhode Island Locomotive Works in Providence. In 1895 he had joined the machinists' union and climbed fairly quickly in the organization; he was elected in 1905 as head of the important New England District 19 and in 1909 president of District Lodge 44, which comprised all the East Coast machinists in government employ. As president of the IMA Johnston continued to advocate the cause of industrial unionism, and his support must have provided a major encouragement to the insurgent forces within the Metal Trades Department, although it is not clear to what extent Johnston supported the steps being taken to set up district councils.[67]

The seriousness of this development was underscored by the fact that during the same year the amalgamation movement threatened to spill over into other AFL sectors. The Toledo Metal Trades Council, which had been in the forefront of the agitation within the Metal Trades Department, issued in September 1912 a circular that was also endorsed by the Detroit and the Grand Rapids councils. It was addressed to all the Metal Trades Councils, Printing Trades Councils, Building Trades Councils, Central Labor Unions, State Federations, Railway System Federations, and delegates to the AFL in general:

It has been demonstrated time and again that it is absolutely necessary for the workers to be more closely united in order to more successfully combat the combinations of the employing class: therefore, be it resolved, That we declare for an amendment to the constitution of the A. F. of L. That Art. II, Section 2, be amended by adding the following: National and International Trade Unions shall have the right to amalgamate; such amalgamation must be endorsed by a referendum vote of the organizations affected. A two-thirds affirmative vote of the members voting on such amalgamation in each organization, shall be necessary to make the amalgamation legal and binding.

A new organization created by amalgamation shall have the right to assume a name appropriate to the industry of which it is a part and shall have full control of the jurisdiction which before amalgamation was conceded to the different national and international trade unions forming the new organization.

We request that all bodies and organizations use their influence of Delegates to the coming convention of the A. F. of L. to support the above amendment.[68]

The initiative taken by some of the metal trades councils and their efforts at mobilizing labor forces from other industrial sectors provide an
important historical background to the protracted agitation that took
place at the 1912 AFL national convention over the issue of industrial
unionism. On that occasion, over one-third of the convention's delegates
voted in favor of a resolution for industrial unionism sponsored by the
United Mine Workers of America, an event that marked one of the highest
points in the agitation for industrial unionism within the AFL.

By the end of 1912 it was clear that the problem of amalgamation
and industrial unionism had become the most important issue within the
Metal Trades Department, threatening its stability and raising serious
questions about the department's future role. But the inroads made by
militant metal trades forces went beyond the level of mere agitational
work. At the 1913 departmental convention, in fact, they concentrated
their efforts on amending the department's constitution so as to
make joint strike action more effective. Backed by the entire delegations of the Metal Polishers, the Machinists, the Blacksmiths, and the
Sheet Metal Workers, this move was successful. Under the amended
constitution, the department had to sanction a strike once the majority
of the local as well as national affiliated unions had voted in favor of joint
strike action. As one delegate put it, this change would put an end to the
problem of "hav[ing] one organization prevent us from moving ahead."[69]
The wide support that this action received stemmed from the dissatisfaction existing among many metal tradesmen with the poor performance of
the department in initiating, or even supporting, joint strike actions.

The few joint strikes in which the department had gotten involved up
to that point had in fact ended in failure. In some cases this was because
of the lack of support from some of the affiliated metal trades unions.[70]
In other instances, the affiliated unions failed to give the strikers the
necessary leadership and financial backing. This was the case with the
Bethlehem Steel Company strike in 1910, which involved 8,000 workers,
many of them metal craftsmen. The metal trades unions seemed more intent on recruiting new members from among the strikers than on providing the much needed financial support to make the strike successful.[71]

The only joint strike that did exhibit a degree of coordination, support,
and militance was that initiated by the Los Angeles Metal Trades Council
in June 1911 over the eight-hour demand. Unfortunately the strike ran
into widespread public hostility because of the social tension created by

the noted *Los Angeles Times* building explosion—a factor that had a determining effect on the failure of the strike.[72]

The victory of the militant metal trades forces over the amendment of the department's constitution did not, however, substantially alter the situation, primarily because it proved to be a short-lived victory.

During the following year, in fact, the conservative forces within the metal trades unions were able to mobilize support against the new amendment on the ground that it violated the constitutions of national and international unions. They were able to take the issue outside the confines of the Metal Trades Department and make it a major policy problem affecting the AFL as a whole, thus gaining the support of other sectors of the federation.[73] This strategy proved successful, for at the 1914 convention of the department the amendment was rescinded, and the conservative forces were back in control of the department's machinery. This control would never be seriously challenged during the following months and would in fact become consolidated once American industry began to feel the impact of war production—an event that opens a new chapter for U.S. labor relations as a whole.

Six years of agitation and struggle over the MTD's structure, aims, and policies reflected the ambiguity that had characterized the department from the beginning. On the one hand, it appeared to many metal tradesmen to be a vehicle that opened the way for effective organizational change in the direction of industrial unionism; on the other hand, it had functioned as a pure bureaucratic decentralization aimed at perpetuating traditional AFL policies and containing more effectively internal pressures from radical elements.

Apart from the tension between the radical and conservative forces the ambiguous character of the department was also reflected in the indifference that AFL affiliated metal trades unions had shown toward it from its establishment. Very little effort was invested by these unions to publicize the department locally or, more significantly, to organize local trades councils.[74] Conversely an attitude of indifference was shown by local metal trades unions, which in many cases acted as if the department did not exist. At the 1914 departmental convention, for instance, it was reported that in no fewer than twenty-eight cities, eligible local unions (in some cases up to six) had failed to affiliate with the local council of their respective cities.[75]

Whether the department was "a farce,"[76] as a frustrated metal tradesmen delegate called it, or "industrial unionism of the upper stratum," as John Commons characterized it,[77] its experience reflects the organizational crisis confronting the American trade union movement in the face of the sweeping transformation occurring in industrial organization.

NOTES

1. Cf. especially Marion D. Savage, *Industrial Unionism in America* (New York, 1922); James O. Morris, *Conflict within the AF of L* (Ithaca, 1958); Philip S. Foner, *The Policies and Practices of the American Federation of Labor, 1900-1909* (New York, 1964), chaps 8 and 14; and John Laslett, *Labor and the Left* (New York, 1970).

2. Cf. especially William Dick, *Labor and Socialism in America: The Gompers Era* (Port Washington, N.Y., 1972), chap. 4.

3. *Iron Moulders' Journal* (January 1901): 23 (hereafter *IMJ*).

4. Ibid.

5. Quoted in *Machinists' Monthly Journal* (December 1900): 658.

6. *IMJ*, 23.

7. Ibid.

8. *Report of the Proceedings of the 21st Annual Convention of the American Federation of Labor* (Washington, D.C., 1902), 18.

9. *IMJ* (January 1901): 23-24.

10. *International Socialist Review* (April 1901): 655.

11. For a contemporary analysis of this agreement, see Ernest L. Bogart, "The Machinists' Strike, 1900," *Yale Review* 9 (November 1900): 302-13.

12. For a detailed account of this strike see Marguerite Green, *The National Civic Federation and the American Labor Movement* (Washington, D.C., 1956), 21-24; Mark Perlman, *The Machinists: A New Study in American Trade Unionism* (Cambridge, Mass., 1961), 25-28.

13. Laslett, *Labor and the Left,* 157.

14. *IMJ* (January 1902): 15-16.

15. Ibid. (September 1901): 549.

16. *The Journal* (official organ of the Polishers, Buffers, Platers, Brass Moulders and Brass Workers International Union of North America) (May 1902): 3-4.

17. Ibid.

18. Cf. p. 112 of this chapter.

19. The UMWIU's history (or rather the lack of one) provides a good illustration of how historians are by no means immune from the "guilt-by-association" fallacy. In his thorough history of the IWW, historian

Melvyn Dubofsky, trying to establish the corrupt performance of C. Sherman as IWW president, calls the UMWIU "a paper union"—a statement that clearly is intended to say more about Sherman than about the UMWIU and its experience in the industrial and labor scene prior to its merger into the IWW; cf. Melvyn Dubofsky, *We Shall Be All* (Chicago, 1969), 106-07. The *International Metal Worker,* the union's official organ, has provided the main source through which this short history of the UMWIU could be reconstructed (hereafter cited as IMW); information about Sherman's earlier labor activities can be found in *Proceedings of the Founding Convention of the IWW* (New York, 1969), 132; cf. also Debs's article in *IMW* (August 1905): 66, and *IMW* (January 1903): 1.

20. Ibid. (January 1903): 1.

21. Ibid. (January 1903): 28.

22. Ibid. (September 1903): 77.

23. "About Our Local Unions," *IMW* (April 1903): 38, (September 1903): 78-79.

24. *Proceedings of the Metal Trades Conference Held in Pittsburgh, January 8, 1905* (n.p., n.d., copy in the Wisconsin State Historical Society), 7.

25. *IMW* (January 1903): 16.

26. Quoted in Foner, *Policies and Practices,* 209.

27. AFL Convention, 1903, *Proceedings,* 18, 19.

28. "About Our Local Unions," 38.

29. *IMW* (July 1903): 63.

30. Ibid., 61.

31. Ibid., 62.

32. For a full account of this strike, cf. Robert Ozanne, *A Century of Labor-Management Relations at McCormick & International Harvester* (Madison, 1967), 46-51.

33. *IMW* (July 1903): 62.

34. Ozanne, *Century of Labor-Management Relations,* 50-51.

35. In February 1903 the union's journal reported that out of a membership of 10,000, "9,000 of them come from the unorganized ranks and the other 1,000 are members who were turned over to the UMWIU by the AF of L"; *IMW* (February 1903): 21.

36. "That Pittsburgh Conference," *IMW* (February 1903): 23.

37. *Proceedings of the Metal Trades Conference Held in Pittsburgh, January 8, 1903* (n.p., n.d.), 10.

38. *IMW* (July 1903): 57.

39. *Proceedings of the Conference of Metal Trades, Held in the City of Washington, January 25-28, 1904* (n.p., n.d.); cf. also "Conference at Washington," *IMW* (March 1904): 30.

40. *IMW* (November 1904): 98.

41. Ibid., 97.

42. Ibid. (March 1905): 30.

43. "The Chicago Strike," *IMW* (July 1904): 66.

44. *IMW* (September 1904): 81.

45. Ibid. (May 1905): 46; AFL Convention, 1904, *Proceedings,* 65-67.

46. Ibid. (November 1904): 97, (March 1905): 30.

47. "The Parting of the Ways," *IMW* (January 1905): 10.

48. *IMW* (May 1905): 46; *Proceedings of the Founding Convention of the IWW, June 27-July 8, 1905* (New York, 1969), 3-7.

49. See, for instance, Lewis L. Lorwin, *The American Federation of Labor: History, Policies, and Prospects* (Washington, D.C., 1933), 93-94; Philip Taft, *The A.F. of L. in the Time of Gompers* (New York, 1957), 213-24; Foner, *Policies and Practices,* 214-18; Dick, *Labor and Socialism,* 90.

50. Laslett, *Labor and the Left,* 159.

51. See, for instance, AFL Convention, 1906, *Proceedings,* 149; AFL Convention, 1907, *Proceedings,* 159.

52. Philip Foner, *The Industrial Workers of the World, 1905-1917* (New York, 1965), 62-68.

53. See, for instance, Alfred D. Chandler, Jr., "Management Decentralization: A Historical Analysis," *Business History Review* 30 (1956): 111-74.

54. For a comprehensive analysis of the functions of the departments, which, however, fails to place it in the context of the organizational crisis in the U.S. trade union movement, see Albert T. Helbing, *The Departments of the American Federation of Labor* (Baltimore, 1931).

55. AFL Convention, 1908, *Proceedings,* 70.

56. AFL, *Industrial Unionism in Its Relations to Trade Unionism, Being a Report of the Executive Council of the AF of L to the Rochester Convention, 1912* (Washington, D.C., n.d.), 2.

57. *ISR* 8 (December 1907): 372.

58. Ibid. 9 (January 1909): 540.

59. Quoted in Laslett, *Labor and the Left,* 26, 27.

60. "Constitution and By-Laws of the Metal Trades Department of the American Federation of Labor," in *Proceedings of the First Annual Convention of the Metal Trades Department, March 15 and 16, 1909,* 17-22 (hereafter cited as *MTD Convention Proceedings*).

61. Perlman, *The Machinists,* 37.

62. Ibid., 15-31, 44.

63. *MTD Convention Proceedings* (1909), 6-9.

64. Ibid. (1910), 5, 9, 10.

65. Ibid. (1911), 28.

66. Ibid. (1912), 10.

67. Laslett, *Labor and the Left,* 163; Perlman, *The Machinists,* 39.

68. *MTD Convention Proceedings* (1912), 10-11.

69. Ibid. (1913), 46-49.

70. For a brief survey of these strikes, see Helbing, *The Departments of the AFL,* 51-55.

71. Robert Hessen, "The Bethelehem Steel Strike of 1910," *Labor History* 15 (Winter 1974): 3-18.

72. For a detailed account of the strike, see Robert E. Knight, *Industrial Relations in the San Francisco Bay Area, 1900-1918* (Berkeley, 1960), 224-35.

73. AFL Convention, 1914, *Proceedings,* 446-57.

74. See, for example, the secretary's report at the 1910 convention, *MTD Convention Proceedings* (1910), 10-11.

75. Ibid. (1914), 20-21.

76. Ibid. (1913), 42.

77. Quoted in Savage, *Industrial Unionism,* 37-38.

PART 3

The critical years

7

INDUSTRIAL RATIONALIZATION AND THE EROSION OF THE TRADE AGREEMENT

The organizational impasse within the American trade union movement acquires a greater historical significance in view of the fact that the trends in the organization of production and work described earlier intensified at a considerable pace during the second half of the Progressive era, bringing out continuous transformations in the patterns of industrial and labor relations. In this context, the 1907 economic panic stands as a major turning point in the industrial history of the Progressive years. Unlike the short recession of 1903-1904, it set off a protracted crisis that, except for two short revivals, dragged on until the conversion of the U.S. economy into war production.[1] The crisis provided the framework in which American capital accelerated and extended the process of restructuring the organization of industry and of work.

The impact of the struggle at the point of production, which American capital had launched in the early 1900s, became in fact much more visible during the years of industrial readjustment following the 1907 panic. The concern with rationalizing labor relations and increasing productivity became more widespread among American businessmen, showing much more distinctively its character of an antilabor strategy.

One does not have to read Marx to realize the important role crises played in the strengthening of capital's control over the working class, thus setting the stage for a new cycle of development.[2] During the early stages of the post-1907 depression the editors of the influential *Engineering Magazine* made this point clearly:

A time of recession in business is indeed emphatically the best time of all
for progression in efficiency. Extravagances which were unnoticed or
which were necessary when the works were running at high pressure now
become evident and call for cure. Wasteful methods that could not be
changed during the rush of an overcrowded season can be replaced by
economical ones without seriously disturbing the routine of work on
hand. Machines known to be in bad condition and costly to run, but impossible to spare when the plant was overloaded, may be laid off and
remodeled or replaced by new. Improvements in power plant, trans-
mission, or special applications are not only feasible but imperative, if
they will save money and increase the percentage of net earning.[3]

The editors were clear and to the point about how these changes would
affect the workers:

Workmen realize that when the payroll becomes an object of anxious
study, the most efficient employee is the surest to keep his job. Managers find that when orders must be sought with diligence, instead of
turned away from already overflowing doors, it is imperative to improve
their organization and methods, so as to compete with the keenest and
most skillful rivals.[4]

The time had finally arrived for U.S. businessmen to set their own
houses in order for the crisis was providing an "opportunity long sought
but long denied in the foregoing years of overpressure upon forces and
facilities." U.S. businessmen, therefore, needed to become receptive to
the "new Gospel of Efficiency," which more than ever appeared as "a
foretaste of possibly the strongest industrial hope of the Twentieth Century."[5] To aid in this process, the magazine decided to devote its pages—
during the following months and years—to the study, discussion, and propagation of the most recent techniques of efficiency and organization.
Some years later the editors expressed the hope that manufacturers were
continuing to make good use of "the interval of quietness to set their
works in order, to effect improvements in organization, in equipment, in
efficiency."[6]

That this hope was founded and that U.S. businessmen heeded this
kind of call is reflected in the rapid inroads that "scientific management"
techniques and company welfare programs made during this period in
U.S. industry. These were in fact the years when U.S. businessmen were
swept by what historian Samuel Haber has called "the efficiency craze."[7]

Haber's study, however, by stressing the phenomenal dimension of this development and trying to characterize its cultural matrix, fails to show the degree to which this pursuit of efficiency was part of the operational exigencies of large sectors of U.S. industry at that specific economic and political conjuncture.[8] Iron and steel, textile, machine tool, transportation equipment, rubber, coal mining, clothing, railroad and maritime transportation—these were some of the key sectors where the reduction of operating costs through the promotion of new efficiency schemes became most markedly visible.

The key economic indicators for that period show that the overall performance of U.S. industry in the post-1907 years was marked by a tendency toward readjustment and rationalization, as opposed to the almost reckless expansion and growth of the pre-1907 decade. There was an absence of any substantial merger activity in contrast with the dramatic wave of mergers at the turn of the century and in the early 1900s. From 1907 to 1915, in fact, the annual average merger activity was less than one-fourth what it had been in the preceding ten years, and it would prove to be the lowest of any comparable period up to 1955.[9] This tendency of readjustment can also be deduced from the slowdown of total capital in manufacturing industries, which during the 1909-1914 period increased by only half the rate of increase experienced during the previous ten years.[10] Similarly, the physical output for all manufacturing during the 1909-1914 period registered an increase that was one-third lower compared to the increase of the previous five-year period.[11]

Of course, these aggregate data should not cloud the important differences often marking the performance of various industrial sectors. In steel, for instance, where major technological innovations had come to an end around 1904, the increase in physical output for the years 1909-1914 was well below the average increase for all manufacturing (a meager 9% compared to an increase of 51% for the 1904-1909 years). After the 1907 panic, rationalization in this sector primarily took the form of closer intraindustry cooperation under the lead of U.S. Steel and a massive reorganization of work. In 1909 U.S. Steel proclaimed officially the open shop in its mills and moved to drive out the last remnants of unionism, embarking at the same time on a program of sweeping new labor policies designed to boost productivity and reduce labor costs.[12] The transportation equipment sector, on the other hand, registered between 1909 and 1914 a spectacular increase in physical output of nearly 100 percent compared to that of the preceding five years. This performance reflected primarily the rise of the new automotive industry, where rationalization of labor policies was coupled with massive spending in technological innovations, best exemplified by the assembly-line model of production Ford instituted in these years.[13]

But it was in the area of labor-market policies that the impact of this process of industrial rationalization became most evident. The problem of trade-union control over the supply of labor had increasingly forced American capital to seek a solution in the optimal conditions of the market. The expansion of the labor market was in fact an essential prerequisite to the strategy of industrial rationalization and reorganization of work. And it was natural that U.S. businessmen would find in immigration the instrument most readily available to effect this operation. Despite their earlier advocacy of restriction of immigration, U.S. business spokesmen increasingly reversed their position, promoting and lobbying for increased immigration. The first sign of this shift in business attitudes had come in 1904 when the National Board of Trade had opposed the literacy test for prospective immigrants. Soon after, the leading U.S. business publications took a similar position, often emphasizing, as the *Commercial and Financial Chronicle* did, the need for unskilled labor that unrestricted immigration would fulfill. And in 1907, the National Association of Manufacturers, which had long championed the cause of immigration restriction, joined the chorus of what by then had become a general business consensus in favor of increased immigration.[14]

This relaxation in the already mild immigration controls then in effect was actually a labor-market policy. It was designed to make the supply and demand of labor power more fluid to ensure the existence of a reserve army of labor and thus increase the availability of the labor force in the face of the industrial restructuration. From a quantitative point of view, this policy soon produced clear results: the already high tide of arrivals that had begun in 1900 became even higher after the shift in attitude of U.S. business. Between 1907 and 1914 an average of one million arrived compared to 700,000 per year during the previous eight years.[15] It is important to look at this process also from a qualitative point of view because of the debate around immigration that took place in those years. By essentially revolving around questions of culture and ethnicity (assimilation, integration, degradation), the debates clouded the more important labor-market function that immigration was designed to fulfill.[16]

It is true that by 1909 the so-called new immigrants, people coming from Austria-Hungary, Italy, Russia, and the Balkan nations (considered culturally inferior nationalities, and a threat to the quality of life in the United States) made up more than half of the entire labor force of the principal industries of the country.[17] But it is also true that according to the 1911 data gathered by the Immigration Commission, 82.6 percent of the immigrants who arrived between 1899 and 1909 were of ages between fourteen and forty-four and therefore were, as the Immigration Commission called them, "producers rather than dependants"; moreover, over three-fourths of the new immigrants were male. And it is also true that figures from 1908 to 1910 show that 38 percent of the new immigrants returned to their country of origin.[18] But these were the qualities that explain the close relationship existing during those years among immigration, labor market, and industrial reorganization. By being highly mobile, interchangeable, and willing to respond to the job market demand, immigrant labor power provided the fluidity in the labor market needed by industry for its continuous technological and organizational leaps. Seldom as in these years had immigration permitted the use of the reserve army of labor as a political instrument through which capital could seek to impose a new relation of power to the working class.

With an annual average rate of unemployment in the nonfarm work force of 12.5 percent for the years 1908 to 1915 (compared to 8.8 percent for the years 1900 to 1907), the optimal condition in the labor market seemed to have been reached.[19] A leading business publication in the building trade, *The American Lumberman,* editorialized: "It is possible now to secure more and better work for the same price than at any time within the last two years. Materials are cheaper, labor is cheaper, anxious for employment and earnest in its desire to give full value. These certainly are factors which the wise investor should take into account."[20]

The state of the labor market therefore gave businessmen and efficiency experts the necessary maneuvering space to introduce new methods of work and production and new wage structures and to select the workers who were most readily willing to adapt to them or, to put it in the common business jargon of the time, to perform "the weeding out of the less efficient workmen."[21] In addition, welfare experts and personnel managers could more freely put into operation programs designed to adjust their work force, stabilize their labor relations, and boost the productivity of their enterprises.

Given these conditions, it should become clear that the efficiency drive of these years was an industrial strategy designed to maximize the unusually favorable conditions existing in the labor market and thus accelerate the process of rationalization and reorganization of work required by U.S. industry. The results of this strategy were not long in coming, judging from the dramatic increase in labor productivity reached in these years. Between 1907 and 1915 the output per unit of labor input in U.S. manufacturing increased at an annual rate of 33 percent, compared to an annual average increase of 9.9 percent between the years 1900 and 1907.[22]

This process of rationalization had a decidedly anti-working class character. In spite of the phenomenal rise in labor productivity, there corresponded no significant rise in the real wages of the manufacturing work force; and in the unskilled and unorganized sectors, there was actually a decline.[23] The data give us, in fact, only a partial picture of this process. The full social impact generated by it has to be sought elsewhere.

The often brutal intensification of work and the harshness of managerial command over the work force required by this efficiency drive set off a new wave of labor conflict that severely shook the U.S. industrial world. Historian David Montgomery has recently characterized the outbreak of this wave of conflict in the summer of 1909 as "the beginning of a decade of strikes of unprecedented scale and continuity," showing in particular the resistance mounted by skilled workers against the introduction of new efficiency schemes and the degree of control that this sector of workers sought to gain in their work places.[24] This was particularly the case with the Illinois Central Railroad and other lines controlled by the Harriman interests, where shopmen's resistance to new efficiency methods resulted in one of the longest and bitterest strikes of this period, thus underlining the difficulties of the railroad industry in countering the rise in operating costs and the sharp decline in investments with a policy of labor rationalization.[25]

What constitutes the most important novelty, both from a historical and a social standpoint, was the reaction manifested by the mostly unskilled and unorganized workers in the mass production sectors. Labor historians, in fact, have not sufficiently underlined the degree to which the recomposition in the working class brought about by the dramatic process of rationalization accelerated the emergency of the mass-production worker as a new social figure and a new protagonist of capitalist development.[26] To characterize this type of worker as merely unskilled or semiskilled is not enough. Unskilled and semiskilled workers have always been part of industrial capitalism's development, and they were certainly not an invention of the new techniques of rationalization. But in previous cycles of development the unskilled worker had been to a large extent peripheral in relation to a work process that revolved around the skills of a certain stratum of the work force; his function in the production process and his relation to capital's command were largely mediated by the central function performed by skilled workers in that process.[27] On the other hand, the mass production worker of these years is a type of labor power which is the object of a constant retraining process carried out directly by managerial decree and designed to integrate his functions scientifically into the machinery and the new division of labor. His function in the production process, therefore, becomes increasingly central because it is on his labor power that the organic recomposition of capital and hence the new organizational leap are largely founded.[28] New and unmediated, therefore, is also his relationship with capital, as the labor developments of these years demonstrate.

John Commons, an acute observer of industrial affairs, realized how the new efficiency techniques were "doing exactly the thing that forces labor to become class-conscious." "When [the worker's] individuality is scientifically measured off in aliquot parts," Commons observed, "and each part is threatened with substitution by identical parts of other men . . . he and his fellow-workmen compete with each other . . . as units of output. Both are then ripe to recognize their solidarity, and to agree not to compete. And this is the essential thing in class conflict."[29]

Commons was writing these words before the rationalization of work and production had acquired dramatic dimensions; he therefore felt that employers had at their disposal a variety of tools with which to defuse or circumvent the potentiality of conflict. One of these tools, Commons felt, was the increasing use of "immigrant and women's labor at the bottom . . . of industry," which had the effect of "undermining class solidarity."[30]

To some extent, Commons's speculations were accurate. Management and efficiency experts were in fact careful to counter the inherently homogenizing tendencies of the new labor processes with policies that reproduced new hierarchies among their work force and in the labor force at large.[31] Despite this, however, many elements driving the new mass production workers into a common lot persisted, and the results would soon become painfully evident. When in the summer of 1909 McKees Rocks erupted right in the heart of the U.S. steel industry (a strike that most labor historians view as signaling the beginning of mass production workers' militancy), Progressive America seemed to be caught by surprise that more than 3,500 unorganized, mass production workers from sixteen different nationalities were taking on that bastion of U.S. corporate power, U.S. Steel. The workers were revolting against the inhuman working conditions produced by the company's efficiency drive. In fact, soon after the 1907 economic crisis and in the midst of severe unemployment, management had hired teams of efficiency experts and had reorganized the work process by introducing a mass production line and a new piecerate system that had resulted in speed-ups and a reduction of take-home pay for most of the workers.[32] The editor of the *Survey,* Paul Kellog, who had covered the strike, expressed the concern of many other observers when he wrote that the strike signaled "a revolution within the labor movement." For Kellog, this strike had "a prophetic character. It shows the forces that during the next decade might determine the standard of life of immigrant workers in the Pittsburgh area."[33]

Commons himself seemed to have had second thoughts a few years later when he privately expressed his concern that "a movement of the unskilled" was dominating the American industrial scene.[34] It was a concern that had quickly become widespread among observers and practitioners of industrial affairs, especially since the Industrial Workers of the World had begun their organizing drives in the mass production sectors, setting off the most dramatic series of strikes among the "unorganizables" in the industrial heartland and becoming the most feared workers' organization in the United States, despite the relatively small number of their membership.

Clearly this was the other face of the process of working class recomposition brought about by the efficiency drive, and it was again forcing the labor problem to center stage—only in a more complex form. It became increasingly difficult in these years to distinguish the "labor problem" from the "immigration problem,"[35] especially for many reformers who could not see, or did not want to see, how the recomposition of the working class made possible by unrestrained immigration was functional to the attainment of their much cherished efficiency and technical progress.[36] More importantly, however, the struggles in the mass production sectors not only constituted a direct challenge to the new model of industrial development and progress; they also underlined the inadequacy of the existing institutional machinery designed to prevent industrial conflict, thus raising again the crucial question of the political mediation of class conflict in progressive America.

It is against this background that one has to view the new impetus manifest among reformers and industrial experts searching for new formulas to regulate industrial disputes and calling for more direct government intervention at both the state and national levels. And it is this historic context that also highlights the erosion of the political mediation operated in the previous years by the AFL-NCF entente through their trade agreement program.

The AFL's inability to resolve the organizational problem in the face of the rapid recomposition of the working class meant not only that increasing sectors of the U.S. labor force remained outside its sphere, totally subject to the employers' initiative in matters of industrial and labor relations; it also meant that when industrial conflict erupted in those "unorganizable" mass production sectors, the AFL was ill prepared, if not unwilling, to throw its weight as a mediating power. The new "class alignment" that such a move would have entailed—to use Commons's expression—was too dear a price for the AFL leadership to pay.

Even in sectors of traditional trade union strength where collective bargaining had become an established practice, the effects of the employers' initiative were becoming apparent. Between 1907 and 1909 about half the number of national and district collective bargaining systems that had been established during the heyday of the trade agreement were dissolved.[37] Some of these agreements had been looked upon by advocates of the trade agreement as models of stable employer-employee relations. A case in point was the agreements between the International Longshoremen's Association and the various carriers and docks associations, established years earlier under the direct influence of such National Civic Federation luminaries as Marcus Hanna and Daniel Keefe.[38] The explanation that H. G. Dalton, one of the dock managers, gave to the NCF president, S. Low, is illuminating: "For years," Dalton pointed out, "we made Trade Agreements with dock men, and were glad to do so: and it was only when it became impracticable and impossible for continued successful operation of the docks, that we were forced to discontinue it." The underlying reason, Dalton emphasized, was the adoption of "very costly and complicated machinery used on the docks," necessitating that the control of operations be totally in management's hands.[39] Confronted by such an operational imperative, the NCF men could only tell the incensed longshoremen's officers that "the indications are that we shall not be able to change the position taken by the Lake Carriers' Association or that of the dock managers."[40]

A statistical survey of union membership trends made in 1910 by Harvard economist C. H. Parker clearly showed the negative impact that the 1907 economic crisis had on union growth and reflected the critical stage into which collective bargaining had entered.[41] Although after 1910 total union membership often tended to fluctuate upward somewhat, by 1915 unionization appeared to have become effectively checked, especially in the groups that made up the bulk of the manufacturing industries and that (except for the conspicuous growth in the garment sector) actually showed a marked decline.[42] Parker's conclusion that "collective bargaining on a large scale in the United States seem [ed] to be for the moment upon the decline" was not without foundation.[43] This becomes especially clear from the difficulties encountered in those years by the Trade Agreement Department of the National Civic Federation, the agency that had led the movement for the diffusion of the trade agreement.

In August 1908 John Mitchell became the full-time director of the Trade Agreement Department. Mitchell, who had just relinquished the presidency of the miners' union, accepted the new job offer with great enthusiasm. As he wrote to his brother David, "the work will be in line with my highest and best conception of the industrial peace movement."[44] Although Mitchell was to aid in strengthening the various facets of the federation, his main function was to develop "the idea of the trade agreement," using all the organizational channels and resources the NCF could muster to generate interest among employers regarding the beneficial effects of the trade agreement.[45]

The outcome of this renewed effort was dismal, clearly reflecting the downward trend characterizing the trade agreement in those years. The promotional and educational work, for instance, did not seem to get off the ground. Mitchell instead found himself involved in a number of disputes, acting in a mediating and arbitrating capacity—a function that was not contemplated in the Trade Agreement Department's new plans but that the NCF could not turn down.[46]

Even when, in August 1909, it was decided to strengthen the department by creating an executive committee composed of employers and union leaders, the result was discouraging. Of the nearly thirty employers who were asked to serve on this committee, only nine accepted, and they all belonged to sectors where the use of the trade agreement had long been established (such as building and printing) or where the people had been officers of the NCF for many years. Of the employers belonging to manufacturing industries, only two indicated a willingness to consider the invitation, and the rest expressed a disinterest in the matter or declined to answer.[47] This cold response from the employers had serious effects on the ability of the department to finance itself. The projected $5,000 per year, which was expected to come from employers, did not quite materialize, and soon the department fell into deficit.[48]

Employers were not the only ones to respond negatively to this effort. A sense of pessimism seemed to exist among trade union officials. Abe Rosenberg of the International Ladies' Garment Workers Union, for instance, in declining an invitation to serve on the Trade Agreement Department's committee, was outspoken about his feelings. He told Mitchell, "Our manufacturers do not believe in trade agreements. I have not yet come across a single one that does, and I have had dealings with most of them. They only sign an agreement with us when they are pressed to the wall by the organization, and as soon as they sign one, they do all they possibly can to violate it. . . . We must constantly apply the force of our organization to make them live up to it."[49]

Rosenberg's prescription actually would soon result in the most astonishing, though unique, labor success of these years in the two major garment centers of the nation, Chicago and New York City. A number of factors—so well analyzed by Melvyn Dubofsky—contributed to this success, not least of all the militance and determination of the mostly immigrant garment workers, the able leadership provided by union officers coupled with their willingness to adopt a semi-industrial union structure, and the highly competitive nature of the industry, which led the employers to recognize that a strong union would bring stability to their strike-ridden industry, would help establish common standards, and would eradicate the sweatshop plague that afflicted the garment industry. The result was an elaborate machinery of industrial relations known as the Protocol of Peace, which for the few years it was in operation generated a great deal of interest and publicity.[50] But this development, which took place totally outside the sphere of influence of the NCF (and was actually looked upon with a mixture of skepticism and envy by Easley), had the effect of emphasizing the difficulties besetting the NCF's Trade Agreement Department.[51]

That the Trade Agreement Department was not meeting the expectations of those who had counted on it is also reflected in the feelings that Mitchell expressed privately. According to his biographer, Mitchell's new work was "a let-down," and he often felt that "he was being sidetracked."[52] Writing to Gompers in August 1910, Mitchell admitted candidly his lack of interest in the work that he had undertaken with great enthusiasm two years earlier. He explained in that letter that most of the work he was doing in the Trade Agreement Department was in the nature of conciliation of disputes; consequently he had been unable to break any new ground in extending the trade agreement to new organizations or new trades. "In the well organized trades," Mitchell pointed out, "the representatives of the union and the employers' interests have been able to work out their own problems, and it is much better of course that they should do so than that there should be an intervention on the part of outside forces." Mitchell then went on to explain the failure of the department to make new inroads in trades that were partially organized or where the unions were not strong. Here, the main obstacle Mitchell was encountering was the employers' insistence on the open shop. Although Mitchell justified his lack of success on the grond that "it was well known among the employers that [he was] in favor of the union shop," it is significant that an agency such as the NCF Trade Agreement Department, with all its experience in the field and its reputation among wide sectors of the employers' class and led by such a respectable public figure as John Mitchell, would be met with such a cold reception from employers.[53]

In 1911 a major crisis beset the NCF, affecting drastically the work of the Trade Agreement Department. As a result of forces mounting in the United Mine Workers of America against the NCF, a resolution was passed at the miners' national convention prohibiting members of the UMW to hold membership in the NCF. Forced to choose, Mitchell decided to resign from his post with the NCF.[54] Losing Mitchell meant in effect the abandonment of those grandiose goals that the NCF executive—and Easley in particular—had hoped to achieve through the Trade Agreement Department.

Easley did try to relaunch the department by considering the appointment of two cochairmen, Herman Ridder and James Lynch, who represented, respectively, the employer and the labor side of a sector (printing) where perhaps the most exemplary system of trade agreement prevailed. Easley was convinced that this move would lay the basis for "a tremendously strong department in the interest of collective bargaining."[55] But when Gompers was consulted on this proposed course of action, he vetoed it. Gompers's reaction is indicative of the atmosphere existing in industrial and labor circles regarding the possibilities of extending the use of the trade agreement through traditional vehicles. His objection centered on the fact that the appointment of another labor man—after the Mitchell event— to the executive council of the NCF would most likely set off another crisis within the AFL. He wrote to NCF President Seth Low, "it would not be wise for some time to come to subject active men in the labor movement to what may be perverted to be a new opportunity for attack by the vicious and the unthinking."[56]

Clearly, the NCF, which had provided the framework for the capital-labor entente through the promotion of the trade agreement, had now reached a major crisis point. And with it, the very possibility of further extending the trade agreement.

The NCF leadership must have been aware of this state of affairs. While its Trade Agreement Department was encountering increasing difficulties, its Welfare Department—promoting an alternative model of industrial relations—was experiencing a spectacular growth and success, thus reflecting the drastic impact that the process of industrial rationalization was having on labor relations practices.

NOTES

1. See the recent revision of the traditional periodization of U.S. economic development by economists Baran and Sweezy, where the years 1907-1914 stand as a period of its own. Paul Baran and Paul Sweezy, *Monopoly Capital* (New York, 1966), 218-34. See also R. A. Gordon's description of the pattern of business cycles for the years 1897-1914, where the three cycles running from June 1897 to June 1908 show an average length of expansion of twenty-six months as against eighteen months of contraction; for the two cycles running from June 1908 to December 1914, the average length of expansion is 15.5 months, as against 23.5 of contraction; R. A. Gordon, *Business Fluctuations* (New York, 1952), 216; cf also, Willard L. Thorp, *Business Annals* (New York, 1926), 137-42; the most thorough work is still W. Schluter, *The Pre-War Business Cycle, 1907-1914* (New York, 1916).

2. For a classic, theoretical statement of this question see Joseph A. Schumpeter, *Business Cycles* (1939), and the recent, perceptive discussion by Antonio Negri, "Note sul Ciclo e la Crisis," in Sergio Bologna et al., *Operai e Stato* (Milan, 1972).

3. *Engineering Magazine* 35 (1908) : 257.

4. Ibid., 95.

5. Ibid., 596.

6. Ibid., 37 (1909) : 982.

7. Samuel Haber, *Efficiency and Uplift: Scientific Management in the Progressive Era* (Chicago, 1964), 52. Cf. also *Report of the U.S. Commissioner on Industrial Relations* (Washington, D.C., 1916), 1 : 763-1024 (hereafter cited as CIR, *Final Report*); U.S. Congress, House of Representatives, *Hearings before the Special Committee of the House of Representatives to Investigate the Taylor System and other Systems of Shop Management* (Washington, D.C., 1912); Frederick W. Taylor, *Principles of Scientific Management* (New York, 1911); Milton Nadworny, *Scientific Management and the Unions* (Cambridge, Mass., 1955); Hugh G. J. Aitken, *Taylorism at Watertown Arsenal: Scientific Management in Action, 1908-1915* (Cambridge, Mass., 1960). The literature on scientific management has grown considerably in recent times; see Bradley Rudin, "Industrial Betterment and Scientific Management as Social Control, 1890-1920," *Berkeley Journal of Sociology* 17 (1972-1973): 59-77; Judith A. Merkle, "The Taylor Strategy, Organizational Innovation and Class Structure," *Berkeley Journal of Sociology* 13 (1968); Daniel Nelson and Stuart Campbell, "Taylorism Versus Welfare Work in American Industry," *Business History Review* 46 (Spring 1972); Harry Braverman, *Labor and Monopoly Capital* (New York, 1974).

8. One important aspect of this economic and political conjuncture—recently analyzed by Burton Kaufman—was the urgency reflected among U.S. manufacturers to improve the country's foreign trade in the face of the severe competition that had been recently mounting, especially from Germany. As future Secretary of Commerce William C. Readfield put it in 1911, successful improvement of foreign trade made it imperative that every concerned U.S. industrialist reappraise "his plant, his methods of management, of production, of handling men, his costs, his overhead charges." Burton I. Kaufman, *Efficiency and Expansion: Foreign Trade Organization in the Wilson Administration* (Westport, Conn., 1974), 46, and esp. chap. 2.

9. Ralph Nelson, *Merger Movements in America* (Princeton, 1960), 34-35.

10. Daniel Creamer, *Capital in Manufacturing and Mining: Its Formation and Financing* (Princeton, 1960), 22, 25.

11. Solomon Fabricant, *The Output of Manufacturing Industries, 1889-1937* (New York, 1940), 60, 61; cf. also John W. Kendrick, *Productivity Trends in the United States* (Princeton, 1961), 465.

12. Fabricant, *The Output,* 61; David Brody, *Steelworkers in America: The Nonunion Era* (New York, 1969), 33, 125, 152.

13. Fabricant, *The Output,* 61; Keith Sward, *The Legend of Henry Ford* (New York, 1972), chaps. 1 and 2.

14. John Higham, *Strangers in the Land* (New York, 1973), 115-16; Robert H. Wiebe, *Business and Reform* (Chicago, 1968), 182-83.

15. Harold Faulkner, *The Decline of Laissez Faire* (New York, 1951), 101; Jeremiah Jenks and W. Jett Lauck, *The Immigrant Problem* (New York, 1913), 465-66.

16. Typical in this regard was the reasoning put forth by the Immigration Commission; despite the attention it devoted to this problem, the commission declined to reach a conclusion on the relationship between immigration and industrial growth: "*Coincident* with the advent of these millions of unskilled laborers there has been an unprecedented expansion of the industries in which they have been employed. Whether this great immigration movement was caused by the industrial development, or whether the fact that a practically unlimited and available supply of cheap labor existing in Europe was taken advantage of for the purpose of expanding industries, cannot well be demonstrated." The commission, however, concluded that "southern and eastern European immigrants have almost completely *monopolized* unskilled labor activities in many of the more important industries," thus suggesting that the degradation of labor conditions in those industries had to be imputed to the immigrants themselves. *Report of the Immigration Commission* (Washington, D.C.), 1 : 37 (emphasis added). Cf. also John Commons, *Races and Immigrants in America* (New York, 1907).

17. *Report of the Immigration Commission,* 1 : 37. Faulkner, *Decline,* 103.

18. *Report of the Immigration Commission,* 1 : 97, 4 : 41; Faulkner, *Decline,* 104.

19. Stanley Lebergott, *Manpower in Economic Growth* (New York, 1964), 512.

20. Quoted in *Engineering Magazine* 35 (1908) : 595.

21. Quoted in Montgomery, "The 'New Unionism,' " 512.

22. Kendrick, *Productivity Trends,* 465.

23. Paul Douglas, *Real Wages in the United States, 1890-1926* (Boston, 1930); Albert Rees, *Real Wages in Manufacturing, 1890-1914* (Princeton, 1961).

24. Montgomery, "The 'New Unionism,' " 511.

25. Ibid.; CIR, *Final Report,* 10: 9697-10048; Albro Martin, *Enterprise Denied: Origins of the Decline of American Railroads, 1897-1917* (New York, 1971), 129-36, 374-75.

26. A beginning attempt has been made in Gisela Bock, Paulo Carpignano, and Bruno Ramirez, *La Formazione dell'Operaio Massa negli USA, 1898-1922* (Milan, 1976).

27. See especially H. J. Habakkuk, *American and British Technology in the 19th Century* (London, 1962); David Montgomery, "Workers Control in Machine Production in the 19th Century," *Labor History* (Fall 1976); Katherine Stone, "The Origins of Job Structure in the Steel Industry," *Radical America* 7 (1973) : 19-64; *Eleventh Special Report of the Commissioner of Labor, Regulation and Restriction of Output* (Washington, D.C., 1904).

28. Despite the terminological confusion, a study done by the U.S. Department of Labor in 1910 described quite well the process in question in regard to the steel industry: "The semi-skilled among the production force consist for the most part of workmen who have been taught to perform relatively complex functions, such as the operation of cranes and other mechanical appliances, but who possess little or no general mechanical or metallurgical knowledge. . . . This class has been developed largely within recent years along with the growth in the use of machinery and electrical power in industry. The whole tendency of the industry is to greatly increase the proportion of the production force formed by this class of workmen. They are displacing both the skilled and the unskilled workmen." U.S. Commissioner of Labor, *Conditions of Employment in the Iron and Steel Industry in the United States* (Washington, D.C., 1913), 3 : 81. Cf. also the perceptive analysis by Stone, "The Origins." I am also indebted for this discussion to the very perceptive analyses by Gisela Bock, "L'Altro' Movimento Operaio negli Stati Uniti," and Paulo Carpignano, "Immigrazione e Degradazione," both in Bock, Carpignano, and Ramirez, *La Formazione.*

29. John Commons, *Labor and Administration* (New York, 1913), 75.

30. Ibid., 78.

31. See especially Stone, "The Origins."

32. Cf. especially John N. Ingham, "A Strike in the Progressive Era: McKees Rocks, 1909," *The Pennsylvania Magazine of History and Biography* 90 (1966) : 353-77.

33. Paul U. Kellog, "The McKees Rocks Strike," *The Survey* 12 (1909) : 665.

34. Commons to W. B. Paker, May 14, 1912; Commons Papers, box 2, Wisconsin State Historical Society, Madison, Wisconsin.

35. Cf. especially the discussion by Isaac Hourwich, *Immigration and*

Labor: The Economic Aspects of Immigration to the United States (New York, 1912), 35; Jenks and Lauck, *The Immigrant Problem.*

36. Typical was the reasoning put forth by the Immigration Commission: "The immigrants' numbers are so great and the influx is so continuous that even with the remarkable expansion of industry during the past few years there has been created an over supply of unskilled labor, and in some of the industries this is reflected in a curtailed number of working days and a consequent yearly income among the unskilled workers which is very much less than is indicated by the daily wage rates paid; and while it may not have lowered in a marked degree the American standard of living, it has introduced a lower standard which has become prevalent in the unskilled industry at large." *Reports of the Immigration Commission,* 1 : 39. When, some years later, the prevailingly immigrant textile workers of Lawrence, Massachusetts, struck against that "lower standard," organs such as the *New York Evening Sun* did not hesitate to label the strike a threat to "the solidarity of the Nation," charging that "the first considerable development of an actually revolutionary spirit comes today, and comes . . . among the un-American immigrants from Southern Europe." *Literary Digest* 47 (1913) : 197.

37. George Barnett, "National and District Systems of Collective Bargaining in the United States," *Quarterly Journal of Economics* 26 (1912) : 427-28.

38. Ibid.; *NCF Monthly Review* (June 1904) : 1-3.

39. H. G. Dalton to Seth Low, June 19, 1909, box 104, NCF Papers, New York Public Library.

40. Mitchell to T. V. O'Connor, June 28, 1909, box 104, NCF Papers.

41. C. H. Parker, "The Decline in Trade Union Membership," *Quarterly Journal of Economics* 24 (May 1910) : 564-69.

42. Leo Wolman, *Ebb and Flow in Trade Unionism* (New York, 1936), 172-92.

43. C. H. Parker, "The Decline," 566.

44. John Mitchell to David Mitchell, September 16, 1908, Mitchell Papers, Catholic University of America, Washington, D.C.; cf. also *NCF Review* (September 1908) : 1, 10.

45. *NCF Review* (September 1908): 1, 10.

46. "Disputes settled, given consideration by, or brought to the attention of the Trade Agreement Department: brief history of," memorandum, box 151, NCF Papers.

47. "Proposed Trade Agreement Committee," memorandum, box 151, NCF Papers.

48. Marguerite Green, *The National Civic Federation and the American Labor Movement* (Washington, D.C., 1956), 318.

49. Rosenberg to Mitchell, November 16, 1908, box 104, NCF Papers.

50. CIR, *Final Report,* 1 : 697-705; Melvyn Dubofsky, *When Workers Organize* (Amherst, 1968).

51. "Proceedings of the Thirteenth Annual Meeting of the N.C.F. Executive Council, January 28, 1913," box 187(1), NCF Papers.

52. Gluck, *John Mitchell,* 227.

53. Quoted in ibid.

54. Green, *National Civic Federation,* 153-58; John Mitchell to editor of the *United Mine Workers' Journal,* March 29, 1911, box 87, Mitchell Papers.

55. Easley to Gompers, March 6, 1911, box 79a, NCF Papers.

56. Gompers to Low, March 9, 1911, box 79a, NCF Papers.

8

WELFARISM VERSUS COLLECTIVE BARGAINING

Among the various techniques devised by the U.S. employing class during the Progressive years to deal with the labor problem, welfarism has not received the same amount of attention by historians as, for instance, Taylorism has. In part this is because of the quick acceptance that welfarism gained among wide sectors of the American public, including the AFL establishment, which contrasts sharply with the controversial character surrounding Taylorism. Moreover, because of its strong humanitarian aura, welfare work was perceived more as an employer's attitude and show of goodwill than as a distinct business policy designed to rationalize labor and industrial relations. Unlike scientific management, welfare work did not produce a body of coherent theory—at least not during the period under review—and although its humanitarian philosophy was widely publicized, its managerial assumptions were seldom articulated publicly and in the main were kept within the confines of business meetings and conferences.

Another important factor accounting for the historians' general neglect stems from the very character of welfare work, which involved a whole range of programs depending entirely on the resources, ambitions, and capabilities of individual employers, thus making it difficult to gain a comprehensive view of both the extent of this trend and its specific contents. One employer explained at the end of an early welfare conference, "Each one had an idea that his welfare work was an individual effort in his particular locality, and was surprised to find out that a great deal of his work was being done throughout the United States."[1]

An early picture of the extent and character of welfare work in the

United States is provided by a confidential report prepared in 1902 by
Gertrude Beeks in her capacity as welfare manager for the McCormick
Harvester Company—a corporation that pioneered in this field.[2] The report
was written after an extensive tour from coast to coast that Beeks undertook in 1901 and 1902, visiting some two dozen companies that had
adopted welfare programs. Most of the companies she surveyed were in
manufacturing sectors, and ranged in size from medium to large. Several
were engaged in serial and mass production, employing in the main unskilled or semiskilled labor—much of it female and immigrant.

The welfare measures varied a great deal from case to case, but a certain degree of uniformity was apparent. They were aimed at three major
areas: (1) improvement of working conditions by making life in the plant
more satisfying to the workers by adding sanitation and health facilities,
proper ventilation and lighting, lunchrooms, cafeterias, and lockers, to
name a few; (2) wage policies, designed to make the workers feel that their
earnings were as good as, if not better than, what they could get working
elsewhere. Some of these policies included profit-sharing and various in-
centive schemes, based normally on productivity and merit. Some of them
were aimed strictly at female labor, such as the attendance pay provision
adopted by the American Manufacturing Company, which entitled a worker
to an extra day of pay for every twenty-four days of continuous work;[3]
(3) organization and planning of workers' free-time activities, including
training programs, such as courses in home economics for female workers,
cultural facilities, such as libraries and reading rooms, and entertainment
facilities and programs, ranging from clubs and summer cottages to elaborate planning of tours, picnics, and parties.

Two years later, a leading business publication gave the following definition of welfare work: "Welfare work involves special consideration for
physical comfort wherever labor is performed; opportunities of recreation; educational advantages; and the providing of suitable sanitary homes;
its application to be measured by the exigencies of the case. Plans for
saving and lending money, insurance and pensions are also included in
welfare work."[4]

Thus, when the leaders of the National Civic Federation decided to set
up a Welfare Department in 1904, welfare work or industrial betterment—
as it was also known at the time—was not a novel idea. In addition several
NCF officers were employers who had adopted welfare work in their establishments. The NCF enlisted Gertrude Beeks, who became the depart-

ment's secretary and a driving force in this sphere of activity.[5] The creation of this department had the effect of crystallizing a growing trend
among American employers and of turning it into a unified national movement. To the trial-and-error method that individual employers were following independently in implementing welfare programs, the NCF was
offering a framework through which employers could compare their
experiences, analyze common problems, and improve their programs. The
spectacular success that the Welfare Department began to enjoy in the
following years evidences not only how timely the move establishing the
department had been, but also how widespread the employers' sentiment
was in favor of welfare work.

At the time of its establishment, the department counted twenty-seven
prominent employers as its officers and had a membership of 125.[6] Two
years later, it had 250 members and a number of local committees had
been established to publicize its welfare work.[7] Soon the department was
able to count on a permanent staff of welfare work experts, thus offering
consulting services to employers and even installing welfare programs
upon request free of charge. The NCF moreover decentralized its welfare
activities through the creation of its Woman's Welfare Department, "composed largely," as the *Review* put it, "of women who are themselves stock-
holders or who, through family relationships, are financially interested in
industrial organizations . . . and who therefore should be interested in the
welfare of workers of enterprises from which they draw their profits."[8]
But it was during the post-1908 years—years of intense industrial restructuring and reorganization—that the welfare movement made its most
dramatic inroads. By 1911, in fact, the NCF's stepped-up campaign had
found many more receptive ears; the department could now boast 500
members.[9] A few years later, it was clear that the welfare movement had
taken root among wide sectors of U.S. employers. A survey taken by the
NCF in 1914 showed in fact that there were some 2,500 employers across
the country adopting welfare programs in their establishments.[10] The movement, moreover, had spread into other industrial sectors, including coal
mining, department stores, and even insurance companies.[11]

The leadership role that the NCF provided to the welfare movement
meant more than merely advocating and popularizing the work among
employers; it also involved the articulation of a philosophy underlying
welfare work and its translation into a series of tenets designed to make
the work more effective and more acceptable to the workers and to the

public. Central to this philosophy was the acknowledgment of the educational function that industry had with respect to the work force, and thus the need for employers to manage this educational process in the first person. The *NCF Review* asked its readers, Was it not "the duty of every captain of industry, who controls the lives of men, women, and children to find some method of work and education that can be applied to his community to educate his employees, to make better citizens of them and to inspire them toward higher standards?"[12] "Education" did not imply strictly the imparting of technical knowledge as, for instance, through training programs—though these too were often part of welfare programs. It was indispensable also to instill in workers the virtues and values that would promote in them an attachment to work and a sense of loyalty to the enterprise.

The rationale expressed by one welfare manager, as he commented on the saving programs introduced by his company, was typical: "The encouragement of thrift or saving should . . . form part of our factory welfare plan. These workers who save some portion of their earnings are the most valuable ones to keep, as being careful of their own goods, and having learned the value of economy they are apt to be also more careful of their employers' materials and time, than the improvident or those who save nothing."[13] Other companies were more outspoken about the educational objective of their welfare programs. The Atchison, Topeka & Santa Fe Railway Co., for instance, made it explicit that "the company's motive in instituting [welfare] work was to surround the employees with educating influences; to develop them and increase efficiency."[14] The company provided fifteen employees' reading rooms and clubhouses, with an inscribed motto saying, "Give a man a bath, a book, and an entertainment that appeals to his mind and hopes by music and knowledge, and you have enlarged, extended and adorned his life; and as he becomes more faithful to himself he is more valuable to the company."[15]

Much of the educational influence contemplated to these programs was directed toward "developing the human side of work"— to use a common expression in the welfare work jargon. In effect this meant promoting among workers the type of life-style and social relations that made them more responsive to the exigencies of production.

Social relations, in other words, both in the plant and in the community, were as important for the productivity of the enterprise as the individual unit of labor power expended by the worker in the work process. These relations therefore had to be regarded as more than a mere by-product of the organization of work: they had to be subjected to rational planning so as to eradicate any potential source of conflict or tension that could hamper the harmonious growth of the enterprise. Hence the NCF recommended that welfare managers should have special qualities: "a knowledge of industrial subjects," plus "tact, executive ability, common sense, acquaintance with local jealousies and sometimes with racial prejudices."[16]

This benevolent attitude on the part of the employer, however, as well as the money involved to administer these programs, could arouse the suspicion of the workers and be interpreted as paternalism at their expense. Gertrude Beeks acknowledged this problem—"any effort at welfare work may be regarded as more or less paternalistic—but proposed a few guidelines to deal with it.[17] The employer had to make sure that he paid at least "the market wage" to his worker to "create in the mind of the worker confidence in the justice and fair dealing of the employer. This confidence," Beeks added, "[was] absolutely essential to the prosecution of welfare work, which must fail whenever the workers are led to suspect that its cost is taken from their work."[18] In any case, Beeks made clear, paternalism was not always bad: "A resort to paternalism . . . is necessary or desirable for recent immigrants who in their native lands have been accustomed to the guardianship of superior authority." In one way or the other, the essential rule was to gain the workers' confidence: "When their confidence has been gained, employees will generally prefer to entrust the direction of welfare work to the employer."[19]

Behind a facade of humanitarianism and philanthropy, welfare work was increasingly emerging as a technique of industrial relations whose value was measured in most cases on the basis of the increased productivity and profits it yielded. The slogan popularized by National Cash Register's president, John Patterson—"it pays"—was reflected in more circumspect, though not less candid, statements from other businessmen.[20] A General Electric officer explained at an NTC Welfare Department meeting, "The General Electric Company does not believe in spending anything in a purely sentimental way; it is a cold business proposition behind it every time. If that was not the case I would not help in the work."[21] According to C. U. Carpenter, the man responsible for setting up the welfare program at the National Cash Register Company, welfare work had proved very effective in combating the workers' restriction of output. As a result of their new welfare policies, Carpenter explained to some fellow businessmen, "our labor cost (of course this is confidential) has been reduced twenty-three per cent, and in one case, forty-nine per cent; so we feel that we could afford to do it."[22] An officer of the J. H. Williams and Co.'s Shops—where one of the main features of their welfare program was the installation of showers and other hygienic facilities— stated that "these things are done . . . as a source of profit. It pays," he said, adding that "a clean man produces more in the long run than a dirty man."[23]

One of the main reasons why welfare policies resulted in higher labor productivity was their stabilizing effect on the work force. In this sense, as an industrial relations technique, welfare work was designed to cope with one of the major problems plaguing employers, especially in the mass-production and mass-service sectors: the high rate of turnover of the work force. The intrinsic characteristics of this type of labor—its mobility, interchangeability, and lack of job consciousness—made the function of management arduous and costly, especially because of the frequent, though short-lived, outbreaks of conflict characterizing these sectors.[24] Most of the employers adopting welfare policies felt that this approach helped them considerably to minimize this problem. A U.S. Steel officer explained that before his company implemented welfare programs, "employees came and went constantly; many of them used to work from one pay to the next." In this particular case, the main feature of U.S. Steel's welfare policy was a banking system designed to encourage and assist workers in saving some of their earnings. As a result, management was able to "secure a more permanent set of employees."[25] Similar experiences were recorded by the officers of two of the major mass-production companies adopting welfare policies: Westinghouse Electric Company and National Cash Register. The welfare manager of the Westinghouse Lamp Company in Bloomfield, New Jersey, felt that welfare had effectively reduced the rate of turnover in their plant, and "enable [ed the company] to command a higher class of workers; [moreover]," she added, "they stay with us, which is quite important, as breaking in new help is a large item of expense to the management."[26]

Stabilizing the work force and securing "a higher class of workers" involved necessarily a process of selection based on loyalty and commitment to the goals of the enterprise, which in effect were part of welfare policies. The welfare office of the John Wanamaker Company—a leading Philadelphia department store—had worked out a system that "[gave] complete records of the home conditions of the employees, as well as other matters which assisted the company materially in maintaining a stable work force."

In order to make the system operative, it was necessary for the company to "investigate each home" and thus keep in constant touch with the lives of its workers and their families.[27] These features of welfare work were clearly summarized in a report prepared by the NCF in 1916, which stated that the main benefits of these programs consisted in their "attracting a higher grade of labor, building up a more permanent force and thereby improving the efficiency of the plant."[28]

In a recent article, business historians Daniel Nelson and Stuart Campbell try to compare welfarism and Taylorism as two trends within the management movement during the Progressive era. The distinguishing criterion the authors adopt is that Taylorism's focus was "entirely within the plant," and welfare work was almost entirely on "outside activities."[29] Not only is it doubtful that this "inside-outside" criterion correctly characterizes Taylorism, but it also obscures some of the essential characteristics of welfare work.

Apart from the fact that some of the welfare policies applied directly to the work place (such as wage incentives, sanitation measures, and employee representation schemes), this criterion misses the fact that the chief characteristic of the welfare approach was to posit a direct relationship between "inside" and "outside" activities. Welfare work, in fact, represents capital's conscious discovery of the direct link existing between work and leisure, between work place and community, between the worker viewed as merely labor power and the worker as part of a network of social relations extending from the work place to the community—and its attempt to subject this relation to rational planning. It was this extended control over the workers—both as labor power and as members of a work community—that was the result of and necessitated the exclusion of any source of authority for the workers other than management's.

In the case of labor unions—the most immediate source of alternative authority for the workers—the effects of these policies were crucial. Although NCF Welfare Department spokesmen and spokeswomen publicly took the position that welfare work was supplementary to any work done by labor unions, in practice one of the main goals of welfare policies was to eliminate labor unions in establishments where they existed or to undermine the possibility of their existence through the gamut of benefits that management granted their employees.[30]

Indeed, in many cases the reason that had led employers to initiate welfare work stemmed from their attempt to halt the impact of unionism in their plants. This is one of the main conclusions emerging from the survey Gertrude Beeks prepared in 1901-1902. The officers of the Heinz Company—a pioneer in the mass production of canned food—explained, for instance, that the secret of the company's success with welfare work was that they "do not employ a single union man." Another company surveyed in the Beeks report, the Willamette Iron and Steel Works, had begun adopting welfare programs immediately after the machinists' strike of 1901 in an attempt to tighten control over the work force and ensure more stable labor relations. The case of Philadelphia's Enterprise Manufacturing Company was similar; management had introduced welfare programs after a nine-month strike. One company officer explained that welfare work had proved "one of the best investments ever made by the Company."[31]

In many cases, the work of preventing the growth of unions was facilitated by the creation of workers' committees, which were considered part of welfare policies. Created with the pretext that they allowed a more active participation by the workers in the activities of the enterprise, in effect these bodies were a vehicle through which management could exert more effective control over the work force—the forerunners of company unions that in later years spread considerably in many sectors of U.S. industry.[32] At an NCF Welfare Department meeting, one employer gave a vivid and detailed description of the workers' committee he had set up in his plant as the main feature of his welfare program and explained how he had been able to "get rid of the union" through this device.[33]

Another such employer was C. E. Mackay, president of the Postal-Telegraph Cable Company, who after a strike had set up a company union as the main feature of the company welfare program. When an officer of the Commercial Telegraphers International Union—the union affected—complained to John Mitchell about the matter, the latter could only reassure him that there were "hopeful signs," on the ground that "the Welfare Department and the Trade Agreement Department [were] closely allied."[34]

Perhaps the most revealing illustration of the antiunion objective of welfare work comes from a corporation with one of the most elaborate systems of welfare programs and whose officers and owners were among the most influential leaders in the NCF: the McCormick International Harvester Company. The company's welfare manager thought the role of the Labor Department was to program and administer welfare policies in the company's plants:

One of the principal objects of this [labor] department should be to create and promote among the employees a feeling of loyalty for and confidence in the management.

It should convince the employees that they can get what they most want without the necessity of paying anyone for it.

It should endeavor to secure for the employee just what he most desires from the union. It should secure for him those results which labor organizations declare are their basic objects; namely, higher wages and shorter hours.

It should provide means by which employees can have their grievances heard and adjusted without the necessity of joining a union.

It should keep thoroughly posted on all matters pertaining to labor organizations, keeping fully informed of the wages and hours demanded by the different trades.

It should have general supervision of betterment, education and recreation work.

It should strive to surround employees with conditions that will conduce to better work.

It should compile statistics showing the rate of wages received and hours worked by the various crafts in all large manufacturing concerns.[35]

From its inception, therefore, welfare work was not just an alternative to unionism; it was also an overt antiunion policy. Clearly, welfarism and collective bargaining could not coexist in the same establishment. In instances where the union shop prevailed and the workers had mounted a determined opposition to newly introduced welfare policies, the program had ended in failure. One such illustration was provided by the Walker & Pratt Manufacturing Co., in Watertown, Massachusetts. A Labor Department researcher studying the case pointed out that the welfare programs had failed because "the laborers are highly organized. Union labor has steadfastly opposed itself to employers' welfare work, holding that the aim and tendency of such work are to shackle labor with gratitude and to diminish its freedom in the bargaining process."[36]

How did the American labor leadership view this development in industrial relations? Were they aware of the implications that this trend had for the future of labor relations in U.S. industry, as well as for the AFL's organizing policies? This question is all the more important because the welfare movement was led by the NCF, an agency that included among its officers the top leaders of organized labor. The attitude they displayed can be characterized as one of tacit consent. Within the NCF, they accepted, for instance, the policy of excluding labor leaders from the Welfare Department—the only department abiding by this policy.[37] Publicly they preferred not to address themselves to the issue, and the few times some of them did, it was in favorable terms. The fullest statement on the subject came from J.W. Sullivan of the typographical union in a pamphlet written for the NCF Welfare Department, which in effect came to represent the official AFL view on the subject. The position he expressed was that welfare work was beneficial to the workers and had to be regarded as supplementary to the activities carried out by unions. Therefore, welfare work had to be accepted in the context of a division of labor in which employers and trade unions would perform different functions, but all in the direction of promoting the well-being of the workers.[38] To a large extent, this attitude of consent was facilitated by the fact that the sectors in which welfare work predominated lay outside the direct area of influence of AFL unions, employing in the main mass-production and mass-service workers, most of them women and foreign—clearly sectors that were not high on the organizing agenda of AFL unions.

The AFL's tacit consent of welfare work, however, gave substantial sectors of capital a free hand in consolidating a model of labor relations that ran counter to collective bargaining. In a context where the administration of labor relations rested entirely in the employers' hands and where the very basis for an autonomous organizational initiative by the work force was undermined at the outset, there was no place for collective bargaining. The very concept of contractual relation was made obsolete by labor policies that were based on workers' unqualified loyalty, obedience, and participation in the goals of the enterprise.

Consequently collective bargaining was losing its claim to universality as the welfare work approach gained a foot in many sectors of U.S. industry, especially during the second decade of the century, and it increasingly appeared to employers as a formidable alternative to the framework provided by collective bargaining. Nowhere was this contrast clearer than within the NCF, the organization that sought to advance both models of labor relations—a contrast dramatized by the spectacular success and growth of its Welfare Department on the one hand and by the gradual decline of its Trade Agreement Department on the other.

The AFL leaders' ability to reconcile their support of two models of labor relations that in practice were mutually exclusive undoubtedly bears witness to their diplomatic skills. It remains, however, one of the major contradictions in AFL policy during the Progressive years—a contradiction destined to bear grave consequences on the industrial front throughout the 1920s.

NOTES

1. *NCF Review* (March-April 1906) : 13.
2. "Report by Gertrude Beeks on Factory Inspection Tours, 1901-02," 3B box 37, Nettie Fowler McCormick Papers, State Historical Society of Wisconsin, Madison (hereafter cited as "Beeks Report").
3. Ibid., 31.
4. *NCF Review* (September 1904) : 15.
5. "How the Welfare Department Was Organized," *NCF Review* (June 1904) : 13-14.
6. Ibid., 14; *NCF Review* (January 1905) : 14.
7. *NCF Review* (March-April 1907) : 11.
8. Ibid. (September 1910) : 24.
9. Ibid. (July 1911) : 22.
10. "Preliminary Report of the Committee on Employers' Welfare Work: Survey of Social Progress," box 188, NCF Papers, New York Public Library.
11. During the war the NCF continued to play a crucial role in this field by mobilizing its Welfare Department's staff and installing welfare programs in 300 plants: minutes of the NCF executive committee meeting, April 29, 1920, box 188, NCF Papers.
12. *NCF Review* (February 1905) : 14.
13. Minutes of the conference of welfare workers, held under the auspices of the NCF, January 1911, box 116, NCF Papers.
14. U.S. Bureau of Labor Statistics, "Employers' Welfare Work," *Bulletin,* no. 123 (May 1913) : 71.
15. Ibid.
16. *Conference on Welfare Work, March 16, 1904* (New York, 1904), vii.
17. Gertrude Beeks, "What Is Welfare Work?" *NCF Review* (August 1904) : 5.
18. Ibid. In one of her speeches, Beeks gave one of the most succinct explanations of the wage policy to be followed in welfare programs: "The successful introduction of any of the features of welfare work depends partly on careful attention to the wage scale that the employees may realize the spirit of the company to be 'fair play,' else all efforts to provide comforts, conveniences, recreation or other betterment features

will probably be regarded suspiciously and a feeling is likely to arise that it would have been preferable to have had the money—expended on these matters—distributed in wages, whereas, if logically considered, it would not only be seen that the sum expended for most efforts of this description would pay the wages of the entire force of the establishment for but a few days or weeks at the most, dependent upon what is contemplated, but that the result of such an expenditure would be the increasing of wages to an almost inappreciable extent. The distribution of such a sum would not add much to the wages. The cost of welfare work should be met by appropriations from the profits of the manufacturer and the wage scale so fairly adjusted that the employees may not feel that it is conducted at their expense." G. Beeks, "Ameliorating the Conditions of Employees: The Relation of the Wage Scale to Welfare Work," typescript, n.d., box 17, NCF Papers.

19. Ibid.

20. John H. Patterson, "Altruism and Sympathy as Factors in Works Administration," *Engineering Magazine* 20 (January 1902) : 579-80.

21. Minutes of the meeting of the NCF Welfare Department, July 24, 1904, 105, box 122, NCF Papers.

22. Ibid., November 15, 1905, 63-64, box 122, NCF Papers.

23. *American Machinist* (April 1901) : 393.

24. For a contemporary analysis of these factors, see Austin Lewis, *The Militant Proletariat* (Chicago, 1911).

25. "Beeks Report," 19.

26. "Welfare Factory Work," statement by Lucy Bannister, 5, box 116, NCF Papers.

27. Beeks to William G Mather, August 31, 1916, box 117, NCF Papers.

28. "The Progress of Labor in the United States," summary of report by the Industrial Economics Department of the NCF (Committee on Labor Conditions), 1916, 69, box 84, NCF Papers.

29. Daniel Nelson and Stuart Campbell, "Taylorism Versus Welfare Work in American Industry: H. L. Gantt and the Bancrofts," *Business History Review* 46 (Spring 1972) : 1, 4.

30. Marguerite Green, *The National Civic Federation and the American Labor Movement* (Washington, D.C., 1956), 274.

31. "Beeks Report," 5, 12, 50.

32. For a detailed discussion on the evolution of employee representation plans, see Stephen Scheinberg, "The Development of Corporation Labor Policy, 1900-1940" (Ph.D. diss., University of Wisconsin, 1967), esp. chap. 5.

33. Minutes of the meeting of the NCF Welfare Department, November 15, 1904, 108-112, box 122, NCF Papers.

34. W. Russell to J. Mitchell, August 24, 1908, J. Mitchell to W. Russell, August 26, 1908: box 104, NCF Papers.

35. Quoted in Robert Ozanne, *A Century of Labor-Management Relations at McCormick & International Harvester* (Madison, 1967), 166.

36. U.S. Bureau of Labor Statistics, "Employers' Welfare Work," *Bulletin,* no. 123 (May 1913) : 10.

37. Green, *National Civic Federation,* 268.

38. J. W. Sullivan, *The Trade Unions' Attitude Toward Welfare Work* (New York, 1907).

9

VOLUNTARISM
VERSUS COMPULSION
IN INDUSTRIAL DISPUTES

If substantial sectors of the employer class seemed to have found in welfarism their way of solving the labor problem and bypassing collective bargaining, even in industrial sectors where collective bargaining had become the accepted framework for the settlement of capital-labor conflict, a number of problems soon began to emerge that threatened the viability of this model of industrial relations. Central among these problems was the question of the arbitration of industrial disputes, especially when arbitration involved the intervention of a third party whose decision would have a determining weight on the result of the dispute and, more important, when this third party was the government. Under what circumstances and on what basis should this intervention become necessary? Should the government intervene on an advisory basis, leaving the final decision to the two disputing parties, or should it use its power to compel the parties to reach a settlement, thereby bringing the dispute to an end? In an era of rapid economic transformations in which the traditional relations of power between capital and labor were subject to constant changes and in which the state's positive role was making major strides, it seemed inevitable that the question of arbitration would transcend the narrow boundaries of industrial relations practice and acquire a wider political significance. The contours of this problem became increasingly visible during the second half of the Progressive era, when industrial strife and violence did not seem to subside despite the wider public acceptance of trade unions as legitimate institutions. The problem was also compounded by the weakening of the labor-employer entente operated through the NCF and which was also reflected in the drastic decline of mediation services the association performed.

It is in this context that the Canadian Industrial Disputes Investigation Act (IDI) of 1907 is of particular historical significance in assessing the development of collective bargaining in the United States, for the intense and ongoing reactions it generated in the country shed much light on the limitations of the prolabor movement forces in coming to grips with this problem. This act, moreover, provides a particular vantage point that makes it possible to enlarge the basis for more comparative studies of the industrial and labor experiences of the two countries during the Progressive era.

To be sure, arbitration had been a major issue of public debate especially during the years of rapid trade union growth and industrial unrest around the turn of the century. The debate had been characterized by the strong advocacy of some compulsory arbitration formula coming not only from business circles but also from leading prolabor figures such as Henry D. Lloyd and William Holt, the noted New York publisher and editor. The NCF-AFL forces had been able to dominate the debate, discrediting the compulsory arbitration approach and arguing in favor of voluntary mediation and arbitration. The NCF could point to its successful work in conciliation and arbitration during its first years of activity as proof that compulsory arbitration was unnecessary. Moreover, the trade agreement rested on the assumption that through discussion and joint conferences capital and labor would discover their common interests and thereby work out a peaceful solution to their dispute. Compulsory arbitration implied instead that the two parties were divided by irreconcilable interests and that the only way to put an end to the dispute was to let an impartial third party render a binding decision.

On this note of clear rejection the debate on compulsory arbitration had subsided, undoubtedly pushed to the background by more vital issues that characterized the U.S. labor scene from about 1903 to 1906. But in 1907 the debate resumed when the Canadian Parliament passed the Industrial Disputes Investigation Act. The act was occasioned by a prolonged strike in the coal mines of Alberta, which threatened the fuel supplies of the prairie provinces and made the outlook for the oncoming winter grim. The most important feature of the act was the provision that the parties in a dispute had to subject themselves to the investigation of a fact-finding board before taking any strike or lockout action. The board was given thirty days to carry out its investigation, and during such time no hostility could be initiated. Only after the investigation was concluded and the facts made public could the parties resort to their coercive weapons. Both parties were subjected to penalties should they violate the truce provision. The act applied to public utilities, industries, and mines (both coal and metal).[1]

The response that this legislative measure generated in U.S. industrial and labor quarters was much stronger than that produced earlier by the New Zealand arbitration act. (This act had been the first instance in which arbitration was made compulsory and binding for the two parties to a dispute.) Partly this response was because of the geographical proximity of the Canadian industrial situation, which also meant that U.S.-based international unions (AFL affiliates) operating in Canada would be directly affected by the act. More important, however, the act had struck one of the notes on which Progressive sentiment seemed to be most sensitive—the ideology of public opinion and the value it embodied in a democratic society. The investigation feature of the act would make the notion of public opinion concrete and operative and transform it from an abstract concept into a positive force in favor of the public interest. The weight of public opinion would in fact be brought to bear by disclosing to the general public the facts that lay beneath the dispute. This would act as a major restraining force, especially for the party that appeared from the investigation as making the most uncompromising demand, in that it ensured public condemnation should this party seek a settlement by resorting to force. The compulsory feature of the act, moreover, appeared in a new light and made it appealing to many who had found a formula such as the New Zealand act much too constraining.[2] The Canadian act, in fact, hit a midway ground between the two extremes, which up to that point had constituted the two open alternatives: its compulsory feature appeared to be more moderate than that provided for by the New Zealand act, for it applied only to the period during which the investigation was being conducted. On the other hand, this compulsory feature was enough to make it depart from the "voluntarist" approach that Gompers and the NCF had preached and practiced over the years.

The appreciation of the act soon became evident in the first official U.S. examination of it, done by Dr. Victor S. Clark for the U.S. Department of Commerce and Labor. The analysis was based on the first twelve months in which the act had been in operation and took into account the immediate responses from various sectors of Canadian society. The evaluation was clearly positive. The act was viewed as "the logical first step toward government intervention in labor disputes"; judging from its first year of operation, it had "accomplished the main purpose for which it was enacted, the prevention of strikes and lockouts in public services industries." In analyzing the act's most innovative feature—the machinery for compulsory investigation—Clark was very careful to emphasize the conciliatory dimension of the process rather than the judicial dimension, thus toning down the element of compulsion underlying the act. This interpretation was greatly facilitated by contrasting the Canadian act to the New Zealand arbitration act whose compulsory aspect was quite far-reaching. This analysis therefore presented the act as a most progressive piece of legislation that pointed the way to industrial peace, a "hopeful example" for the American people that would "prove a guiding star in their difficulties."[3]

If the advocates of the act were careful to contrast it to the New Zealand act by stressing the former's moderate character, the opponents of the act tended instead to view both acts together. From the "voluntaristic" standpoint, with which Gompers and other AFL leaders looked at the act, there was not much point in drawing fine distinctions between those acts. "As soon as the Government steps in," Gompers pointed out, "and says to the workingman . . . : you must work under such conditions as are here stipulated; if you do not work you will go to prison. At that moment slavery has been introduced . . . call it by whatever name you please, compulsory arbitration or compulsory investigation, compulsory work pending the final determination of that investigation. . . [establishes] the system of slavery."[4] For Gompers, the thirty-day, no-strike order—pending the result of the investigation—was enough to make the Canadian act appear as an infringement of the workers' most sacred right, the right to withhold their labor. Hence, the reaction from AFL quarters was immediate. Gompers's opposition to the act became one of overt belligerence, and he welcomed all opportunities to denounce it as a most oppressive and enslaving piece of legislation. He saw the potential that the Canadian act might have in influencing U.S. public opinion in favor of some form of compulsion in the settlement of industrial disputes. Gompers's fears were not unfounded. During the 1908-1909 legislative session two important industrial states, New York and Wisconsin, had introduced in their state assemblies bills that embodied provisions modeled after the Canadian act.[5] Although these early attempts were unsuccessful, some years later the New York State legislature tried again to push through a similar bill. This proposed bill became the principal topic of discussion at the thirteenth annual meeting of the NCF's executive council. Here Gompers, who was the council vice-president, embarked on a pointed speech in which he stressed the danger of arbitration schemes such as the Canadian one and expressed his determination to fight any measure that would take away the workers' right to strike, under whatever guise it presented itself.[6] Gompers's belligerence toward the Canadian act would intensify through the years as other states contemplated similar legislation, and Colorado actually succeeded in passing an industrial disputes law that, except for some slight differences, was essentially a replica of the IDI act.[7]

Of the AFL-affiliated unions, the one that became most vocal in denouncing the IDI act was the United Mine Workers. This seemed obvious since the union was directly affected by the provisions of the act because the Alberta and British Columbia coal miners were organized by that union. At the 1909 annual convention of the UMW in Indianapolis, the miners adopted a resolution condemning the act. A resolution was also passed by the Canadian delegates, advising "our brothers on this side of the line to oppose any such measure of like nature to the utmost of their powers."[8] John Mitchell, who remained one of the most influential figures in Progressive industrial and labor circles even after leaving his position as president of the UMW, attacked the bill as being ineffective, and therefore useless, legislation. To Henry Howard, chairman of the Boston Chamber of Commerce, who had written to Mitchell requesting a personal opinion concerning the Canadian act, Mitchell answered pointing out the clearly antilabor character of such a measure. Howard's interest in the Canadian act stemmed from the fact that a bill resembling the Canadian IDI had been introduced in the Massachusetts legislature.[9] A few years later, when called upon by the U.S. Industrial Relations Commission to give his opinion on the merits of the IDI act, Mitchell called it a "repressive system" and "a species of involuntary servitude, which is repugnant to the law of the land."[10]

If U.S. organized labor was united in denouncing the Canadian act, the same cannot be said of the NCF. Although the leading spokesman of the federation, Ralph Easley, had left no doubts as to his opposition to the Canadian law, some NCF members were ambiguous about the act's fea-

tures; many on the executive council were employers who obviously
looked at the Canadian act from quite a different angle. A leading example
was Marcus Marks. As president of the National Association of Clothiers,
he had been a leading member of the federation for many years and enjoyed a high reputation in industrial circles because of his repeated services as mediator and conciliator for the federation's Conciliation Department. The NCF historian calls him "the star mediator."[11] Besides his
practical knowledge of that field growing from his involvement in hundreds of disputes, he was also a keen student of the subject. His response
to the IDI act was enthusiastic. He wrote Easley that he was "impressed
with it" and took a particular interest in the measure, spending a great
deal of time traveling throughout Canada, talking with arbitrators, labor
leaders, employers, and politicians.[12] He soon became convinced that the
Canadian act pointed the way toward a peaceful solution of the industrial
problem and firmly believed, as he told an NCF audience, that "the principles of that Act [could] be introduced into our States."[13]

Marks gave wide publicity to the principles of the Canadian act in various articles he wrote through the years. One appeared in the *Independent*
in 1910 and was later put into pamphlet form and widely circulated.[14]
The article aroused Gompers's wrath not only for the position Marks took
on the act but also for the position he took on the thorny topic of the
open versus closed shop. Gompers decided to call this whole issue to the
attention of the labor public by reproducing the article in the *American
Federationist* and by refuting its arguments. Referring to the principle
of compulsory investigation that Marks had advocated, Gompers pointed
out that the principle was "repugnant not only to that provision of
the Constitution which guarantees that no man shall be kept in voluntary servitude except as a punishment of crime, but [was] at vari-
ance with every concept of liberty and progress."[15] Another exchange
between the two men took place again in the February issue of the AFL
paper, in which Marks reaffirmed his belief in the principle of compulsory
investigation, and Gompers proceeded again to refute it as being contrary
to the interests of organized labor and useless as far as unorganized workingmen were concerned.[16] Because of the position of prominence that
both Gompers and Marks occupied in industrial circles and in the NCF's
high councils, such a controversy could very well have produced a serious
crisis in the NCF. However, Easley intervened promptly and with his
famous diplomatic skills was able to defuse the tension between the two

men. If the issue seemed to be settled in the short run, it is very likely that the controversy had a crucial role in strengthening the feelings of antagonism toward the NCF that had been mounting in recent years in large segments of the AFL membership and that was to erupt during the United Mine Workers annual convention in 1911; at that time John Mitchell was forced to sever his affiliation with the NCF, and at the AFL national convention that same year, a resolution forbidding AFL members to maintain membership in the NCF was barely defeated.

That the IDI act became a subject of major controversy within the NCF is also witnessed by the repeated times in which the act was hotly debated during NCF-sponsored conferences. One of these took place at the federation's annual convention in January 1911 when a whole session was devoted to the subject of "industrial peace." NCF President Seth Low hoped that the session would become a testing ground for some amendments he had worked out to the New York State industrial disputes law, in the hope that the new law would become a model for other states, thereby generating uniformity while at the same time extending the principle of the Erdman Act (voluntary arbitration in interstate railroads) to disputes involving public service corporations. Instead most of the discussion revolved around the significance of the Canadian IDI act, and most of the speakers pointed to it as a possible solution to the problem of industrial disputes in the United States. For Cornelius J. Doyle, chairman of the Illinois State Board of Arbitration, the principle of compulsory investigation upon which the IDI was founded was "a desirable clause to be inserted into the arbitration laws of every State." He pointed out that that principle grew out of the appreciation of the value of enlightened public opinion and felt that "publicity [was] the strongest weapon that can be used for the maintenance of industrial peace." According to Edward W. Frost, Wisconsin labor commissioner and fervent admirer of the "brilliant young Canadian statesman" Mackenzie King, in the Canadian system of arbitration "there lay the way toward industrial peace." Frost warned the audience that "unless labor and capital stand shoulder to shoulder for some such principle as that, there are very much graver dangers ahead of us, and there is danger of such an uprising of public opinion as will lead us into new ends and into new measures for the solution of this problem." Seth Low's position toward the Canadian act—forced by the course the debate had taken—was quite ambiguous and reflected the contradictory nature of the NCF's activities of having to pursue the interest of capital while at the same time trying not to alienate its labor members. Actually it would be correct to say that Low avoided taking any position. He admitted that the IDI act "seems to work fairly well in Canada" but felt that it should be dismissed from consideration "at the present time"; he thought it unlikely that similar legislation could be adopted in the United States because of the strong opposition from organized labor.[17]

The pro-IDI act statements of Doyle and Frost did not necessarily reflect the opinion of all government arbitrators; they nevertheless indicate the degree of support the act was gaining among this important class of professional arbitrators, especially at a time when agitation among the profession was mounting because of the limitations of state boards on handling industrial disputes of an interstate character.

The centrality of the IDI act in the minds of U.S. industrial relations experts became strikingly apparent in the work of the U.S. Commission on Industrial Relations.[18] When in 1914 the commission began carrying out its massive work of investigating industrial conditions, touring the whole country and interviewing hundreds of employers, labor leaders, government officials, and academics, the Canadian act was one of the main items on the agenda, and the commission members repeatedly brought it into the discussion in an attempt to ascertain the reaction of the American public and to assess the merits of the act in practice. The highlight came when the author of the IDI, Mackenzie King, appeared before the commission to testify and was subjected to extensive questioning, especially by the commissioners representing labor. All the arguments against the act that had emerged since its enactment were presented to King, and he proceeded with great argumentative skill to refute them one by one. One of the main charges against it had been that of portraying it as a "law against strikes and lockouts." American opponents of the act had often neglected to differentiate it from the compulsory arbitration provision of the Australasian acts. King took great pains to point out the difference and to show the characteristic features of the IDI act to prove that the accusation was unfounded. If labor was sincere in its claim that the strike weapon was the very last resort, King argued, now the Canadian government had provided some machinery whereby the state would assume all the expenses of investigating industrial disputes. Therefore the Canadian act, King pointed out, was "tak[ing] away no right from labor that it desires to have." Instead it had provided "one other means of obtaining justice" for the working people. King then proceeded to defend the act from the allegation that it had been a failure in Canada. This allegation had been repeatedly used by U.S. labor leaders who opposed the act; they pointed to the various occasions when large numbers of striking workers had violated the act without incurring any penalities, because of the sheer impossibility of prosecuting several thousand striking workers. King's answer was that under the act the government was not so much concerned in initiating prosecutions as it was in trying to render a service to the community. The act assumed that both parties were sincere in allowing the machinery of the state to bring out the facts with a view to reaching a just settlement. Both organized labor and organized capital had expressed their willingness to this effect. "The penalty feature of the Act," King thus concluded, "had to be regarded as quite a secondary feature."[19]

Although King intended this emphasis on the conciliatory rather than on the judicial aspect to tone down the element of compulsion contained in the act, he was finally forced to admit that compulsion was indeed one of the characteristic features of the legislation. He discussed the principle of compulsion, which in effect underlay the whole philosophy of the act. The principle of law and order—so essential if the state was to ensure social justice—made it necessary for people to give up a certain amount of their rights for the good of society as a whole. Therefore, both capital and labor had to surrender their rights to society. This restraint was necessary to "gain a wider measure of liberty from and for society as a whole."[20] In the long run, King argued, the act was providing an extension of the bounds of liberty of labor rather than a restriction.

In an earlier appearance before the commission, King had been forced to discuss the political significance that the compulsory investigation legislation had taken on in Canada in relation to the labor-capital conflict. King had admitted that the penalty provision was aimed primarily at ensuring "continuous operation of the utility . . . concerned" and that this had been a sort of "understanding" between the state and the employers. In exchange for this concession, labor had in turn been given a concession: "the right to have their own member on a board."[21] This admission that King made to the U.S. Industrial Relations Board commissioners is, of course, of vast historical importance. It dissolves the intricate ideological verbiage that he so masterfully put forth to the commissioners as an apologia of the IDI act and points to the actual political bargaining surrounding the enactment of that labor legislation. It also provides the key to gaining a clearer historical understanding as to why the compulsory investigation provision had met the support of a wide sector of the Canadian labor bureaucracy when a similar one would instead have met the outright opposition of U.S. organized labor and would become branded as antilabor legislation.[22]

When the commission completed its investigations, the final reports it issued reflected the degree of division existing among its members in regard to the principle of compulsory investigation that the Canadian act had popularized throughout the past few years. The report presented by the three representatives of labor and by the commission's chairman, Frank Walsh, rejected outright the principle of compulsory investigation and recommended the creation of national boards of mediation and investigation, independent from the Department of Labor, where investigation would be carried out on a purely voluntary basis.[23] The opposite position was taken by the three representatives of capital, who in a dissenting report recommended the adoption of compulsory investigation in public utility industries to be carried out by industrial commissions that would be created for that express purpose.[24] Between these two opposite positions was economist John Commons's report, which received the partial support of the three representatives of capital. In his report Commons dealt at great length with the Canadian act. He commended it for having made capital and labor sensitive to the great value of public inquiry by elevating the principle of investigation—a principle that Commons had carefully studied over the years and that had become central to his theory of industrial democracy. In his report, therefore, he recommended the adoption of "a voluntary board of investigation, adapted from the Canadian Act but without its compulsory feature."[25]

Soon the commission disbanded; its massive findings became nothing more than source material for industrial scholars and its recommendations fell on deaf ears. Throughout its search for a solution to the problem of industrial conflict, the IDI act had been a constant reference point and a base for analysis and experimentation. More important, the commission had served to crystallize the division of opinion existing in the United States in regard to compulsory investigation; it had made clear that the principle served primarily the interest of capital and that it worked against the interest of organized labor.

Only a few months had passed before the debate over compulsory regulation of industrial disputes became the center of industrial and political affairs. Late in the summer of 1916 the four railroad brotherhoods threatened a nationwide strike that could have paralyzed the country. What is more significant is the fact that the brotherhoods had grown dissatisfied with the arbitration machinery (voluntary investigation) provided by the Newlands Act to settle disputes in the railroads. In their demands for the eight-hour day and for wage increases, they had no intention of submitting to arbitration. It became evident that some new legislation had to be enacted if a period of major economic chaos was to be averted in the country.

It was in the midst of this feeling of impending industrial and labor crisis that the compulsory investigation and arbitration features began to be viewed again in many quarters as possible solutions. This became the object of serious consideration in organizations such as the U.S. Chamber of Commerce and the American Academy of Political Science (which totally supported compulsory arbitration). Easley, who had met privately with Dr. Samuel McCune Lindsay, president of the academy, found to his great dismay that among the members of the academy there was "not a man who is against compulsory arbitration . . . they are all for it."[26] The issue generated enormous tension among the NCF executive council members, which characterized the October 23 emergency meeting called to discuss the subject. Once again Gompers used the occasion to denounce all forms of compulsory government intervention in industrial matters, but this time he got a cold reception from some prominent members, including August Belmont and economist B. Seligman. They were beginning to display clear signs of annoyance with Gompers's intransigence on the matter. In their view, this was no time for rigidity. The situation demanded a careful assessment of the limitations that the present machinery embodied and a search for some alternative that would preclude the enactment of more extreme measures.[27] In reality, these objectives were going right to the heart of Gompers's philosophy of voluntarism. That the labor impasse was about to precipitate a crisis in the NCF can also be seen from Easley's response to the situation. He had to admit that the labor crisis had raised the all-important question as to whether "collective bargaining point[ed] the way out." He wrote to a leading railroad president: "if the most intelligent unions and the largest capitalists, under a model collective agreement, can reach a stage where one has the power to say to the other—and says it— 'unless you yield, we will destroy you,' then those employers who oppose collective bargaining have had placed in their hands a very formidable weapon."[28]

As the debate on compulsory regulation of industrial disputes intensified, the features of the Canadian IDI act were increasingly emerging in the minds of many as constituting the proper formula for the solution of the problem at hand. Easley was very well aware of this, and he tried desperately to influence public opinion against the act. In an article he very tactically entitled "The Canadian Compulsory Investigation Act," which appeared in several publications, he set out again to analyze the act and to show how it had failed in its objectives. To the growing number of people who were asking themselves whether the Canadian act would not solve the crisis situation in the railroads, Easley was proving that it did not hold "any promise as a way out for the United States."[29]

The sentiment favoring the Canadian act reached a climax when it became known that President Woodrow Wilson had given very careful consideration to it and that he was attempting to formulate a plan "having in mind the Canadian Investigation Act."[30] But the overwhelming opposition from organized labor to such a plan,[31] the determination of the brotherhoods that the eight-hour day was not negotiable, and the worsening of the crisis on the international front forced Wilson to accede to the brotherhoods' demands by passing what became known as the Adamson Act, thereby averting a major economic and political paralysis.[32]

President Wilson's serious intentions to enact arbitration legislation modeled after the IDI act marks the high point of influence that the act exerted on the U.S. industrial and political establishments. Undoubtedly the situation of crisis surrounding Wilson's design made the Canadian formula appear to be a ready solution to the impending industrial chaos. Nevertheless, the decision was the culmination of nearly a decade of intense debate, during which all the pros and cons of the IDI formula had been carefully scrutinized and argued, with its advocates and opponents taking sides.

World War I not only put an end to this debate, but it also prevented the debate from transforming itself into a power confrontation between organized labor and the employer-government front. The Adamson Act was not only the railroad brotherhoods' historic victory over the eight-hour demands, it was the victory of U.S. organized labor over the principle of compulsory investigation, a victory that shows not only the objective position of power of U.S. labor at that particular historical juncture but also the wider political significance that an industrial relations formula such as compulsory investigation acquired in the context of the capital-

labor conflict in the United States. The event also signaled the success—
however short-lived—that collective bargaining would enjoy during the
war years because of the delicate industrial situation the country was
going through—a factor that had a vital role in conferring on organized
labor a position of power.

NOTES

1. Cf. *Labour Gazette* 7 (April 1907) : 1108-09; U.S. Bureau of
Labor, *Bulletin No. 76,* (May 1908) : 657ff.

2. U.S. Bureau of Labor, "Labor Conditions in New Zealand,"
Bulletin, no. 49 (November 1903) : 1142-1281.

3. Victor S. Clark, "The Canadian Industrial Disputes Investigation
Act of 1907," U.S. Bureau of Labor, *Bulletin,* no. 76 (May 1908) :
657-740.

4. U.S. Commission on Industrial Relations *Final Report and Testimony* (Washington, D.C., 1916), 1 : 721 (hereafter cited as CIR, *Final
Report*).

5. U.S. Bureau of Labor, "The Canadian Industrial Disputes Investigation Act of 1907," *Bulletin,* no. 86 (January 1910) : 21.

6. Proceedings of the thirteenth annual meeting of the executive
committee of the NCF, January 28, 1918, box 187(1), NCF Papers,
New York Public Library.

7. *Monthly Review* (U.S. Bureau of Labor Statistics) 1 (December
1915) : 10-12.

8. U.S. Bureau of Labor, "The Canadian Industrial Disputes Investigation Act of 1907," *Bulletin,* no. 86 (January 1910) : 15.

9. John Mitchell to Henry Howard, February 7, 1910, box 156,
Mitchell Papers, The Catholic University of America, Washington, D.C.

10. CIR, *Final Report,* 1 : 421, 422.

11. Marguerite Green, *The National Civic Federation and the American
Labor Movement* (Washington, D.C., 1956), 300.

12. Marcus M. Marks to Ralph Easley, January 22, 1912, box 79a,
NCF Papers.

13. *Proceedings of the Eleventh Annual Meeting of the National Civic
Federation, New York, January 12, 1911* (New York, 1911), 283.

14. Marcus M. Marks, "The Employer and the Labor Union," *Independent* 68 (May 26, 1910) : 1112-15.

15. Samuel Gompers, "Labor's Differences with Mr. Marcus M. Marks
et al.," *American Federationist* 17 (October 1910) : 884.

16. "Isn't it wiser," Marks asked Gompers, "to investigate while the men are earning wages, the company doing business and the public being accommodated rather than take up these questions after a strike has been declared?"—a question that summed up the feeling of many employers toward the Canadian act. *American Federationist* 18 (February 1911) : 109, 110.

17. *NCF Proceedings, 1911,* 250-67.

18. For a thorough analysis of the history and the activities of the U.S. Commission on Industrial Relations in the context of Progressive politics, see Graham Adams, Jr., *The Age of Industrial Conflict* (New York, 1966), and James Weinstein, *The Corporate Ideal in the Liberal State, 1900-1918* (Boston, 1968), 172-213.

19. CIR, *Final Report,* 9 : 8834-42.

20. Ibid., 8843.

21. Ibid., 1 : 716.

22. King told the commissioners, with a certain amount of pride, that "the leading officers in the labor organizations at that time were not opposed to [the legislation]" and that in particular "the Trades' Labor Congress of the Dominion indorsed it." Ibid., 716. On the immediate reaction from the Canadian Labor movement, cf. also Clark, "Canadian Industrial Disputes Investigation Act," 672ff.

23. CIR, *Final Report,* 1 : 120-24.

24. Ibid., 233.

25. Ibid., 210.

26. Proceedings of the executive council meeting of the National Civic Federation, October 23, 1916, 8, Box 189, NCF Papers.

27. Ibid.

28. Ralph Easley to Vincent Astor, September 12, 1916, box 188, NCF Papers; letters similar in tone were sent to other prominent railroad presidents.

29. Copy of the article in box 76, Mitchell Papers.

30. *NCF Proceedings, October 23, 1916,* 4.

31. See Gompers's editorial "Freedom Must Not Be Surrendered," *American Federationist* 24 (January 1917) : 45-46. The opposition of the railroad brotherhoods to compulsory investigation was well articulated by Austin B. Garretson, "The Attitude of Organized Labor Toward the Canadian Industrial Disputes Investigation Act," *Annals of the American Academy of Political and Social Science* 16 (January 1917) : 170-72.

32. "R.R. Workers Win Eight Hours," *American Federationist* 24 (April 1917) : 282-84.

10

THE INSTITUTIONAL IMPASSE: THEORY AND PRACTICE

In the debate over investigation and the Canadian IDI Act there was much more at stake than might have appeared on the surface. Clearly organized labor had succeeded in preventing a measure based on the state's compulsory intervention from being adopted as a way of dealing with the problem of labor-capital conflict. On the other hand, the voluntaristic attitude of organized labor served as a serious obstacle to any attempt aimed at fixing the relations between labor and capital on a firmer institutional basis. The voluntarist approach based on the trade agreement had undoubtedly allowed labor unions to gain the recognition of wide sectors of public opinion; but this approach had remained limited to sectors where the function of labor unions was considered essential for the stability of the industry or where unions were in a position to force employers to accept the contractual relation. Moreover, nothing could prevent employers from terminating a trade agreement when the opportunities presented themselves.

During the years of uncertainty in labor-capital relations that marked the second half of the Progressive era, not a few prolabor reformers grew aware of the fact that increasing the memberships of unions was not enough, especially since the increase was giving clear signs of slowing down; rather, they realized that it was necessary to find some method through which labor-capital relations could be somehow prescribed by the intervention of the state—an intervention based on the acknowledgment of the collective demands of workers in a dispute and that would

guarantee that such demands would become the object of bona-fide
bargaining by the employers.

This awareness was dictated not only by the search for a more democratic approach to industrial relations but, more importantly, by the re-
surgence of widespread industrial conflict in both the organized and unorganized sectors. Historian David Montgomery has very ably analyzed
the wave of strikes that occurred from 1909 to the war period—showing
both the intensity of the conflicts and their impact on industrial relations
practice.[1] From a somewhat different angle, Graham Adams, Jr., has
focused on the years 1910-1915 and has described the acute concern
existing among politicians and reformers over the widespread industrial
violence.[2] Historians, however, have not sufficiently brought out the
extent to which this concern expressed itself in a search for a firmer institutional basis regulating labor-capital relations. Ultimately, it seemed,
a lasting solution to the labor problem hinged on this, and it was in this
spirit that some of the leading experts on industrial relations embarked
on the greatest attempt of the age to get at the root of the question. The
creation of the U.S. Commission on Industrial Relations, in fact, had been
occasioned by the violence associated with the bombing in 1910 of the
Los Angeles Times and was supposed to provide some answers to the
problem of industrial violence; but the experts who staffed it, especially
after Woodrow Wilson's election, looked much further.

Despite their different outlooks on industrial matters, they all acknowledged the legitimacy of labor's and capital's interests, and they shared a
commitment to making the two parties more responsive to the public interest. To the extent that industrial disputes affected the public interest in
various degrees, they could not be left to the whims of the two parties involved but necessitated the creation of some machinery designed to stabilize the relations between capital and labor, safeguard their mutual interests, and protect the public interest—an ambitious project. One man among
the commissioners whose career had been so intimately linked to the development of industrial relations seemed to possess both the qualifications and
the determination to make this project a reality. Known to historians as
the father of American labor history and to economists as the founder of
the institutional school in economic theory, John Commons was also the
leading expert on industrial relations in America and the man who sought
to provide the most thorough answer to the labor problem in those years.
His search for a solution must be analyzed in conjunction with the views

and aspirations of a small but influential body of professionals and experts of industrial relations—the state mediators and arbitrators—to give a more complete picture of the difficulties encountered in the attempt to institutionalize labor-capital relations.

Like his former colleagues in the National Civic Federation who had schooled him in the work of conciliation and mediation, Commons believed that collective bargaining would provide the key mechanism through which capital-labor relations could be worked out democratically. But unlike them, Commons had gradually come to the conclusion that what brought labor and capital to war against each other was not the failure to see a harmony of interest but rather the existence of conflicting interests that at best could become the object of compromise. By the end of the first decade of the century, hardly anybody who was at all familiar with industrial affairs would dispute this fact, but Commons made this a key tenet in his attempt to rescue collective bargaining from its uncertain future.

Collective bargaining, in its last analysis, is based upon the coercive power of antagonistic classes organized for aggression and defense. The bargaining power of either side is the power to use the strike against the lockout, the boycott against the blacklist, the picket against the strikebreaker, the closed shop against the closed nonunion shop, and so on. These are essential weapons, and no plausible verbiage or double meaning of words should blind us to the fact that these weapons are coercive, and are intended to be coercive, and, in the last analysis, will be used, secretly or openly, as coercive, by either side. Their objective is similar to legislation regulating the individual labor contract except that they regulate it through joint agreements backed by their coercive weapons, instead of fines and imprisonment.[3]

Throughout his career as a historian, economist, and mediator of industrial disputes, Commons had been an ardent believer of the trade agreement approach publicized by the NCF and practiced by the AFL.[4] For him the trade agreement and the process whereby the parties involved arrived at it and worked out its provisions represented the best expression of industrial democracy. In fact, this principle remained basic to Commons's conception of industrial relations. In 1915 he wrote: "Modern trade agreements are almost complete codes of labor law for a particular industry, and if voluntary collective bargaining could become universal and effective for all employers and employees, then the State or Government might not need to enact many labor laws."[5]

To the extent that this voluntary approach had resulted in a limited adoption of the trade agreement at a time when industrial conflict was mounting, this formula was proving to be inadequate to solve the labor problem and needed major revisions. A student of Commons's, Richard Gonce, comments that by approximately 1907 "Commons was growing in the conviction that voluntary collective bargaining between unions and employers was inadequate."[6] "I went too far in my generalizations on collective bargaining instead of legislation," Commons would in fact admit in later years.[7] The trade agreement approach therefore had to be supplemented by some machinery instituted by the state that would ensure not only a more widespread adoption of collective bargaining but would also allow a more responsible use of the coercive weapons available to both parties.

It is to this end that Commons directed his efforts in the ensuing years —efforts that culminated in 1915 in the recommendations he presented as a member of the U.S. Commission on Industrial Relations:

1. A new organism of a quasipolitical nature should be created, to obviate the state of political corruption in administering labor legislation; to be entrusted with all the detailed and complex tasks of research and investigation to enable the legislative branch to legislate effectively in the area of industrial relations; and to make sure that all interests—labor, capital, and the public—be equally represented and have a voice in the formulation and administration of labor legislation.

This organism would be the Industrial Commission; Commons supplied all the necessary guidelines for its organization and functioning. Through the means of an advisory representative council, the commission would make sure that all conflicting interests would participate, through consultation, in its findings and recommendations. The underlying assumption in Commons's recommendation was his distinction "between the enactment of law which is political in its nature and hence must be fought out in the Congress and in the Cabinet, and the administration of law which is nonpolitical and should be administered by disinterested parties in cooperation with representatives of capital and labor." "It is because executive officials are mainly partisans," Commons charged, "that the administration of labor laws in this country has broken down."[8]

2. After recommending the solution for the problems of legislation and administration of labor laws via the Industrial Commission, the ground-

work was laid for his recommendations on collective bargaining. Collective bargaining, Commons recommended, must become the machinery through which two conflicting interests of capital and labor come together to work out a compromise. As such, collective bargaining must not only be recognized and extended to all industry but also be protected and made more functional so that it would become the basis of the industrial relations apparatus.

To facilitate this process, Commons recommended that the Industrial Commission be empowered to set up a national system of mediation that would consolidate the services then provided by the Newlands Act and by the Department of Labor and that would coordinate its efforts with state boards of mediation.[9]

Clearly Commons's industrial relations scheme was the best that Progressive enterprise could offer: it was based on an acknowledgment of the institutional evolution that had occurred in the field of labor and employers' organizations; it was extremely sensitive to the positive function that public opinion could play on the issue of labor-capital relations; and it envisaged a state intervention immunized from the dangers of political partisanship, being solely guided by scientific criteria and administrative expertise.

In later years Commons prided himself that the principles advocated in his recommendations had been largely adopted in the New Deal program: "Eighteen years after that Commission's report the labor organizations of the national find themselves compelled, but without experience in the field of collective bargaining, under government administration, to participate in the formulation of codes, the working rules of the National Industrial Recovery Administration."[10] For the moment, however, Commons's scheme was not accepted or supported by the other members of the commission. The dissent recorded by the three members of the commission who represented organized labor must have been bitter to the reformer who had always prided himself with being a friend of labor.[11] It must have been even more embarrassing to Commons that the only support his recommendations received, however partial, came from the three members representing the employers. However strongly Commons had tried to emphasize the voluntary features of his scheme (for instance, in his combined national-state mediation system) to allow for labor's outspoken voluntarism, the labor members stood unconvinced and distrustful.

Two of them charged in their dissenting statement that the "elaborate machinery" prescribed in Commons's recommendations, "while without definite compulsory features . . . [would] of necessity exercise an influence in that direction"; it would give the officers in charge of the new agencies "powers far in excess of those exercised by the President of the United States, or the Governor of any State." In short, this would be "Bureaucracy run made, and a subversion of Democracy dangerous to the civil and social liberty of all citizens."[12]

If the labor members were quick to criticize Commons and dismiss his recommendations, they were not as quick in presenting an alternative. The existing governmental agencies, they felt, were sufficient to ensure a better development of industrial relations. In their view, the only alternative was the promotion of labor organization. Their argument deserves to be quoted in full not only for its eloquence but also because it reveals so clearly the nature of the impasse encountered in institutionalizing labor-capital relations:

> Instead of any elaborate machinery for the prevention of strikes or lockouts we are convinced, from the testimony gathered by this commission, that the most effectual course that can be pursued to bring about general contentment among our people, based upon a humane standard of living is the promotion of labor organization. The most casual investigator will soon discover that in those lines of industry where organization of labor is the strongest, there is the least danger of industrial revolt that would endanger the fundamental principles of our Government and the maintenance of a nation with respect for law and order.[13]

One could hardly say that the tune played by these labor representatives was outworn, judging from the enormous mass of workers who still lacked the protection of an organization. But coming as it did after two years of intense investigations and deliberations, it had all the aspects of a chicken-or-egg argument; and as it happens with these arguments, they do not lead very far. In fact, the commission had misfired even before making its recommendations public, and labor could afford the luxury of playing its tune in the highest industrial and political places.

If trying to devise some machinery to institutionalize labor-capital relations at the national level was proving to be an impossible task, things did not look much more hopeful at the state level, judging from the experience of state boards of mediation and arbitration in their attempts to stabilize industrial relations. State boards had been in existence in some key industrial states for quite some years, but it was during the first decade of the twentieth century that they multiplied rapidly in many other states. By 1911 no fewer than twenty-five states, including all the leading industrial ones, had in one form or another bodies providing mediation and arbitration services.[14]

This growth reflected the increasing influence exerted by organized labor at both the national and the state level and represented, at least in principle, an important step in the process of government intervention in industrial relations. The services provided by these boards in the settlement of industrial disputes meant in fact that the government was being given a function that had been traditionally considered the private domain of employers and labor (though in most cases government aid was invoked only after private efforts had failed). Even more important, the work of these boards represented a state sanction of collective bargaining to the extent that most state arbitrators felt that unionization and written agreements were essential prerequisites of successful mediation efforts.[15]

As the number of these boards grew and as they were increasingly brought into contact with one another, state mediators emerged as a distinct body of professionals whose influence in industrial relations matters was significant. The occasions bringing them together were certainly not lacking. One occurred in 1909 as a result of the long and bitter strike of the seamen on the Great Lakes when the arbitration and mediation boards of six states bordering on the lakes were unable to deal effectively in a concerted way with that crisis because of the diverse powers given by law to those boards.[16] By 1910 state arbitrators were gathering as a distinct professional body in Washington to hold their first national conference and to examine the common problems encountered in their work.[17] At this convention, concrete organizational steps were taken, and by January 1911 an organization called the International Association of State Boards of Arbitration and Mediation was meeting in New York City.[18] As one of its officers—Illinois state mediator C. Doyle—explained, "the principal work" of the organization was "to advance the cause of arbitration [so] that each State shall have a separate bureau dealing specifically with these problems, and that each State shall possess within its law as much uniformity as possible with the sister States of the Union."[19]

Superficially this statement of purpose may sound like a mere plea for nationwide professional recognition; yet, in effect, it betrayed frustrations that had been building up for years. Despite the noble purpose that many state arbitrators felt their work was supposed to accomplish, there was a common feeling among these men that their work had not received the public recognition it deserved and that they were not sufficiently empowered to meet the rising need existing in the country. In some states, for example, these boards were not permanent and were created only when a major labor crisis called for state intervention. In others these boards were burdened with tasks other than mediation and arbitration, or, as Doyle put it, they were "mixed up with other bureaus dealing with industrial questions."[20]

Even in major industrial states where state mediation had long been an established practice and was performed by better-equipped agencies, mediation officers could find ample reason for complaint. In New York State, for instance, where after 1901 a separate mediation and arbitration bureau existed within the Labor Department, its work had been "rather slow"; the main reason, according to its chief mediator, was the "lack of understanding and appreciation of the purposes and possibilities of the work."[21]

The fact that employers and labor organizations had paid "too little attention" to these state boards can be explained in part by the fact that during the years in which the trade agreement enjoyed its golden age, the mediation work of these boards had been overshadowed by the spectacular volume of mediation performed by the NCF. It is not surprising, however, that as the mediation activities of the NCF began to subside, as the NCF came increasingly under attack from both labor and business quarters, and as a new wave of industrial conflict hit the country, state mediators would become more acutely aware of the importance of their function and of the inadequacies of their boards in meeting the growing need for which they had been legislated into existence. And as soon as they began agitating for more recognition and for improved machinery, it would soon become apparent that the obstacles they were running against were much more complex than it might have seemed on the surface.

One such obstacle most commonly pointed to was the boards' difficulties in getting advance knowledge of a threatened strike or lockout. Wisconsin labor commissioner Frost complained that "we rarely hear that there is a strike, that there is to be a strike, until the strike has taken place," and by that time it was too late to influence the parties; it was like trying "to stop a fight between two small boys . . . after the first blow had been struck."[22] As late as 1914 New York State chief mediator William Rogers complained that his board had found "no method by which we can rely on getting immediate or advance information on strike." This meant that state mediators had to depend on haphazard means to know when and where industrial strife was about to erupt. In the case of New York State, "newspaper reports" were one of the main sources of information. Mediation officers also had to rely a great deal on "friends, both in the labor movement and in the associations of employers who," explained Rogers, "keep us informed of the conditions of the trade in their localities."[23]

Another major problem state mediators encountered was the lack of uniformity in the powers that the various state boards had to intervene in labor disputes. This problem was most acute in labor disputes affecting work sites located in different states, for it prevented the state boards involved from intervening in a concerted fashion. Recounting one such case, Illinois mediator C. Doyle explained how "the powers conferred on the board of one State were greater than in another, and where the laws of one State might have authorized an independent investigation the laws of others did not"; the result was that although the boards involved were "ready and anxious to try and effect a settlement," in effect they were "absolutely powerless to do so."[24] In fact, this had been the major issue that had brought state mediators together as a national body and around which they agitated most assiduously—however meager the results of their efforts would prove to be.[25]

The difficulties that weakened the effectiveness of these boards might have been overcome—at least in principle—through proper legislative measures. That state mediators believed so is suggested by the acute interest with which many of them clamored for the adoption of some modified form of the Canadian IDI act and by the support many of them gave to the Newlands Act, which had established permanent mediation machinery in railroad transportation affecting interstate trade. But there were other sorts of problems that did not lend themselves so easily to legislative solutions and that demanded that state mediators "enter upon a long and difficult course in the education of public opinion."[26]

One of the most central of these problems concerned the ability and professional qualifications of state mediators. Doyle showed himself to be quite aware of this fact when he stated that one of the key objectives of the newly formed association was to find ". . . men who are especially qualified by training and environment to administer [mediation] laws intelligently."[27] But did he imply that state boards of mediation were staffed by people who were not particularly qualified for the job or that it was extremely difficult to find enough people who were qualified for this profession? Most likely, he meant both.

One of the high points in the inquiry conducted by the U.S. Commission on Industrial Relations came when mediator John Williams testified. Williams was a former coal miner who had a keen interest in labor matters; he had been able to pull himself free from that trade and develop an expertise in industrial relations affairs that made him one of the most respected mediators in the country. Williams is credited with being the first to conceive of the idea of the preferential shop (as an alternative to the closed versus open shop impasse), which had become a practice in some sectors of the clothing industry.[28] In fact, by this time Williams was shuttling between Chicago and New York City, serving in both as a full-time mediator in the clothing industry.[29] To be sure, Williams did not entirely fit the description of a typical state mediator; his job was part of the industrial relations arrangements worked out privately by the employers and unions of the particular industry. His testimony, however, shed much light on some important problems surrounding the activity of mediation.

In his testimony, Williams lectured the commissioners on the causes of industrial unrest and discontent, on the great educational value of trade unionism, on the need to "create some new force or institution" to regulate the relations between capital and labor while at the same time protecting the public interest, and the high degree of "dignity and self-respect" involved in a profession such as his. Williams spoke of mediation as constituting the "missing link" that would "bridge the wide chasm" between capital and labor. Clearly he impressed the commissioners deeply, for near the end of the testimony the acting chairman, John Commons, congratulated him for being the first truly "competent mediator" that had appeared before the commission. Congratulations apart, however, it remained that there were very few of these competent mediators, and what concerned the members of the commission was finding some way to promote "the development of a business of that type, which would be not simply the accident of one man . . . who is particularly qualified, but how can we find such men, to make it a professional business?" Although Williams agreed that there were few competent mediators, he felt that there were "many individuals who could be found that would possess the qualities needed to make [the profession of mediation] a success . . . as soon as it [would] be known that it was possible to have it institutionalized." But how to go about doing it? When Commons asked about the type of legislative enactment needed or the viability of a method such as civil-service examination, Williams could only reply that he was "not prepared" as this question represented a "new development." The best he could offer then was to reaffirm his faith in the "human spirit as a mediating force."[30]

That this question was one of high priority in the commission's inquiry is reflected by the insistence with which the commissioners pursued it with other mediators who testified. The picture that emerged from that investigation is revealing; it shows the difficulty encountered in finding criteria based on technical expertise as a way to professionalize a function that previously had relied heavily on charismatic qualities.

Mediation officers who testified gave their opinions on the major qualities that made for successful and competent mediators. According to New York chief mediator, William Rogers, it was essential for a successful mediator to be "a man of tact and quick judgment." The situation of haste and heated emotions often surrounding his intervention required that "the man that can meet the greatest emergency [is] the type of man that is most desirable for the purpose." This meant that even where a man "might be good under ordinary conditions," he "would be useless" if he were unable to operate under conditions of "strain and tenseness" where quick judgment was of paramount importance. These qualities had to be augmented by the virtue of determination: the mediator must "not [be] easily discouraged." Former New York State mediator John Lundrigan held that the courage "to take the responsibility for criticizing the position, attitude, or contention of either or all parties to the controversy" was another important quality. The mediator also had to be tactful to overcome the feelings of mistrust present among the parties and thus be able to "inspire and retain the confidence of both parties to a dispute."[31] This was particularly true in cases where the mediator had not only "to overcome the reluctance of one or both parties in meeting the other in conference" but also had "to keep them from still further irritating each other when they come together."[32] In fact, in states like Ohio, where antiunion sentiment was very strong among employers, mediators had to exercise a great deal of tact; often they had to act as "confidential intermediaries between the parties" to bring about a settlement without the two parties meeting in joint conference.[33]

According to Williams, getting the confidence of the workers was much more important—it was actually "indispensable to success"; being able to generate in the worker "the belief . . . that he is going to get a fair deal is an indispensable condition for the success of mediation." Williams explained that "it is relatively easy to satisfy the employer, because he [the mediator] has immediate access to him, and he [the employer] knows the business and there are few of him in number; while the satisfaction of the laborers is much more difficult. They stand at quite a distance removed from it, they do not understand the business, and it is hard to get their confidence. I may say here that it is my judgment that nothing is worthwhile that does not get the moral support of the worker. However much force you may put behind the decision, it would not get any distance in establishing peace unless you have the real assent of the people to whom it must apply." This is why Williams felt that the mediator needed "to be a thorough believer in unionism"; this was the one area where the mediator could afford not to look "disinterested or impartial."[34] When asked what particular training the mediator should have, William Rogers answered that although he felt that it was "largely a matter of personality," it "would be a very valuable training for a man to have had executive experience in labor organizations." Such experience, according to Rogers, helped the mediator not only in his relations with workers but also with the employers. This, he explained, was because "mediators who are former labor leaders have had so much experience as labor leaders that if they have any prejudices along the lines of the labor movement they are able to conceal or subordinate such prejudices at an appropriate time . . . . The labor leader has gained a capacity by his very leadership of dealing with the representatives of the employers."[35]

The opinion Rogers expressed here did in fact reflect a trend that had characterized the development of state boards of mediation: state mediators were chosen much more frequently from the ranks of organized labor than from the ranks of the employers. The most conspicuous example was New York State where for a number of years the office of chief mediator had been held by men who had previously been trade union officers. In addition, the four assistant mediators of that state had also been officially connected with labor organizations.[36] The explanation for this trend is not difficult to find. Besides trade unionists, people having an adequate knowledge of industrial relations matters could be found only among businessmen or among public figures (scholars, lawyers, journalists, professional reformers) who for one reason or another had developed a knowledge of

the field. But one could hardly have conceived of a Brandeis, a Holt, a
Weyl, or even an Easley abandoning a prestigious, if not lucrative, career
to become a full-time civil servant, however highly they might have thought
of the purposes served by state boards of mediation. Similarly it was unrealistic to expect that a well-established and experienced employer—the
kind who had developed an expertise in adjusting disputes with labor
unions—would leave his business to pursue a civil service career of the
mediation officers' caliber.

It should not be surprising, therefore, that former trade union officials
served most frequently as state mediators. Besides possessing a great deal
of experience in the field, trade unionists could also view the position as
an opportunity to perform a valuable public function that permitted them
at the same time to rise in social and economic status. For some former
trade unionists, their experience in state mediation work could even become a stepping-stone for more remunerative positions in related fields.
John Lundrigan, for example, who had left one of the railroad brotherhoods to become state mediator in New York, became general superin-
tendent of the industrial department of the International Paper Company
after he had mediated a long and bitter strike involving several of this
company's plants.[37] This case is even more interesting since Lundrigan
had been one of the most active and outspoken state mediators when the
profession began to agitate for reforms and one of the central figures in
the creation of a national mediators' association.[38]

This trend had some effect on the image of these state boards as impartial agencies of industrial peace. What Rogers and other mediators
saw as a positive factor—the trade-union experience of state mediators—
also had serious negative effects. In fact, when pressed by one of the
members of the Industrial Relations Commission, even Rogers had to
admit that a man who came from the ranks of organized labor was "handi-
capped as a mediator."[39] The problem was more serious than Rogers indicated; whether or not state mediation laws had been passed largely as a
result of the political influence exerted on state legislatures by organized
labor, the predominant presence of former trade unionists in these agencies had nourished the suspicion that the positions of the members of
the boards or bureaus were "party jobs," and the mediators were a sort
of party spoilmen.[40] Whether or not political patronage was in fact the
criterion adopted for the selection of state mediators, this question had
become a serious problem, and many state mediators had become pain-

fully aware of it. However strongly New York State mediator John Lundrigan stressed, in his address to the first National Convention of State Mediators, the importance of possessing the quality of personal integrity ("It goes without saying that no one who has the appearance of prejudice or bias or whose personal or official integrity is even doubtful can engage successfully in work of this character"),[41] state mediators were constantly running against the suspicion "prevailing in many quarters as to the ground of their selection and the motives which guide them in their intervention."[42] Illinois mediator C. Doyle noted that state mediators were confronted by "the inherent objection of employers and employees alike to trust the settlement of their differences to men who are looked upon as politicians."[43] In the case of Michigan, this problem had become so acute that in 1911 the statute providing for the workings of the state board was repealed because "the board became an instrument for the convenience of partisan politicians rather than an agency for industrial peace."[44] Here, it seems, was a problem overshadowing all the others associated with the personal qualities of mediators and that ultimately weakened the boards' effectiveness considerably. In their survey of state Mediation Agencies, in fact, Barnett and McCabe reached the conclusion that it was "very difficult even for mediators of proved ability, fairness, and tact" to operate properly under those circumstances.[45] And Doyle put it even more strongly when he stated that "it makes no difference whether the members of a board may be especially qualified to fulfill the duties for which they are appointed; they are often treated with little consideration by the parties engaged in industrial disputes."[46]

Clearly the difficulties encountered by state boards of mediation contained all the characteristics of an impasse. It was difficult to found the profession of mediator on criteria of technical expertise so as to permit the access of a larger number of qualified candidates; and this difficulty was compounded by the fact that the very function of state mediation seemed to be suffering from decades of widespread industrial conflict and from the years of intense labor and businessmen crusading that had so politicized the relations between capital and labor and undermined the role of these impartial state agencies of industrial peace.

In this context one can better appreciate the growing interest that many state mediators shared with John Commons in the possibilities of investigation. As Commons had theorized, investigation was a technical-scientific procedure rather than a political one—something the government had to

provide freely and that organized capital and labor could avail themselves
of whenever the need arose. Its great value, therefore, lay not merely in
the fact that it allowed for government intervention in the arena of industrial conflict but also that it provided the necessary technical machinery
to ascertain the causes of industrial disturbances, thus laying the groundwork for a reasonable solution.[47] To many state mediators, therefore,
investigation offered the way to bypass the problem of class bias or political partisanship through the adoption of a fact-finding procedure based
on scientific criteria.

But if most people could agree with the principle of investigation, it
was quite another thing to find agreement on how investigation was to be
applied. Organized labor's fierce opposition to the adoption of compulsory
investigation procedures proved to be an insurmountable obstacle to making investigation an effective instrument to solve industrial relations problems. In addition labor's stance on this issue represented an implicit challenge to the argument advanced by Commons and other reformers according to which problems of power relations between labor and capital could
be solved through the application of scientific-administrative criteria and
the institution of a depoliticized model of industrial relations. But if
labor's challenge was implicit, Commons's argument was both explicit and
eloquent, and it adds another dimension to this institutional impasse.

What is most striking about Commons's theory of collective bargaining
is not only its comprehensiveness but the degree to which it is based on a
keen awareness of the social and political milieu confronting Progressive
America. The recognition of a state of "social warfare" and "class antagonism" marking American society was in fact the starting point for Commons's theoretical elaborations. As he wrote years later, "in dealing with
the momentuous conflict of 'capital and labor' . . . I was trying . . . to save
Wisconsin and the nation from politics, socialism or anarchy."[48]

The subversive potential that class antagonism embodied—especially if
left unchecked—was a concern that Commons shared with other leading
reformers of his day, particularly the NCF leaders. But if his academic
poise kept him from embarking on public antisocialist crusades, his theoretical work was no less aimed at checking the inroads of socialism than
was the strategy pursued by his friends in the NCF. For Commons, socialism was clearly not the answer to America's economic and social evils,

primarily because of its denial of private property and ownership, which, as he increasingly emphasized, constituted the foundation of Western civilization. Capitalism had to be led "on its good behaviour"; its basic institutions had to be readjusted to new historical circumstances through a process of vigorous reforms based on the application of scientific and technical knowledge that had become available to society.[49] He asked, "Is it not better . . . to recognize in advance the foundations of capitalism, than to turn out eventually disillusioned, hopeless, reactionary, revolutionary, or contented with 'natural law' instead of better organized collective action?"[50]

Collective bargaining, as Commons envisioned it, would have the function of thwarting these dangers through the depoliticization of industrial relations—a process that had to begin with the depoliticization of the labor movement. In recounting the disagreements among the members of the U.S. Commission on Industrial Relations, Commons saw the problem dividing them as "whether the labor movement should be directed toward politics or toward collective bargaining." He then added, "I wanted them to avoid politics and to direct their energies toward what I knew was the policy of Samuel Gompers in building strong organizations of self-governing unions able to meet the employers' organizations on an equality, and freed from the interference of politicans."[51]

In this perspective, the task of the labor movement was to build up the organizational apparatus, making it possible that the collective sale of labor power occurred on the best possible terms for the workers. For Commons, a political turn by the labor movement meant not only producing a fertile soil for the inroads of socialism but also clouding the industrial front with issues that were alien to a process that essentially was of a technical-organizational character. Collective bargaining, as Commons posited it, provided the framework through which the interests of the working class could be represented in the process of an equitable distribution of the fruits of production, thus making recourse to political action useless and unnecessary.

In Commons's theory was a precondition that was essential if the industrial order he envisioned was to become operative: that collective bargaining "become universal and effective for all employers and employees"—an assumption that makes one wonder to what extent Commons's theoretical elaboration took into account the historical reality surrounding him.[52] The industrial events of the last two decades had pointed in the opposite direction; the American employers' class was unwilling to grant any power to labor, let alone institutionalize a relation of equality through the mechanism of collective bargaining. To try to resolve the problem of class antagonism through the scientific planning of institutional relations meant not only transcending the industrial and political reality of those years but also misconceiving the very character of those relations. The institutionalist hypothesis Commons theorized seemed to ignore the fact that at the origin of the existing institutional relations between capital and labor was their relation of power at the level of production. And it was at this level that capital had proved unwilling to tolerate any interference.

If, for instance, in 1915 (when Commons was formulating his recommendations) collective bargaining was confined to only a few sectors of industry and affected a small minority of American workers, how much was due to a malfunctioning in the development of the U.S. institutional apparatus, and how much was it instead the result of deliberate antilabor policies pursued by capital? And how much, one might add, was it the result of deliberate organizational policies pursued by the AFL? Commons's ambivalence in dealing with the link between relations of force at the level of production and relations of force at the institutional level prevented him from grasping the historical significance of the massive reorganization of work and production that capital had carried out throughout the Progressive era.[53]

A typical illustration of how in Commons the institutional relations overshadowed the relations of force at the level of production is found in the way he viewed the rise of employers' associations. He considered them a positive development in the attainment of industrial government and thought it was essential that their growth be promoted so that every employer in the country would be included in them. As he put it in his final report recommendations, "an employer who stays out of his organization is as culpable as a laborer who stays out of his union. Employers should organize 100 per cent just as the unions endeavor to reach that mark."[54]

Commons's insistence in casting this development in capitalist organization into a symmetrical institutional framework obscured the essential characteristic of employers' associations—their attempt to restructure the organization of work by taking the control of industrial and labor relations in their own hands. Only by looking at the employer-employee relations as essentially an act of exchange, as an "economic" transaction whose character was "politically neutral," was it possible to posit, at a higher level, an institutional equilibrium between capital and labor, but with the result of obscuring what the past decades had so clearly demonstrated—that it was at the point of production that the relations of power were often determined and it was there that capital had sought to gain a greater domination and control over the work force.

But even when looking at the working class and the trade unions, Commons's theoretical scheme rested on a dubious assessment of the reality surrounding the working class in America. Just as he had posited collective bargaining as a universal model of industrial relations, similarly the category of worker was invested with the character of universality. From this institutionalist angle, the process of unionization was reduced to an essentially functional problem, depending on the organizational effectiveness of labor unions and on the level of social maturity of the workers. Thus Commons could impute culpability to "a laborer who stays out of his union."[55] In reality, however, the type of worker on which Commons and most mediators postulated their institutional scheme was the organized, disciplined trade unionist—powerful but responsible, militant when necessary but corporatist, hardly the typical wage worker of Progressive America.

What was overlooked in this scheme was the reality of divisions existing within the working class in America—divisions resting on differences in skills, race, sex, and ethnicity. And moreover, these divisions were not accidental factors in the makeup of American society, but because of their use by employers and of trade unions' policies, they were a reflection of relations of power among different sectors of the working class and prevented that process of workers' organizational unification so essential to Commons's vision of the new industrial order.

Labor mediators knew very well how useless their function was in disputes where workers were unorganized or where the employers refused to bargain with unions or mediators because they did not want to "give the power to anybody else to interfere with their business." Where employers "would not transfer their power," where they "would not part with their power"—stressed mediator John Williams—"is not the place for a mediator. That is the place for fighting."[56]

And in the years 1909 to 1916 the belief that industrial relations problems could be solved only by all-out confrontation was far from being dormant. Many employers had long acted on this assumption, with quite encouraging results. From the ranks of labor, one organization in particular, the Industrial Workers of the World, made this belief central to its philosophy and organizational practice and in so doing heightened even further the institutional impasse of those years.

NOTES

1. David Montgomery, "The 'New Unionism' and the Transformation of Workers' Consciousness in America, 1909-22," *Journal of Social History* (Summer 1974) : 509-24.

2. Graham Adams, Jr., *Age of Industrial Violence, 1910-1915* (New York, 1966).

3. U.S. Commission on Industrial Relations, *Final Report and Testimony* (Washington, D.C., 1916), 1 : 207 (hereafter cited as CIR, *Final Report*).

4. John Commons, *Myself* (New York, 1934); Bruno Ramirez, "Collective Bargaining and the Politics of Industrial Relations in the Progressive Era, 1898-1916," (Ph.D. diss., University of Toronto, 1975), 275-303.

5. CIR, *Final Report,* 1 : 188.

6. Richard Gonce, "The Development of John R. Commons System of Thought" (Ph.D. diss., University of Wisconsin, 1966), 222.

7. Commons, *Myself,* 123-24.

8. CIR, *Final Report,* 1 : 173ff.

9. Ibid., 121-24.

10. Commons, *Myself,* 175.

11. CIR, *Final Report,* 1 : 121-24.

12. Ibid., 164.

13. Ibid., 165.

14. Carl H. Mote, *Industrial Arbitration* (Indianapolis, 1916), 191-214, provides a good summary of the mediation agencies existing in the various states.

15. "Tentative Plan for Local Boards of Conciliation and Arbitration of Industrial Disputes Suggested by New York State Bureau of Mediation and Arbitration," in CIR, *Final Report,* 2 : 1960; John Lundrigan, "Address Before the National Convention of State Arbitration Boards at Washington, D.C., March, 1910," in ibid., 1958.

16. Ibid., 1954.

17. Ibid.

18. Reference to this New York meeting is found in *Proceedings of the Eleventh Annual Meeting of the National Civic Federation, New York, January 12, 1911* (New York, 1911), 257 (hereafter cited as *NCF Proceedings, 1911*).

19. Ibid., 259.

20. Ibid., 261; for a detailed description of the organization of the various state boards see Mote, *Industrial Arbitration,* 215-38.

21. CIR, *Final Report,* 2 : 1932.

22. *NCF Proceedings, 1911,* 251.

23. CIR, *Final Report,* 2 : 1933, 1934.

24. *NCF Proceedings, 1911,* 260.

25. CIR, *Final Report,* 2 : 1954.

26. *NCF Proceedings, 1911,* 251.

27. Ibid., 262.

28. Donald O. Clark, "John E. Williams. Peacemaker: A Study of the Life of an Early Illinois Mediator and Arbitrator and His Impact upon the American Labor Movement" (Master's thesis, University of Illinois, 1957), 52; see also Michael O'Byrne, *History of La Salle County, Illinois* (Chicago, 1924), 3 : 509-12.

29. CIR, *Final Report,* 1 : 697-98.

30. Ibid., 697-713.

31. Ibid., 2 : 1935, 1940, 1956.

32. George Barnett and David McCabe, *Mediation, Investigation, and Arbitration in Industrial Disputes* (New York, 1916), 16.

33. Ibid., 24, 27.

34. CIR, *Final Report,* 1 : 699, 700, 709.

35. CIR, *Final Report,* 2 : 1935, 1938.

36. Barnett and McCabe, *Mediation,* 56.

37. CIR, *Final Report,* 2 : 1907-11.

38. Ibid., 1916, 1954.

39. Ibid., 1939.

40. Barnett and McCabe, *Mediation,* 53-54; Mote, *Industrial Arbitration,* 255.

41. "Lundrigan Exhibit," in CIR, *Final Report,* 2 : 1956.

42. Barnett and McCabe, *Mediation,* 53-54.

43. *NCF Proceedings, 1911,* 261.

44. Mote, *Industrial Arbitration,* 255.

45. Barnett and McCabe, *Mediation,* 54.

46. *NCF Proceedings, 1911,* 261.

47. Ramirez, "Collective Bargaining," 275-303.

48. Commons, *Myself,* 170.

49. Quoted in Gonce, "The Development," 361.

50. Quoted in ibid., 452.

51. Commons, *Myself,* 167-68.

52. CIR, *Final Report,* 1 : 188.

53. See Gisela Bock, Paolo Carpignano, and Bruno Ramirez, *La Formazione dell' Operaio Massa negli, USA, 1898-1922* (Milan, 1976).

54. CIR, *Final Report,* 1 : 219-20.

55. Ibid.

56. Ibid., 1 : 710.

11

THE IWW AND
THE NEGATION OF THE
TRADE AGREEMENT

Despite the several recent attempts to put the definite seal upon the history
of the Industrial Workers of the World, there are many aspects of the IWW
experience that still need to be analyzed and that are of great historical importance for any study of the industrial relations of that period.[1] Through
the IWW experience it is in fact possible to reconstruct—from within the
American workers' movement itself—a radical critique of the institutional
mechanisms that were designed to regulate industrial conflict, first among
them the trade agreement. Most importantly, this critique does not ex-
haust itself in empty and abstract polemics; rather, it rests on a relentless
organizational practice and seeks to take into account the concrete conditions of the American working class—as the Wobblies saw them.

Central to any assessment of the IWW's role in the context of the capital-
labor confrontation of the Progressive era is the Wobblies' concern for the
unskilled segments of the American working class. Judging from the proceedings of the founding convention of the organization, one would say
that an all-inclusive view of the working class prevailed among the delegates of the nascent organization. Bill Haywood's famous dictum hurled
out in one of his speeches at the convention—that the IWW was to include
"everyone who works for wages"—clearly seems to reflect this orientation.[2] Yet behind this seemingly universalistic stance there lies an extremely dynamic view of the working class—a class subjected to continuous
changes and recomposition by the revolutionizing transformations in

capitalist production, the whole reflecting a process that not only created divisions within the working class but also crystallized these divisions into relations of power.

Along with this awareness of class divisions was also the IWW's singling out of a new sector of the working class—which they saw emerging as a specific product of the new processes of production of those years. It was the mass-production and mass-service worker who generally lacked skills, was highly mobile, was largely of immigrant origin, and was increasingly female. It was to this sector that the IWW largely directed its organizing efforts, especially during the years when its impact was most felt on the American industrial front.

In attempting to organize the growing mass of unskilled and semiskilled workers, the Wobblies were in effect launching the bluntest challenge to American capital. This was the kind of labor force that American employers could more easily mold in order to undermine the restrictive practices of the craft unions. Moreover, it was the type of labor force on which the entrepreneurial dynamism of the mass-production sectors largely rested, and thus it was an essential element to the innovative processes marking the capitalist development of those years. Whether employed in enlightened enterprises—where various forms of welfare programs were in effect—or in industries such as steel and textile where the employers' absolutism was reflected in the harshest wages and working conditions, this sector of the labor force had become the uncontested domain of capital, especially since the AFL-affiliated unions had abandoned the field.

Only by ignoring this historical and structural context can one draw the conclusion that the IWW's organizing drives among the unskilled mass-production workers had no revolutionary content on the ground that the main concern was "higher wages and shorter workdays . . . improved conditions of life and job security,"[3] or on account of the fact that the IWW was "fighting for the immediate interest of workers as workers, rather than as revolutionaries whose purpose was to destroy class society."[4] But this is not the only aspect of the IWW's experience that historians have criticized on dubious ground.

In a recent historic-political assessment of the IWW's role in the American workers' movement, James Weinstein makes the correct assertion that the IWW concentrated its organizing efforts on "the unskilled industrial and migratory workers," and on this ground he draws the conclusion that the IWW adopted "a narrow conception of the working class."[5] Weinstein's criticism ignores the keen awareness demonstrated by the IWW (and some left-wing socialists attracted to the organization) about the structure, composition, and trends in the American working class. What is even more significant, his criticism fails to grasp the strategic factors that led the IWW to concentrate on the unskilled.

In the most minimal sense, the unskilled mass-production and mass-service workers had to be organized because, as the IWW saw it, it was impossible to conceive of a program of industrial unionism without taking into account this growing sector of the labor force. Second, because no other labor organization was showing the ability or the willingness to organize them, the IWW felt impelled to do so. This aspect was ably captured by labor journalist John Fitch on the occasion of the famous Paterson strike. Writing in the *Survey*, he noted,

Had John Golden of the U.T.W. . . . . come to Paterson on February 25th, undoubtedly he could have organized the workers in his union. Instead came Haywood, Elizabeth Flynn, Quinlan, Tresca—empty-handed, with neither money nor credit nor with the prestige of a 2,000,000 membership, but willing to work and go to jail. They have put into the 25,000 strikers a spirit that has made them stand together with a united determination for a period that must have tried the souls of the strongest.[6]

It was, indeed, the concern that the organizational vacuum existing in many sectors of the mass-production work force might soon be filled by the IWW that made the Wobblies the most feared workers' organization in employers' circles. In a letter that Easley wrote to Brandeis in 1912, after lamenting that unionization in the U.S. Steel plants had been effectively halted, he expressed his concern that the organizational vacuum existing in that sector would soon be filled by the IWW: "If the men [steelworkers] are not organized by the American Federation of Labor, an organization standing for American Institutions, they will sooner or later be organized by the Industrial Workers of the World."[7] Gertrude Beeks, secretary of the NCF Welfare Department, sought to put pressures on southern textile employers to enter into agreements with the United Textile Workers of America—an AFL affiliate—"to prevent the IWW from duplicating their work at Lawrence, Massachusetts." In view of this potential danger, Beeks argued, textile employers should change their traditional aversion to unionism, especially because the UTW "is a conservative body to ward off the IWW."[8] She believed that "the AF of L is the greatest fighting force in the country against Socialism and the IWW's."[9]

Another key aspect explains the strategic significance of the IWW's choice to concentrate their organizing efforts on the unskilled mass-production workers. It is an aspect that emerges with dramatic clarity and coherence especially after the series of spectacular organizing drives in the industrial East begun in 1909 with the McKees Rocks strike. To critics who advanced the thesis of the unorganizability of these sectors of the working class, the IWW drives were demonstrating that not only could these workers be organized but also that their struggles displayed a remarkable degree of initiative, militance, and determination. Wobbly leaders were quick to point out that in many cases the IWW was called to the scene of the strike after the struggle had begun; its role consisted therefore of giving leadership to the spontaneous self-activity of the workers and their sudden rebellion against inhuman working conditions.[10] In this sense Socialist party leader Morris Hillquit was more than correct when he told the members of the Commission on Industrial Relations, "the Industrial Workers of the World mean more than 14,000 men organized in Mr. St. John's organization. It means a certain new spirit in the American labor movement. It means Lawrence, it means Paterson. It means Little Falls, it means McKeesport Rock [sic]. It means this new phase of the labor movement which has risen within the last few years. How are we to account for it?"[11] It is on this ground that IWW organizers and spokesmen saw the militant potential of the unskilled and semiskilled mass-production workers and saw them emerging as a mass vanguard in the working class struggle against the capitalist organization of production. Reporting on the Lawrence strike, Luis Fraina (later to become the leading American theorist of the mass strike) expressed this point very clearly: "The situation here, and the spirit of the meetings, strengthens the belief that the non-skilled worker is the revolutionary force in capitalist society. The skilled workers are wavering, the non-skilled are solid to a man. It is this non-skilled mass, produced by the machine process, that must be molded into shape, and out of it to make the new, Socialist World."[12]

It was the experience of the IWW-led mass strikes in the East that led Austin Lewis—a California left-wing socialist who became intimately associated with the IWW serving often as the organization's attorney—to articulate some of the most perceptive observations on the changing composition of the American working class and the vanguard role of the unskilled mass-production workers.[13] Utilizing some of Thorstein Veblen's abstractions on the revolutionizing efforts of the "machine process," Lewis was able to translate them into a series of propositions that not only reflected closely the organizational practice of the IWW but also constitute one of the most original contributions to the analysis of the working class under capitalist development.

Among the four major sectors into which Lewis divided the American working class—"the slum proletariat," the "highly paid, well-skilled craftsmen," "the intellectual proletariat," and the "unskilled and migrant workers"—it was the last group that was emerging as the agent of revolutionary social change in American society. This nucleus of the working class—a "machine proletariat" as Lewis called it—was "the special and essential product of modern industry," and as such it embodied intrinsic characteristics that made it prone to revolutionary action. The machine process—of which mass-production and mass-service workers were such an essential part—produced in them a "revolutionary state of mind . . . which is the most fruitful immediate source of revolutionary action."[14] This nucleus of the class is found "in the basic industries" and as such "it hold[s] the strategic position." The standardization process to which the machine process subjected them daily had erased in them any residue of professional or work ethics—if one ever existed. On the contrary, it had the effect of creating "an identity of interest with each other," a material basis for their organization.

The machine industry rules the mass of unskilled proletarians. It drives them to work in unison. It forces them to keep time with the industrial machine and in so doing teaches them the goose step of industrial organization, for organization by the employer is the first step to self-organization of the employed. . . . [These] facts themselves force him to revolt. Facts also teach him the method of revolt. This method takes more and more the form of spontaneous mass action. This is the reflex upon the mind of the workers who have nothing in common and never have had anything in common except the fact of common environment, a common subjection to the machine industry. This is the reason that the unskilled are goaded into mass action wherever the machine industry has become established.[15]

Several years earlier, the IWW founders had described the emergence of the mass worker as arising from the employers' attacks on the power of the working class. As they put it in their manifesto, "The worker, wholly separated from the land and the tools, with his skill of craftsmanship rendered useless, is sunk in the uniform mass of wage slaves. . . . Shifted hither and thither by the demands of profit-takers the laborer's home no longer exists. In this helpless condition he is forced to accept whatever humiliating conditions his master may impose."[16] Now, after the industrial efficiency drive and the wave of struggles led by the unskilled workers, Lewis saw how that very process of mass production had created the conditions making possible a new attack on the capitalist organization of work. "It will soon be easier to organize the masses of the so-called unskilled than it was only a few years ago to organize the carpenters, who worked by threes and fours in small shops scattered here and there under various competing employers."[17] It was in this new sector of the working class—*Solidarity* editorialized in 1910—that "the hope of industrial unionism is to be found."[18]

But if the Wobblies and their spokesmen had found in the unskilled sector of the working class the new revolutionary force, the fact remained that in the context of the reorganization of work produced by the capitalist development of those years, this type of labor power was the most vulnerable to attacks by capital. They were, as *Solidarity* described them, "the victims of unrestrained exploitation," embodying "most keenly the degradation of wage slavery."[19] Their unorganized state was both a symptom and a cause of their position of weakness against capital—a weakness reflected in the working conditions and wage policies to which they were subjected and resting largely on their lack of skills. Lacking skills meant, in fact, being deprived of a material basis to use as a lever of power and around which to organize to wrest improved conditions from capital. If for Gompers the distinction between skilled and unskilled was academic and, in his own words, "a matter of gradation," for the IWW the distinction was not only a most sharp one, it also lay at the basis of the relation of power existing between organized and unorganized labor.[20] It is this original view of social conflict—where power is conceived not merely as affecting the relation between capital and labor but as affecting also relations between different sectors of the working class—that adds new meaning to the IWW's program of industrial unionism and to their critique of the AFL.

In a most fundamental way, the industrial unionism the IWW advocated meant organizing all wage laborers, but starting with the weaker sectors of that class. This process of equalization from below was viewed as the only guarantee to institute a true workers' democracy; it would unify the working class and at the same time undermine the position of privilege and power of the organized few over the unorganized many. This point was clearly articulated in 1913 by William E. Walling, at that time still a close fellow traveler of the IWW: "The new unionism for the first time introduces democracy into the labor movement; for the organization of the skilled and unskilled into a single industrial union means that everything is placed absolutely in the hands of the unskilled majority. And as democracy is taken seriously by the workers, this means the gradual annihilation of all the advantages of the skilled."[21] But this strategic vision was already contained essentially in Bill Haywood's speech at the IWW founding convention. As he put it,

I do not mean that this organization is going to improve the condition of purely skilled workers, but I mean we are going to get at the mass of the workers and bring them up to a decent plane of living. I do not care a snap of my fingers whether or not the skilled workers join this industrial movement at the present time. When we get the unorganized and the unskilled laborer into this organization the skilled worker will of necessity come here for his own protection. As strange as it may seem to you, the skilled worker today is exploiting the labor beneath him, the unskilled man, just as much as the capitalist is."[22]

During the following years, as the IWW embarked in its organizing drives, its critique of the AFL and of craft unionism in general became more radical. No longer could the IWW afford to ignore skilled workers and their organizations, waiting until they came to their fold: craft unions had in fact become "an instrument of capitalism."[23] Not only had they outlived their usefulness in the struggle for the emancipation of the working class, they were now emerging as a barrier to such emancipation. Their organizational rigidity and their exclusiveness had become a useful instrument for capital, through which the unification of the working class could be prevented. The weakness of the unorganized, unskilled sectors was therefore perpetuated by the practice of the skilled craft organizations. As W. E. Walling put it in 1913, "In proportion as the unskilled workers and machine operatives attempt, in industry after industry, to improve their lot, they find that these owners of jobs oppose them almost as bitterly as the capitalists do." In this process of "class struggle within the working class," Walling saw, as many Wobbly spokesmen did, a direct correlation between the position of power and privilege of the unskilled craft organizations, and the position of weakness of the unskilled, unorganized workers. "Until this policy [the craft unions'] is followed," Walling pointed out, "the capitalists, by making concessions to skilled labor and by turning the rest of the . . . manual workers and intellectual workers against each other, will be able to prevent either economic or political advance of the masses."[24]

But even in instances where the AFL was making some attempts to organize unskilled and semiskilled workers, IWW spokesmen saw this as a move forced on the craft organizations to exert a more direct control over unskilled labor and thus to perpetuate the existing relations of power. Austin Lewis, for instance, analyzed at length the attempts made by the California State Federation of Labor to organize migrant and unskilled laborers—attempts that he felt were destined to failure because of the impossibility of integrating unskilled workers into craft unions. For Lewis, the motives behind this organizing campaign were clear:

The unskilled, for the most part, are products of the machine industry and operate in terms of the new system. The crafts are tottering before the assaults made upon them by the machine industry. . . . Therefore the unskilled must be organized to form a screen between the crafts and the operation of the machine industry. The unskilled must remain classified as unskilled, in order that the crafts may maintain their prestige as skilled, and their pay in proportion.[25]

Most striking in this critique of the AFL is the absence of any moralism; it focuses exclusively on the class conditions produced by capitalist development in America.

Just as the consciousness of the unskilled, mass-production workers had been analyzed in terms of the material conditions they occupied in the organization of production, in a similar view IWW spokesmen tried to explain the skilled craftsmen's propensity for conserving their position of power vis-à-vis other sectors of the working class. For W. E. Walling, "the conservative position taken by the 'aristocracy of labor,' both in politics and labor union matters . . . [was] a *permanent and fundamental* characteristic of all skilled labor."[26] For Lewis, this conservative attitude of skilled workers was commonsensical, and it would be absurd, he claimed, to expect otherwise. "Why should a trade unionist," Lewis asked, "put himself to the inconvenience of a strike to benefit a poorly paid and generally negligible member of the unskilled proletariat, with whom he has no intimate relations? . . ." To Lewis the answer seemed obvious: "the skilled workmen will not strike on behalf of the unskilled, nor will they make any other sacrifices in his behalf as long as they hold an economic position which they regard as secure." On this basis, to maintain that the skilled workers have "an identity of interest" with the unskilled workers was erroneous and self-deceiving. "When a matter of property is involved," Lewis pointed out, "even if it be only the transient and uncertain property in skill, interests become differentiated and there can be no united or really purposeful action."[27]

The organizational implications that the Wobblies and their spokesmen drew from this state of affairs within the working class were crucial. As an unsigned article in *Solidarity* put it, "If Gompers and Mitchell, Morrison, Lewis, etc., would ALL withdraw from the AF of L and would be succeeded by 'socialists' of the S. P. type the AF of L would just be as yellow as it is today."[28] The problem, therefore, was not one of leadership sell-out—though this kind of accusation is not absent in IWW pronouncements—but rather the specific negative function that craft unions played in the working class's struggle for emancipation because of the particular corporatist interest they represented. Therefore it was not only wrong but strategically suicidal to expect that the initiative for the unification of the working class would come from these organizations. Lewis explained, "The crafts will not move for [the unskilled]. It is necessary therefore that they move the crafts. They can only do this by forcing the crafts which will not strike on their behalf into such a position that they must cease work whether they will or not. In other words, the unskilled must be so organized that they can compel the highly paid workers to share in their fight." On the basis of all these points, Lewis articulated the important principle of unskilled workers' autonomy, a principle that had increasingly become the organizational practice of the IWW:

The unskilled must help themselves and the only way that they can do so is by forming an organization apart and distinct from that of the skilled workers, one which is in fact the antithesis of that of the skilled worker in concept and design. The unskilled must constitute themselves the nucleus. They cannot be grafted on to the existent form: they must take a form for themselves. Their organization must be representative of common unskilled labor and not of accidentally skilled labor. Therein lies their power. The realization of that power will come from the inherent and unavoidable hostility of the skilled trades.[29]

Clearly, industrial unionism for the IWW was more than an organizational model; it was a class perspective whose implementation had to start with the destruction of the existing power relations within the working class. Only by failing to grasp this dimension can one advance the thesis, as J. Conlin has recently done, that the organizing work of the IWW was "supplementary" to that of the AFL unions. "The union sought out the workers," states Conlin, "that the AFL ignored."[30] However commendable is Conlin's attempt to exonerate the IWW from the accusation of "dual unionism," his interpretation misses entirely the antithetical directions characterizing the two movements, as well as the real significance of the historical factors that brought them into conflict.[31]

If there was one point on which the IWW was in total agreement with American trade-unions spokesmen, this was that "the trade agreement"— to use John Mitchell's famous expression—"was the essence of trade unionism." However total their agreement on this premise might have been, the implications drawn from it were radically different. Historians have generally referred to the IWW's proverbial aversion to the so-called time agreements and its refusal to be bound to agreed-upon conditions for any specific length of time. But it was not only the time clause that the IWW repudiated; the very concept of trade agreement was subjected to a radical critique —a critique growing out of the IWW awareness of the power relations existing between sectors of the working class, as well as out of the centrality of unskilled workers in the IWW program. For the IWW trade agreements were a reflection of the hierarchy of power existing between different sectors of the working class; their only function was to legitimize the position of privilege that the "aristocracy of labor" occupied vis-à-vis the unorganized masses of the labor force.

While acknowledging that in earlier periods the right of craft organizations to enter into agreement with employers had been won at the cost of long and bloody battles, under the new industrial regime trade agreements had outlived their usefulness as objectives of the class struggle. At best, they were tantamount to institutionalizing the workers' struggle against capital, thus accepting capital's most favorable terms. As Lewis put it, "A [labor] contract is a legal document, to be construed in legal terms, subject to the operation of legal technicalities. The employer is quite at home here, for the bourgeois always cheat one another in the name of the law."[32]

Wobblies scoffed at the very idea that workers' labor power could be the object of a contractual relation between equal parties. "In law," wrote the *Industrial Worker*, "a contract to be binding must be between equal contracting parties. Now who will contend that the men who have nothing to sell but their labor are equal to the owners of the tools they use when the two try to strike a bargain as to wages, hours, and conditions of labor."[33]

The rejection of the notion of an equal exchange between capitalist and wage earner is a theme that runs through the IWW literature. It grew out of the Wobblies' belief that the employer-employee relationship was fundamentally one of force between two irrepressible parties. The point of production, far from being a marketplace, was the arena where the worker "meets the enemy" and where the "[class] issue must be fought out."[34] It was therefore on this relation of force that wages and working conditions hinged, not on any abstract law of supply and demand. "Why make contracts with bosses," editorialized *Solidarity*, "when industrial organization will enable us to dictate terms?"[35] Similarly, wage scales, the heart of the trade agreement, were a reflection of this relation of force. To the famous trade unionist slogan, "a fair day's wage for a fair day's work," the *Industrial Worker* responded, "the amount of money we'll get will depend on our power at the shop."[36] In an editorial in the same Wobbly paper, this principle was described more fully: "The wage scale of a union, to be anything but a joke, must be a scale that is established and enforced by the union and this of course requires sufficient organization to control the work. The IWW stands for the full product of the workers' work, but we have no wage scale, unless STRONG enough to ENFORCE it."[37]

In a context of permanent conflict—as the Wobblies saw the work place —no truce could be contemplated by the workers; and signing a contract with the employer would mean violating this basic rule of class warfare. Such a move, Vincent St. John explained to the members of the Industrial Relations Commission, "prevents the workers from taking advantage of any favourable opportunity that might arise during the term of the agreement, by which they could get better conditions."[38]

This conception of permanent warfare inevitably led to a radical questioning of the one weapon contemplated by the trade agreement: the strike. According to the Wobblies, in fact, the new conditions of industrial warfare had rendered the traditional strike obsolete. It allowed the employer to anticipate it, thus making the necessary preparations for the confrontation. It also was expensive; only a craft organization with a huge war chest could afford it. As an IWW spokesman writing on the subject put it, "the employer can better afford to fight one strike that lasts six months than he can fight six strikes that take place in the same period."[39]

Lewis was able to articulate this new development in industrial warfare, linking it to the material conditions characterizing the unskilled, mass-production workers whom the IWW was seeking to organize. If these methods of institutionalizing industrial conflict—through trade agreements and official strikes—were possible weapons for skilled craftsmen's organizations because of their superior "economic position, . . . these agreements and delays," Lewis noted, "mean death to the unskilled worker, who is compelled by the necessities of the case to strike rapidly and hard. His life is so uncertain, he always stands so perilously near the edge, that he can waste no time."[40] Under such conditions, it was imperative that new weapons and new tactics of struggle be devised to render the action of the unskilled workers effective.

One of these methods was the mass strike. What characterized this type of strike—at least in the IWW experience—was not merely the large number of participants it drew but rather the fact that the strike involved the whole community—women, children, sympathizers, and others.[41] But apart from this more dramatic and intermittent form of struggle, other new tactics had to be sought to enable unskilled, mass-production workers to engage in daily warfare at the work place. It is no coincidence that a whole gamut of tactics—known under the various names of direct action, sabotage, passive resistance, and striking on the job—occurred during the years when the diffusion of scientific management techniques in the United States had become most widespread—the post-1909 years—and the organizing drives among the unskilled mass-production workers reached its highest point.

The violent controversy that such tactics of industrial warfare caused in socialist circles has been described by many historians. Moreover, the historical debate concerning the alleged syndicalist parentage of some of these tactics still goes on. What concerns us most in this study, however, is the implications that these tactics had for the existing legitimate forms of industrial relations, as well as the immediate purpose they were intended to serve in the context of the material conditions of work and life of those unskilled sectors the IWW sought to organize. The rationale behind these tactics was that of hitting hardest at the employer's profits with the least losses for the workers, in a sort of on-the-job "guerrilla warfare" as now organizer Elizabeth G. Flynn put it.[42] The essential significance that this form of industrial warfare had for low-paid, unskilled workers was clearly expressed in the definition that Wobbly writer W. I. Fisher gave: "doing whatever hinders production or cuts down profits. By attacking the employer's income and at the same time drawing wages is a very effective fighting method, as it keeps us from starving, weakens the financial standing of the employer and thus makes him less able to lock us out for any prolonged period."[43]

Wobbly spokesmen felt that the massive process of reorganization of production was increasingly creating the ideal conditions for practicing those tactics in a more effective way. According to Lewis, in fact, "The conduct of great industrial enterprises . . . where the cost of production is calculated to a nicety and where delay or interruption or the noncoordination of interdependent parts of machinery implies not only an immediate money loss but tends to the annihilation of the business itself, if continually repeated, places the safety of the capitalist property and the making of capitalist profits more and more in the hands of the working class."[44]

Although the IWW displayed a remarkable acumen for trying to harness certain forms of workers' struggles to the changing organization of production, they were not the inventors of these tactics. Restricting the workers' output and withdrawing one's efficiency from work by either working slower or turning out poorer work had become universal practices among industrial workers.[45] In the United States these practices certainly predated the rise of the IWW and were widespread not only among skilled craftsmen (as shown in chapter 5) but also among unskilled immigrant workers. One may even go so far as to say—as the observations of W. Williams in his *What's On the Worker's Mind* seem to corroborate—that rank-and-file immigrants did not need the IWW to tell them about soldiering, slowing down, and other forms of industrial sabotage.[46]

Yet, to conclude that the IWW merely endorsed what immigrant workers practiced would be very simplistic. For in IWW practice and theory, what in most cases had been spontaneous workers' resistance was seized upon and elevated to a central form of anticapitalist struggle to be carried out in a conscious and organized manner. Wobbly writer Walker C. Smith produced the most thorough treatment of sabotage when the topic was most widely debated, describing it as the cutting edge of a new workers' militancy. "Sabotage is to the social war what guerillas are to national wars. If it does no more than awaken a portion of the workers from their lethargy it will have been justified. But it will do more than that; it will keep the workers awake and will incite them to do battle with masters. It will give added hope to the militant minority, the few who always bear the brunt of the struggle."[47]

According to the IWW, therefore, sabotage had to be practiced with a clear objective in mind, namely that of strengthening the power of the working class by enabling "the workman to win in the shop, to improve his economic position, to develop his fighting capacity and build up his organization every step . . . toward ultimate victory."[48]

For IWW leaders the adoption of these practices called for a conscious organizational choice, which involved political risks—risks that in fact were concretized in such consequential developments as the sharp rupture that occurred between the IWW and the Socialist Party precisely on the question of sabotage.

One question that is perhaps of greater historical relevance to the IWW's use of these tactics is the degree to which the political and social context of the time—i.e., the institutional power that businessmen were able to command, the efficiency of the state to curb and repress class conflict, the search for forms of mediation advocated by most industrial reformers— made the tactics of industrial sabotage appear realistic in a broader working class program. Similarly, one may ask to what extent the Wobblies' insistence on these forms of struggle contributed to the decline of their organization and to the failure of their revolutionary project.

Complete answers to these questions would lead us beyond the chronological confines of this study and into a historical topic that has been widely debated by historians. What is important here is the direct relationship between the defeat the IWW suffered by the American capitalist state and their anti-institutional approach best exemplified in their aversion for labor contracts and their insistence on forms of struggle such as sabotage. For if it is true that the Wobblies' uncompromising stance and their refusal of political mediation had often allowed them to give organized expression to the struggles of immigrant and unskilled workers, it is also true that the forms of struggle that their refusal required did not prove sufficient to produce the unification of the working class "from below" that had been postulated by IWW leaders. Despite the fact that at times their organization appeared as the iceberg-tip of a movement whose dimensions were difficult to assess,[49] the IWW failed to function as the hegemonic force within the American labor movement.

In part this can be explained by the fact that—as David Montgomery has pointed out—on the eve of World War I, workers' resistance to the capitalist restructuring of industry proceeded along two distinct currents: One represented the struggles of the unskilled, immigrant, mass-production workers, and the other represented the more skilled sectors who challenged the new managerial despotism by claiming and fighting for a greater share of control within the production process.[50] Whether these two fronts of anticapitalist resistance could have merged into a new and larger body, within which the IWW would have maintained a certain vanguard position, is a matter of historical conjecture. But if such a process could have occurred, and the instances of Wobbly cooperation with non-IWW skilled workers in local strikes were not lacking, it would seem that the IWW ideology and practice risked turning into major organizational liabilities. True, the proverbial Wobbly antagonism toward the skilled crafts and their rejection of the trade-agreement philosophy were not empty radical rhetoric; rather, they grew out of a keen awareness of American industrial and social conditions and of a thorough knowledge of the AFL politics of compromise. Yet the international dimension of the crisis in which U.S. capital found itself at the onset of World War I was opening for the U.S. labor movement new possibilities in political mediation. Under the new circumstances collective bargaining came to provide an institutional shield for larger sectors of the U.S. working class, who used the government-sanctioned contractual relation in their struggle to improve their position of power within the industrial framework. The ability in 1916 of the railroad brotherhoods to prevent their dispute's being settled by compulsory investigation and arbitration and their success in forcing the Wilson Administration to grant them the eight-hour day best symbolizes the changing climate of industrial relations that was brought about by the war—as does the dramatic rise in strike activity, which in 1916 and 1917 reached unprecedented proportions.[51]

In this historical context made even more complex by its international dimension, the refusal of the political mediation practiced by the Wobblies could only become a losing proposition, not only because it clashed frontally with a capital threatened domestically and internationally, but also because it had the effect of putting into question the power that large sectors of the labor movement were increasingly gaining, and for whom collective bargaining appeared as a substantial democratic conquest.

Under these conditions, the Wobblies' attitudes, exemplified in their leader Vincent St. John's statement, could not sound more suicidal: "There is but one bargain that the IWW will make with the employing class—complete surrender of the means of production."[52]

NOTES

1. See especially Philip Foner, *The Industrial Workers of the World, 1905-1917* (New York, 1965); Melvyn Dubofsky, *We Shall Be All: The History of the Industrial Workers of the World* (Chicago, 1969); Joseph

R. Conlin, *Bread and Roses Too: Studies of the Wobblies* (Westport, Conn., 1969).

2. *Proceedings of the Founding Convention of the IWW,* 575 (hereafter cited as *IWW Proceedings, 1905*).

3. Dubofsky, *We Shall Be All,* 486 and esp. 480ff.

4. James Weinstein, "The IWW and American Socialism," *Socialist Revolution* 1 (September-October 1970) : 26.

5. Ibid., 33.

6. John Fitch, "The IWW: An Outlaw Organization," *Survey* 30 (June 7, 1913) : 361.

7. R. Easley to L. Brandeis, November 4, 1914, box 79a, NCF Papers, New York Public Library.

8. G. Beeks to Isma Dooley, August 10, 1914, box 121, NCF Papers.

9. See, for instance, Beeks to Frank Mebane, August 10, 1914, box 121, NCF Papers.

10. *Industrial Worker,* November 23, 1911, 2. This point is also discussed by Conlin, *Bread and Roses Too,* 88.

11. U.S. Commission on Industrial Relations, *Final Report and Testimony* (Washington, D.C., 1916), 2 : 1570 (hereafter cited as CIR, *Final Report*).

12. Quoted in Paul Buhle, "Debsian Socialism and the 'New Immigrant' Worker," in William L. O'Neill, *Insights and Parallels: Problems and Issues of American Social History* (Minneapolis, 1973), 262.

13. Austin Lewis's writings and analysis have not received from historians the attention that they deserve. One exception is ibid.

14. Austin Lewis, *The Militant Proletariat* (Chicago, 1911), 25-37, 51, 66.

15. Austin Lewis, "Organization of the Unskilled," *New Review* (December 1913) : 926, 961.

16. *IWW Proceedings, 1905,* 4.

17. Lewis, "Unskilled," 961.

18. *Solidarity* (June 11, 1910) : 2.

19. Ibid.

20. CIR, *Final Report,* 2: 1576.

21. William E. Walling, "Class Struggle within the Working Class," in William L. O'Neill, ed., *Echoes of Revolt: The Masses, 1911-1917* (Chicago, 1966), 48. This article was reproduced in part in *The Industrial Worker* (February 6, 1913) : 4.

22. *IWW Proceedings, 1905,* 575-76.

23. *Industrial Union Bulletin* (March 16, 1907) : 1.

24. Walling, "Class Struggle," 48.

25. Austin Lewis, "Organization of the Unskilled (part I)," *New Review* (November 1913) : 879. Lewis's description and analysis of the California State Federation of Labor's organizing drives found corroboration in the organizing practice of the machinists' union—the organization that perhaps more than any other was pressed with the problem of expanding its jurisdiction to include semiskilled and unskilled workers. When in 1911 the IAM decided to include helpers in the organization, they were to be subjected to the strict control of the skilled element. For instance, they were to have separate locals, and qualified machinists were forbidden to teach helpers the skills of the trade; more importantly, helpers' locals could not call any strike action without the sanction by the local journeymen's lodge. As the historian of the IAM puts it, the inclusion of "helpers" "was [due] to economic necessity, not democratic sentiment." Mark Perlman, *The Machinists: A New Study in American Trade Unionism* (Cambridge, Mass., 1961), 34, 148.

26. Walling, "Class Struggle," 48.

27. Lewis, "Unskilled," 957, 962.

28. *Solidarity* (June 11, 1910) : 4.

29. Lewis, "Unskilled," 960.

30. Conlin, *Bread and Roses Too,* 20.

31. The same criticism can be applied to Dubofsky, *We Shall Be All,* esp. 482.

32. Lewis, "Unskilled," 957-58.

33. *Industrial Worker* (March 12, 1910) : 4.

34. Lewis, *The Militant Proletariat,* 115.

35. *Solidarity* (December 18, 1909) : 2.

36. Cf. *Industrial Worker,* esp. May 1, 1913, February 6, 1913.

37. Ibid. (April 15, 1909) : 2.

38. CIR, *Final Report,* 2 : 1451.

39. Quoted in *New Review* (January 18, 1913) : 89.

40. Lewis, "Unskilled," 958.

41. In this context it must be pointed out that the participation of women in these strikes—not just as wage earners but as housewives— has not received from historians the attention it deserves. Where factors such as "ethnic behavior"—that is, the greater cohesiveness of the ethnic family—have been adduced, the explanation seems at best partial. When comparisons are made with the average strike actions of the highly paid craft unions, it seems possible to suggest that in the IWW-led mass strikes, the precarious wage conditions characterizing the unskilled, male breadwinner in these mass-production sectors, and consequently the greater difficulty of the housewife in fulfilling her role of managing the house-

hold, made her a participant in the struggle for survival, thus bridging
the gap between work-place struggles and the isolated, daily struggle of
the housewife in the community.

42. Quoted in Mike Davis, "The Stop Watch Versus the Wooden Shoe,"
Radical America 9 (January-February 1975) : 85. This article is a provoca-
tive attempt to analyze IWW on-the-job tactics in relation to Taylorism.

43. W. I. Fisher, "Industrial Unionism, Tactics, and Principles,"
Industrial Worker (March 12, 1910) : 4. See also the series of editorials
on the subject that appeared in the *Industrial Worker* from January to
April 1913.

44. Lewis, *Militant Proletariat,* 121-22.

45. Cf., for instance, the remarks by William Walling in *Progressivism—
and After* (New York, 1914), 301-02.

46. Whiting Williams, *What's On the Worker's Mind, By One Who Put
on Overalls to Find Out* (New York, 1921).

47. Walker C. Smith, *Sabotage—Its History, Philosophy and Function*
(Chicago, 1913), 13 (originally appeared as a series of editorials in the
IWW national paper, the *Industrial Worker*).

48. Lewis, *Militant Proletariat,* 121-22.

49. Cf., for instance, the comments by Socialist party's secretary
Morris Hillquit in CIR, *Final Report,* 2 : 1570; and John Commons in
Commons to W. B. Paker (copy), May 14, 1912, Commons Papers, box 2,
Wisconsin State Historical Society, Madison, Wisconsin.

50. David Montgomery, "The 'New Unionism' and the Transformation of
Workers' Consciousness in America, 1909-22," *Journal of Social History*
(summer 1974), esp. 519.

51. Cf. chap. 9 and Montgomery, "The 'New Unionism'."

52. Vincent St. John, *The IWW: Its History, Methods, and Structure*
(Chicago, n.d.), 12.

EPILOGUE

The economic prosperity that Senator Marcus Hanna had promised the American public at the turn of the century if industrial peace could be maintained had certainly materialized by the middle of the 1910s. But if the American industrial apparatus had undergone one of the major expansions of its history, its results in terms of economic and social benefits had meant little or no change for the majority of the American laboring masses. The reports submitted by the members of the Commission on Industrial Relations in 1915, while disagreeing on a number of policy matters, were in substantial agreement on the social and economic picture emerging from their long and thorough work of investigation.

The scenario was one of a growing disparity between the huge profits and wealth amassed by business and corporations and the material and physical hardship under which the large masses of wage earners lived. Despite "the inexhaustible natural resources of the United States," one report stated, "her tremendous mechanical achievements, and the genius of her people for organization and industry . . . possibly one half of the families of wage earners employed in manufacturing and mining . . . [are] living in conditions of actual poverty."[1]

The labor problem appeared far from being resolved. Industrial violence—this distressing problem that in 1912 had prompted President Taft to appoint the commission—had escalated at a fearful rate even while the commissioners were touring the country to gather information. The problem was compounded by the outbreak of war in Europe and the uncertain future of the United States. Commissioner Basil Manly described very vividly this state of apprehension in his report:

> The lack of a proper industrial relationship and the existence of bad labor conditions is a matter of the most serious moment during times of peace, but the events of the past year have demonstrated how enormously their menace to the welfare of the nation is increased during a period of war. The present European war is being fought on the farms and in the factories as much as in the trenches. The effective mobilization of our industrial resources is as important, simply from the standpoint of war, as is the mobilization of our military and naval forces.[2]

In pointing to collective bargaining as the solution to the existing industrial ills, the Industrial Commission was not prescribing any new formula—despite some new features recommended in the Commons-Harriman report. The commission was essentially appealing to the goodwill of businessmen and policy makers to the end that a model of industrial relations practiced in certain industrial sectors be extended to American industry as a whole. In doing so, these reformers were revealing a limitation that was common among most prolabor reformers in the Progressive era—invoking ideals of economic and social equality as a guide to public policy and in the process ignoring the operational imperatives characterizing various industrial sectors.

For collective bargaining to be elevated to a national industrial relations policy, at least two basic conditions were required: the organizational base of the trade union movement had to be broadened to include large masses of semiskilled and unskilled workers and the state had to intervene in the process of industrial relations, not in situations of emergency, but as a planner and administrator of those relations. Both of these conditions became a reality in the New Deal years, but not without an economic and political crisis that threatened the collapse of American capitalism and not without the most intense and violent cycle of workers' struggles in U.S. history.

During World War I, however, it seemed as if the formula recommended by the Commission on Industrial Relations was being heeded. The war years, in fact, saw an unprecedented extension of collective bargaining in American industry with organized labor being delegated some powers to ensure stability and order over labor relations—a condition essential for the success of war efforts. But to see this arrangement as merely an attempt to "conciliate business and pro-war unions" or as a reward to the AFL for its prowar stance provides only a partial answer.[3] The extension of collective bargaining must also be seen as a result of a new outbreak of workers' struggles that, starting in the months before the U.S. entrance in the war, reached by the end of 1916 dramatic proportions—with a record figure of 3,789 strikes involving more than 1.6 million workers. By the end of 1917 the number of strikes had climbed to 4,450.[4] In this context, collective bargaining was the only mechanism available to policy makers to keep the capital-labor conflict under control within the formality of a democratic institutional framework; but it also was a clear demonstration of the workers' movement's power stemming from its strategic position in the midst of a grave emergency situation. As a commentator has put it, the war situation was giving labor the opportunity to "strengthen [its] organization by exploiting the class adversary's national need."[5]

Only by viewing labor relations as part of the continuing dynamics of capital-labor confrontation is it possible to lay bare the essential historical significance of collective bargaining in the Progressive era: it was both a result of labor's power as well as a vehicle to control workers' struggles and channel them in a path compatible with capitalist development.

In this sense, the parallels between the 1900-1904 years and the war years are not coincidental. Both periods were marked by the highest levels of labor strife and were accompanied by an unprecedented growth in unionization; and in both periods—though in varying degree—collective bargaining came close to being elevated to a national industrial relations policy. The first period saw the trade agreement as providing the framework that facilitated the institutional recognition of labor's newly acquired power and thus staving off the potential economic and political threats that the rising tide of labor strife foreshadowed.

It is this dual character that collective bargaining took on in the Progressive years that helps explain the organizational crisis marking the trade union movement in that period. At a time when the main content of workers' struggles was the demand for organization and unionization, by institutionalizing its position of power organized labor was in effect foreclosing this possibility to a large segment of the American working force. The organizational experience of the IWW and the critique that grew from it shows the extent to which this process rested on a sharp division between the skilled and unskilled sectors of the working class and the extent to which the trade agreement came to represent a right accessible in the main to only the first of those two sectors.

The institutional arrangement that the NCF was able to consolidate around its trade agreement program—particularly during the 1900 to 1904 years—did not prevent important sectors of American employers from seeking alternative forms of industrial relations that were more compatible with the productive exigencies confronting them. In a most important sense, alternative models such as scientific management and welfarism were not complementary to collective bargaining, as several prolabor reformers tended to view them. While in a later historical period these various models would often coexist in one enterprise, the Progressive years provide the clearest historical context for showing how the emergence of scientific management and welfarism occurred in direct opposition to the collective bargaining model. And more significantly, by the middle of the 1910s these alternative models were well on the way to becoming consolidated in some of the most dynamic and propelling sectors of U.S. industry.

It is more than a historical irony that while the Progressive years provided the most successful model through which to contain the tide of workers' struggles in the war years, it had also produced models of industrial relations such as scientific management and welfarism on the basis of which American capital could undertake that "technological path to repression" on which the social peace and prosperity of the 1920s was largely founded.

NOTES

1. U.S. Commission on Industrial Relations, *Final Report and Testimony* (Washington, D.C., 1916) 1 : 22; cf. also 153-55, 158-60.

2. Ibid., 18.

3. James Weinstein, *The Corporate Ideal in the Liberal States, 1900-1918* (Boston, 1968), 216.

4. Florence Peterson, "Strikes in the United States, 1880-1936," U.S. Department of Labor, *Bulletin 651* (August 1937): 38-40. For a recent analysis of this wave of strikes—though under a different periodization—see David Montgomery, "The 'New Unionism' and the Transformation of Workers' Consciousness in America, 1909-22," *Labor History* 17 (Fall 1976); this article represents, in my view, a major contribution to the study of strike activity in the Progressive era.

5. Mario Tronti, "Workers and Capital," *Telos* 14 (Winter 1972) : 38.

BIBLIOGRAPHY

NOTE ON SOURCES

The Archives of the National Civic Federation have been a central source of information for this study. The material contained in this collection provides valuable information on practically all aspects of labor and industrial relations during the Progressive years. The extensive correspondence that NCF officers had with employers and labor officials throws much light on the condition confronting businessmen and unions in various industrial sectors. Of special value are the surveys that the NCF took periodically among employers and labor unions. The files of the Trade Agreement Department and the Welfare Department were most important for this study—especially the latter, which is perhaps the single most important manuscript source on the welfare movement. Unlike the files of other NCF departments, the Welfare Department files are arranged topically, covering virtually all aspects of welfare work. Another valuable source was the federation's *Review,* undoubtedly one of the leading national publications on industrial relations of that period. In addition to ongoing coverage of industrial events and the periodic surveys of industrial conditions, the *Review* featured symposia and semitheoretical articles on a variety of economic and political topics, making it possible to reconstruct the federation's ideological posture toward the labor problem.

Of great value also were the John Mitchell Papers. The correspondence that Mitchell had with major political figures, such as Senator Hanna, President Roosevelt, and Commissioner of Labor Neill—especially during the

1900 to 1908 period—reveals the centrality of the UMW in national industrial affairs and the important mediating role Mitchell played between the AFL and the Republican administration. The Charles Neill Papers served as a supplementary source for this aspect of our investigation.

The papers of Seth Low—reform mayor of New York and long-time president of the NCF—throw much light on the federation's conciliation and mediation work. The collection also contains important material on some of the major industrial disputes prior to Low's affiliation with the NCF.

The papers of Louis Brandeis and John Commons were also a useful source of information for this study. They provided some valuable insights into the activities of two of the major prolabor reformers of the period. Of particular interest was the documentation relating to Brandeis's involvement in the Eastern Rate Case, as well as in the Protocol of Peace, two events that, though not directly treated in this study, raised some important industrial relations issues.

The following manuscript collections were used in a more selective fashion.

Among the government publications, by far the most valuable sources of information were the reports and testimonies of the U.S. Industrial Commission (1900-1902, 19 volumes) and the U.S. Commission on Industrial Relations (1916, 11 volumes). Besides the enormous wealth of information they contain, they make it possible to trace the evolution of labor and industrial conditions during the Progressive years. The reports of the second commission were particularly important for this study because of the investigators' more critical approach and the central focus they placed on virtually all aspects of industrial and labor relations. The reports also throw much light on some of the most important industrial disputes and labor struggles of the period.

The *Eleventh Special Report* of the commissioner of labor on the regulation and restriction of output is an indispensable source for the study of craft-union practices, as well as of the various managerial approaches to dealing with this problem. The report was prepared during a period of major consolidation of trade unions' power (c. 1900-1904), and thus it is an essential starting point for the study of the employers' offensive in the area of industrial relations.

Central to this study were also the monthly bulletins of the U.S. Bureau of Labor Statistics—the most relevant of which are listed below. Although some of their statistical data have been surpassed and updated, the bulletins featured important in-depth studies on a number of industrial relations issues that are treated in this book.

PRIMARY SOURCES

MANUSCRIPT MATERIALS

American Association for Labor Legislation Papers. New York State School of Industrial and Labor Relations. Ithaca, New York.

American Federation of Labor Papers. Wisconsin State Historical Society. Madison.

Louis D. Brandeis Papers. University of Louisville Law School. Louisville, Kentucky.

John R. Commons Papers. Wisconsin State Historical Society. Madison.

Samuel Gompers Copy Books. Library of Congress. Washington, D.C.

Seth Low Papers. Columbiana Collection. Columbia University. New York, New York.

Nettie Fowler McCormick Papers. Wisconsin State Historical Society. Madison.

John Mitchell Papers. Catholic University of America. Washington, D.C.

National Civic Federation Papers. New York Public Library, Annex.

Charles Neill Papers. Catholic University of America. Washington, D.C.

GOVERNMENT DOCUMENTS

Clark, Victor S. "Labor Conditions in New Zealand." *Bulletin of the Bureau of Labor,* no. 49 (November 1903).

——. "The Canadian Industrial Disputes Investigation Act of 1907." *Bulletin of the Bureau of Labor,* no. 76 (May 1908).

Croxton, Fred C. "Mediation of Industrial Disputes in Ohio, January 1914 to June 1916." *Bulletin of the Industrial Commission of Ohio* 3 (1916), no. 4.

Neill, Charles B. "Mediation and Arbitration of Railway Labor Disputes in the United States." *Bulletin of the Bureau of Labor,* no. 98 (January 1912).

Olmsted, Victor H. "The Betterment of Industrial Conditions." *Bulletin of the Bureau of Labor,* no. 31 (November 1900).

Sheridan, Frank J. "Italian, Slavic, and Hungarian Unskilled Immigrant Laborers in the United States." *Bulletin of the Bureau of Labor,* no. 72 (September 1907).

Virtue, George. "The Anthracite Mine Laborers." *Bulletin of the Bureau of Labor,* no. 13 (April 1897).

Weyl, Walter, and Sakolsky, A. M. "Conditions of Entrance to the Principal Trades." *Bulletin of the Bureau of Labor,* no. 67 (November 1906).

U.S. Bureau of the Census. *Abstract of the Twelfth Census of the United States.* Washington, D.C.: Government Printing Office, 1904.

——. *Abstract of the Census of Manufacturers, 1914.* Washington, D.C.: Government Printing Office, 1917.

U.S. Bureau of Labor. *Eleventh Special Report of the Commissioner of Labor, Regulation and Restriction of Output.* Washington, D.C.: Government Printing Office, 1904.

——. *Twenty-first Annual Report of the Commissioner of Labor, Strikes and Lockouts.* Washington, D.C.: Government Printing Office, 1907.

——. *Conditions of Employment in the Iron and Steel Industry in the United States.* Washington, D.C.: Government Printing Office, 1911-1913. 4 vols.

U.S. Bureau of Labor Statistics. "Report to the President on the Anthracite Coal Strike." *Bulletin Whole Number 43* (November 1902).

——. "Report of the Anthracite Coal Strike Commission." *Bulletin Whole Number 46* (May 1903).

——. "Employers' Welfare Work." *Bulletin Whole Number 123* (May 15, 1913).

——. "Conciliation and Arbitration in the Building Trades of Greater New York." *Bulletin Whole Number 124* (June 1913).

——. "Collective Bargaining in the Anthracite Coal Industry." *Bulletin Whole Number 191* (March 1916).

——. "Welfare Work for Employees in Industrial Establishments in the United States." *Bulletin Whole Number 250* (February 1919).

——. "Strikes in the United States, 1880-1936." *Bulletin Whole Number 651* (August 1937).

——. "Conciliation Work of the Department of Labor, March 4, 1913, to June 6, 1916." *Monthly Review* 3 (July 1916).

U.S. Commission on Industrial Relations. *Final Report and Testimony.* Washington, D.C.: Government Printing Office, 1916. 11 vols.

U.S. Congress. House of Representatives. *Hearings before the Special Committee of the House of Representatives to Investigate the Taylor System and other Systems of Shop Management.* Washington, D.C.: Government Printing Office, 1912. 3 vols.

U.S. Immigration Commission. *Reports.* Washington, D.C.: Government Printing Office, 1911. 42 vols.

U.S. Industrial Commission. *Reports of the Industrial Commission.* Washington, D.C.: Government Printing Office, 1900-1902. 19 vols.

CONVENTION AND CONFERENCE PROCEEDINGS
American Federation of Labor. *Report of the Proceedings of the Annual Convention.* 1898-1916.

Chicago Conference on Trusts, Held September 13th-16th, 1899. Chicago: The Civic Federation of Chicago, 1900.

Proceedings of the Conference of Employment Managers' Association of Boston, Held May 10, 1916. In U.S. Bureau of Labor, *Bulletin Whole Number 202* (September 1916).

Federated Metal Trades of North America. *Proceedings of the Meeting of the Executive Board, Toledo, April 2, 1902.* Wisconsin State Historical Society.

Industrial Workers of the World. *Proceedings of the First Convention, Chicago, June 27-July 8, 1905.* New York: Merit Publishers, 1969.

Proceedings of the First Annual Conference of the Coal Miners and Operators of Illinois, Indiana, Ohio, and Pennsylvania, January 17, 1898. Columbus: The Lawrence Press, n.d.

Proceedings of the Metal Trades Conference Held in Pittsburgh, January 8, 1903. Wisconsin State Historical Society.

Proceedings of the Metal Trades Conference Held in Washington, D.C., January 25-28, 1904. Wisconsin State Historical Society.

Metal Trades Department of the American Federation of Labor. *Report of Proceedings of the Annual Convention, 1909-1916.*

National Association of Manufacturers. *Report of Proceedings of the Annual Convention, 1902-1908.*

Industrial Conciliation: *Report of the Proceedings of the Conference Held Under the Auspices of the National Civic Federation, December 16 and 17, 1901.* New York: G. P. Putnam's Sons, 1902.

Industrial Conference, Held Under the Auspices of the National Civic Federation, December 8-10, 1902. New York: Winthrop Press, 1903.

Conference on Welfare Work, Held Under the Auspices of the Welfare Department of the National Civic Federation, March 16, 1904. New York: A. H. Kellogg Co., 1904.

Proceedings of the Eleventh Annual Meeting of the National Civic Federation, January 12-14, 1911. New York: National Civic Federation, n.d.

United Mine Workers of America. *Report of Proceedings of the Annual Convention, 1898-1908.*

LABOR AND BUSINESS JOURNALS

American Federationist.
American Industries.
American Machinist.
Engineering Magazine.
Industrial Union Bulletin.

Industrial Worker.
International Metal Worker.
Iron Molders' Journal.
Monthly Journal (International Association of Machinists).
Machinists' Monthly Journal.
Review (National Civic Federation).
Solidarity.
The United Mine Workers' Journal.

AUTOBIOGRAPHIES AND REMINISCENCES

Brophy, John. *A Miner's Life.* Edited and supplemented by John O. P.
    Hall. Madison: University of Wisconsin Press, 1964.
Columbia University Oral History Project. *The Reminiscences of John
    P. Frey.* 1957.
Commons, John R. *Myself.* New York: Macmillan, 1934.
Gompers, Samuel. *Seventy Years of Life and Labor.* New York: E. P.
    Dutton, 1925.
Hanna, Marcus A. *Mark Hanna, His Book.* Boston: Chapple Publishing,
    1904.
Haywood, William D. *Bill Haywood's Book.* New York: International
    Publishers, 1929.
Jones, Mary. *Autobiography of Mother Jones.* Edited by Mary Field
    Parton. New York: Arno Press, 1969, reprint.
Powderly, Terence V. *The Path I Trod: The Autobiography of Terence
    Victor Powderly.* Eidted by Harry Carman, Henry David, and Paul
    Guthrie. New York: Columbia University Press.

BOOKS, PAMPHLETS, AND ARTICLES BY CONTEMPORARIES

Baker, Ray S. "Employers' Association in the United States." *McClure's*
    21 (June 1904).
Brandeis, Louis D. *Business: A Profession.* Boston: Small and Maynard
    Co., 1914.
Cohen, Julius H. *Law and Order in Industry.* New York: Macmillan, 1893.
Commons, John R. *The Distribution of Wealth.* New York: Macmillan,
    1893.
——. *Labor and Administration.* New York: A. M. Kelly, 1964, reprint.
——. "Representation of Interests." *The Independent* (June 21, 1900).
——. "Trade Agreements." In John R. Commons, ed., *Trade Unionism
    and Labor Problems.* Boston: Ginn & Co., 1905.
——. "Is Class Conflict in America Growing and Is It Inevitable?" *Ameri-
    can Journal of Sociology* (May 1908).

———. "Industrial Relations." In John R. Commons, ed., *Trade Unionism and Labor Problems*. 2d series. Boston: Ginn & Co., 1921.

———, and Andrews, John B. *Principles of Labor Legislation*. New York: Harper and Bros., 1916.

Debs, Eugene. "The Crime of Craft Unionism." *International Socialist Review* 11 (February 1911).

De Leon, Daniel. *Industrial Unionism: Selected Editorials*. New York: Labor News Company, 1944.

Easley, Ralph. "Senator Hanna and the Labor Problem." *The Independent* 55 (March 3, 1904).

Ebert, Justus. *The I.W.W. in Theory and Practice*. Chicago: Industrial Workers of the World, n.d.

Fisher, W. I. "Industrial Unionism—Tactics and Principles." *Industrial Worker* (March 12, 19, 1910).

Fitch, John. "The I.W.W.: An Outlaw Organization." *Survey* 30 (June 1, 1913).

Garretson, Austin B. "The Attitude of Organized Labor Toward the Canadian Industrial Disputes Investigation Act." *Annals of the American Association of Political and Social Science* 16 (January 1917).

Gompers, Samuel. *The American Labor Movement—Its Makeup, Achievements, and Aspiration*. Washington, D.C.: American Federation of Labor, 1914.

———. *Labor and the Employer*. Edited by Hayes Robbins. New York: E. P. Dutton, 1920.

———. "The Limitations of Conciliation and Arbitration." *Annals of the American Association of Political and Social Science* 20 (July 1902).

———. "Strikes, Sympathetic and Otherwise." *American Federationist* (August 1902).

———. "Attitude of Labor Towards Government Regulation of Industry." *Annals of the American Academy of Political and Social Science* 32 (July 1908).

———. *Collective Bargaining: Labor's Proposal to Insure Greater Industrial Peace*. Washington, D.C.: American Federation of Labor, 1920.

———. "From Politics to Industry." *American Federationist* (May 1923).

Halsey, F. A. "The Economics of the Premium Plan." *American Machinist* (May 3, 1900).

Hanna, Marcus A. "Industrial Conciliation and Arbitration." *Annals of the American Academy of Political and Social Science* 20 (July 1902).

Haywood, William. "Socialism, the Hope of the Working Class." *International Socialist Review* 12 (February 1912).

———, and Bohn, Frank. *Industrial Socialism*. Chicago: C. H. Kerr, 1911.

Kellogg, Paul. "The McKees Rocks Strike." *Survey* 12 (1909).

Lewis, Austin. *The Militant Proletariat*. Chicago: C. H. Kerr, 1911.
——. "Organization of the Unskilled, I." *New Review* 1 (November 1913).
——. "Organization of the Unskilled, II." *New Review* 2 (December 1913).
Low, Seth. "The National Civic Federation and Industrial Peace." *Annals of the American Academy of Political and Social Science* 44 (November 1912).
Mailly, William. "The Anthracite Coal Strike." *International Socialist Review* (August 1902).
Marcy, Mary E. "The Battle for Bread at Lawrence." *International Socialist Review* 12 (March 1912).
Marks, Marcus M. "The Employers and the Labor Union." *The Independent* 68 (May 26, 1910).
——. "The Canadian Industrial Disputes Act." *Annals of the American Academy of Political and Social Science* 44 (November 1912).
Mitchell, John. *Organized Labor*. Philadelphia: American Book and Bible House, 1903.
——. *The Wage Earner, and His Problems*. Washington, D.C.: P. S. Ridsdale, 1913.
——. "Recognition of Trade Unions." *The Independent* 53 (August 15, 1901).
——. "The Mine Worker's Life and Aims." *Cosmopolitan* (October 1901).
National Civic Federation. *The National Civic Federation: Its Methods and Its Aims*. New York: National Civic Federation, 1905.
Nicholls, T. D. "The Anthracite Board of Conciliation." *Annals of the American Academy of Political and Social Science* 36 (September 1910).
Orcutt, H. F. L. "Machine Shop Management in Europe and America." *Engineering Magazine* (February 1899).
——. "Effects of Environment on the Efficiency of Workmen." *Engineering Magazine* (March 1899).
Parker, C. H. "The Decline in Trade Union Membership." *Quarterly Journal of Economics* 24 (May 1910).
Patterson, John H. "Altruism and Sympathy as Factors in Works Administration." *Engineering Magazine* 20 (January 1902).
Peters, John, ed. *Labor and Capital*. New York: G. P. Putnam's Sons, 1902.
St. John, Vincent. *The I.W.W.: Its History, Structure, and Methods*. Cleveland: I.W.W. Publishing Bureau, 1917.
Smith, Walker C. *Sabotage—Its History, Philosophy and Function*. Chicago: I.W.W. Publishing Bureau, 1913.
Spargo, John. *Syndicalism, Industrial Unionism and Socialism*. New York: B. W. Huebsch, 1913.

Steffens, Lincoln. "A Labor Leader of Today: John Mitchell and What He Stands for." *McClure's* 19 (August 1902).

Strauss, Oscar S. "Results Accomplished by the Industrial Department, National Civic Federation." *Annals of the American Academy of Political and Social Science* 20 (July 1902).

Sullivan, J. W. *The Trade Unions' Attitude Toward Welfare Work.* New York: National Civic Federation, 1907.

Taylor, Frederick W. *Scientific Management: Comprising Shop Management, the Principles of Scientific Management, Testimony Before the Special House Committee.* New York: Harper, 1947.

Trautmann, William. *Why Strikes Are Lost.* In Joyce L. Kornbluh, ed., *Rebel Voices.* Ann Arbor: University of Michigan Press, 1972.

Veblen, Thorstein. *The Theory of Business Enterprise.* New York: C. Scribner's Sons, 1904.

Walker, Francis. "The Development of the Anthracite Combination." *Annals of the American Academy of Political and Social Science* 111 (January 1924).

Walling, William E. "Class Struggle Within the Working Class." In William L. O'Neill, ed., *Echoes of Revolt: The Masses, 1911-1917.* Chicago: Quadrangle Books, 1966.

——. *Progressivism–and After.* New York: Macmillan, 1914.

——. "Industrialism or Revolutionary Unionism, I." *New Review* 1 (January 11, 1913).

——. "Industrialism or Revolutionary Unionism, II." *New Review* 1 (January 18, 1913).

Warne, Frank J. "John Mitchell, the Labor Leader and the Man." *Review of Reviews* (November 1902).

——. "The Miners' Union: Its Business Management." *Annals of the American Academy of Political and Social Science* 25 (1905).

Weyl, Walter. "The Man the Miners Trust." *The Outlook* (March 1906).

SECONDARY SOURCES

BOOKS

Abbott, Edith. *Women in Industry.* New York: D. Appleton, 1910.

Adams, Graham Jr. *The Age of Industrial Conflict, 1910-1915.* New York: Columbia University Press, 1966.

Aitken, Hugh C. J. *Taylorism at Watertown Arsenal.* Cambridge, Mass.: Harvard University Press, 1960.

Ashworth, John H. *The Helper and American Trade Unions.* Baltimore: Johns Hopkins Press, 1915.

Aurand, Harold W. *From the Molly Maguires to the United Mine Workers.* Philadelphia: Temple University Press, 1971.

Baran, Paul, and Sweezy, Paul M. *Monopoly Capital.* New York: Monthly Review Press, 1966.

Barnett, George. *Chapters on Machinery and Labor.* Cambridge, Mass.: Harvard University Press, 1926.

Barnett, George, and Hollander, Jacob H., eds. *Studies in American Trade Unionism.* New York: H. Holt, 1906.

Barnett, George, and McCabe, David. *Mediation, Investigation, and Arbitration in Industrial Disputes.* New York: D. Appleton, 1916.

Bing, Alexander M. *Wartime Strikes and Their Adjustment.* New York: E. P. Dutton, 1921.

Bloch, Louis. *Labor Agreements in Coal Mines.* New York: Russell Sage Foundation, 1931.

Blum, Solomon. *Jurisdictional Disputes Resulting from Structural Difference in American Trade Unions.* Berkeley: University of California Press, 1913.

Bock, Gisela; Carpignano, Paolo; and Ramirez, Bruno. *La Formazione dell'Operaio Massa negli USA, 1898-1922.* Milan: Feltrinelli Editore, 1976.

Bologna, Sergio et al. *Operai e Stato.* Milan: Feltrinelli Editore, 1972.

Bonnett, Clarence E. *Employers' Associations in the United States.* New York: Macmillan, 1922.

Braverman, Harry. *Labor and Monopoly Capital.* New York: Monthly Review Press, 1974.

Brissenden, Paul F. *The I.W.W.: A Study of American Syndicalism.* New York: Columbia University Press, 1920.

Brody, David. *The Butcher Workmen: A Study of Unionization.* Cambridge, Mass.: Harvard University Press, 1964.

——. *Steelworkers in America: The Nonunion Era.* New York: Harper, 1969.

Carpenter, Jesse Thomas. *Competition and Collective Bargaining in the Needle Trades, 1910-1967.* Ithaca: Cornell University Press, 1972.

Carpenter, Niles. *Immigrants and Their Children.* New York: Arno Press, 1969.

Chandler, Alfred D., Jr. *Strategy and Structure: Chapters in the History of the Industrial Enterprise.* Cambridge, Mass.: MIT Press, 1962.

Christie, Robert A. *Empire in Wood.* Ithaca: Cornell University Press, 1956.

Conference on Research in Income and Wealth, Output, Employment, and Productivity in the United States After 1800. New York: National Bureau of Economic Research, 1966.

Conlin, Joseph. *Bread and Roses Too: Studies of the Wobblies.* Westport, Conn.: Greenwood Publishing, 1969.

Cornell, Robert J. *The Anthracite Strike of 1902.* Washington, D.C.: Catholic University of America Press, 1957.

Creamer, Daniel B. *Capital in Manufacturing and Mining.* Princeton: Princeton University Press, 1960.

Croly, Herbert. *Marcus Alonzo Hanna: His Life and Work.* New York: Macmillan, 1912.

Derber, Milton. *The American Idea of Industrial Democracy, 1865-1965.* Urbana: University of Illinois Press, 1970.

Dick, William M. *Labor and Socialism in America: The Gompers Era.* Port Washington, N.Y.: Kennikat Press, 1972.

Douglas, Paul. *Real Wages in the United States, 1890-1926.* Boston: Houghton Mifflin, 1930.

Dubofsky, Melvyn. *When Workers Organize: New York City in the Progressive Era.* Amherst: University of Massachusetts Press, 1968.

——. *We Shall Be All: A History of the Industrial Workers of the World.* Chicago: Quadrangle Books, 1969.

Erickson, Charlotte. *American Industry and the European Immigrant, 1860-1885.* Cambridge, Mass.: Harvard University Press, 1957.

Evans, Chris. *A History of the United Mine Workers of America, 1860-1900.* Indianapolis, 1918-1920. 2 vols.

Fabricant, Solomon. *The Output of Manufacturing Industries, 1899-1937.* New York: National Bureau of Economic Research, 1940.

Faulkner, Harold. *The Decline of Laissez Faire, 1897-1917.* New York: Rinehart, 1957.

Foner, Philip S. *History of the Labor Movement in the United States.* New York: International Publishers, 1947-1965. 4 vols.

Gilman, Nicholas P. *Methods of Industrial Peace.* Boston: Houghton Mifflin, 1904.

Ginger, Ray. *Eugene Victor Debs: A Biography.* New York: Collier Books, 1966.

Glueck, Elsie. *John Mitchell, Miner.* New York: John Day Co., 1929.

Gordon, Robert A. *Business Fluctuations.* New York: Harper, 1952.

Green, Marguerite. *The National Civic Federation and the American Labor Movement.* Washington, D.C.: Catholic University of America Press, 1956.

Greene, Victor R. *The Slavic Community on Strike.* Notre Dame: University of Notre Dame Press, 1968.

Habakkuk, H. J. *American and British Technology in the 19th Century.* Cambridge: Cambridge University Press, 1962.

Haber, William. *Labor Relations and Productivity in the Building Trades.*

Ann Arbor: University of Michigan Press, 1956.

Haber, Samuel. *Efficiency and Uplift: Scientific Management in the Progressive Era.* Chicago: University of Chicago Press, 1964.

Helbing, Albert T. *The Departments of the American Federation of Labor.* Baltimore: Johns Hopkins Press, 1931.

Higham, John. *Strangers in the Land.* New York: Atheneum, 1973.

Hourwich, Isaac A. *Immigration and Labor–The Economic Aspects of European Immigration to the United States.* New York: G. P. Putnam's Sons, 1912.

Jenks, Jeremia, and Lauck, W. Jett. *The Immigrant Problem.* New York: Funk and Wagnalls, 1913.

Jensen, Vernon H. *Heritage of Conflict.* Ithaca: Cornell University Press, 1950.

Jones, Eliot. *The Anthracite Coal Combination in the United States.* Cambridge, Mass.: Harvard University Press, 1914.

Karson, Marc. *American Labor Unions and Politics, 1900-1918.* Boston: Beacon Press, 1965.

Kaufman, Burton I. *Efficiency and Expansion.* Westport, Conn.: Greenwood Press, 1974.

Kellogg, Paul U., ed. *The Pittsburgh Survey.* New York: Russell Sage Foundation, 1909-1914. 6 vols.

Kendrick, John W. *Productivity Trends in the United States.* Princeton: Princeton University Press, 1961.

Kolko, Gabriel. *The Triumph of Conservatism.* Chicago: Quadrangle Books, 1967.

Korman, Gerd. *Industrialization, Immigrants and Americanization: The View from Milwaukee.* Madison: State Historical Society of Wisconsin, 1967.

Kornbluh, Joyce L., ed. *Rebel Voice: An I.W.W. Anthology.* Ann Arbor: University of Michigan Press, 1972.

Laslett, John H. M. *Labor and the Left.* New York: Basic Books, 1970.

Lebergott, Stanley. *Manpower in Economic Growth.* New York: National Bureau of Economic Research, 1964.

Leiserson, William M. *Adjusting Immigrants and Industry.* New York: Harper & Bros., 1924.

Lorwin, Lewis L. *The American Federation of Labor: History, Policies, and Prospects.* Washington, D.C.: The Brookings Institution, 1933.

Lubin, Isador. *Miners' Wages and the Cost of Coal.* New York: McGraw-Hill, 1924.

McCabe, David A. *National Collective Bargaining in the Pottery Industry.* Baltimore: Johns Hopkins Press, 1932.

Mathewson, Stanley B. *Restriction of Output Among Unorganized Workers.* New York: Viking Press, 1931.

Montgomery, David. *Beyond Equality.* New York: Vintage Books, 1972.

Morris, James O. *Conflict Within the A. F. of L.* Ithaca: Cornell University Press, 1958.

Mote, Carl H. *Industrial Arbitration.* Indianapolis: Bobbs-Merrill, 1916.

Nadowrny, Milton J. *Scientific Management and the Unions, 1900-1932.* Cambridge, Mass.: Harvard University Press, 1955.

Nelson, Ralph. *Merger Movements in American Industry, 1895-1956.* Princeton: Princeton University Press, 1959.

Ozanne, Robert. *A Century of Labor-Management Relations at McCormick & International Harvester.* Madison: University of Wisconsin Press, 1967.

Perlman, Mark. *The Machinists: A New Study in American Trade Unionism.* Cambridge, Mass.: Harvard University Press, 1961.

Rees, Albert. *Real Wages in Manufacturing, 1890-1914.* Princeton: Princeton University Press, 1961.

Roberts, Peter. *The Anthracite Coal Industry.* New York: Macmillan, 1901.

Roy, Andrew. *A History of the Coal Miners of the United States.* Columbus: J. L. Trauger Co., 1907.

Savage, Marion D. *Industrial Unionism in America.* New York: Ronald Press, 1922.

Schluter, William. *The Pre-War Business Cycle, 1907-1914.* New York: Columbia University Press, 1923.

Schumpeter, Joseph A. *Business Cycles.* New York: McGraw-Hill, 1939.

Steigerwalt, Albert K. *The National Association of Manufacturers, 1895-1914.* Ann Arbor: University of Michigan Press, 1964.

Stockton, Frank T. *The International Molders Union of North America.* Baltimore: Johns Hopkins Press, 1921.

Suffern, Arthur E. *Conciliation and Arbitration in the Coal Industry of America.* New York: Houghton Mifflin, 1915.

——. *The Coal Miners' Struggle for Industrial Status.* New York: Macmillan, 1926.

Sward, Keith. *The Legend of Henry Ford.* New York: Atheneum, 1972.

Taft, Philip. *The AFL in the Time of Gompers.* New York: Harpers, 1957.

Taylor, Albion G. *The Labor Policies of the National Association of Manufacturers.* Urbana: University of Illinois Press, 1928.

Thompson, Bertrand C. *Theory and Practice of Scientific Management.* Boston: Houghton Mifflin, 1917.

Thorp, Willard L. *Business Annals.* New York: National Bureau of Economic Research, 1926.

Wagoner, Harless. *The U.S. Machine Tool Industry from 1900 to 1950.*

Cambridge, Mass.: MIT Press, 1968.

Warne, Frank J. *The Immigrant Invasion.* New York: Dodd, Mead, 1913.

Weinstein, James. *The Corporate Ideal in the Liberal State, 1900-1918.* Boston: Beacon Press, 1968.

Wiebe, Robert. *Businessmen and Reform.* Chicago: Quadrangle Books, 1968.

Wolman, Leo. *Ebb and Flow in Trade Unionism.* New York: National Bureau of Economic Research, 1936.

Yellowitz, Irwin. *Labor and the Progressive Movement in New York State, 1897-1916.* Ithaca: Cornell University Press, 1965.

ARTICLES

Barnett, George. "National and District Systems of Collective Bargaining in the United States." *Quarterly Journal of Economics* 26 (1912).

Becker, William H. "American Manufacturers and Foreign Markets, 1870-1900." *Business History Review* (Winter 1973).

Bogart, Ernest I. "The Machinists' Strike, 1900." *Yale Review* 9 (November 1900).

Bologna, Sergio. "Class Composition and Theory of the Party." *Telos* 13 (Fall 1972).

Buhle, Paul. "Debsian Socialism and the 'New Immigrant' Worker." In *Insights and Parallels,* edited by William L. O'Neill. Minneapolis: Burgess Publishing Co., 1973.

Chandler, Alfred D., Jr. "Management Decentralization: A Historical Analysis." Business History Review 30 (1956).

——. "The Beginning of 'Big Business' in American Industry." *Business History Review* 33 (Spring 1959).

——. "The Structure of American Industry in the Twentieth Century: A Historical Overview." *Business History Review* 43 (Autumn 1969).

Davis, Mike. "The Stop Watch and the Wooden Shoe: Scientific Management and the Industrial Workers of the World." *Radical America* 9 (January-February 1975).

Destler, Chester. "On the Eve of the Anthracite Coal Strike Arbitration: Henry D. Lloyd at United Mine Workers Headquarters." *Labor History* 13 (Spring 1959).

Durand, E. Dana. "The Anthracite Coal Strike and Its Settlement." *Political Science Quarterly* 18 (September 1903).

Fraser, F. G. "Anthracite Coal Miners' Wages." *Annals of the American Academy of Political and Social Science* 16 (1900).

Garraty, John. "U.S. Steel Versus Labor: The Early Years." *Labor History* 1 (Winter 1960).

George, J. E. "The Coal Miners' Strike of 1897." *Quarterly Journal of Economics* 12 (January 1898).
——. "The Settlement in the Coal-Mining Industry." *Quarterly Journal of Economics* 12 (July 1898).
Hessen, Robert. "The Bethlehem Steel Strike of 1910." *Labor History* 15 (Winter 1974).
Hicken, Victor. "The Virden and Pana Wars." *Journal of the Illinois State Historical Society* 51 (Spring 1959).
Ingham, John N. "A Strike in the Progressive Era: McKees Rocks, 1909." *The Pennsylvania Magazine of History and Biography* 90 (1966).
Leinenweber, Charles. "The American Socialist Party and the New Immigrants." *Science and Society* 32 (Winter 1968).
Litterer, John. "Systematic Management: Design for Organizational Recoupling in American Manufacturing Firms." *Business History Review* 36 (Winter 1963).
Merkle, Judity A. "The Taylor Strategy: Organizational Innovation and Class Structure." *Berkeley Journal of Sociology* 13 (1968).
Montgomery, David. "The 'New Unionism' and the Transformation of Workers' Consciousness in America, 1909-22." *Journal of Social History* (Summer 1974).
——. "Workers' Control of Machine Production in the Nineteenth Century." *Labor History* 17 (Fall 1976).
Nelson, Daniel. "The New Factory System and the Unions: The National Cash Register Company Dispute of 1901." *Labor History* 15 (Spring 1974).
——, and Campbell, Stuart. "Taylorism Versus Welfare Work in American Industry: H. L. Gantt and the Bancrofts." *Business History Review* 46 (Spring 1972).
Preston, William. "Shall This Be All? U.S. Historians versus William D. Haywood et al." *Labor History* 12 (Summer 1971).
Ramirez, Bruno. "Tensioni Ideologiche nella Storiografia del Progressismo Nordamericano." *La Critica Sociologica* 23 (Fall 1972).
Roberts, Peter. "The Anthracite Coal Situation." *Yale Review* 11 (1902).
Rosenberg, Nathan. "Technological Change in the Machine Tool Industry, 1840-1910." *Journal of Economic History* 23 (1963).
Rudin, Bradley. "Industrial Betterment and Scientific Management as Social Control, 1890-1920." *Berkeley Journal of Sociology* 17 (1972-1973).
Stone, Katherine. "The Origin of Job Structures in the Steel Industry." *Radical Amerca* 7 (November-December 1973).
Tronti, Mario. "Workers and Capital." *Telos* 14 (Winter 1972).

Weinstein, James. "The IWW and American Socialism." *Socialist Revolution* 1 (September-October 1970).

UNPUBLISHED MATERIALS

Clark, Donald O. "John E. Williams (1853-1919) Peacemaker: A Study of the Life of an Early Illinois Mediator and Arbitrator and His Impact upon the American Labor Movement." Master's thesis, University of Illinois, 1957.
Gonce, Richard. "The Development of John R. Commons's System of Thought." Ph.D. dissertation, University of Wisconsin, 1966.
Gowaskie, Joseph. "John Mitchell: A Study in Leadership." Ph.D. dissertation, Catholic University of America, 1968.
Jensen, Gordon. "The National Civic Federation: American Business in an Age of Social Change and Social Reform, 1900-1910." Ph.D. dissertation, Princeton University, 1956.
Pierce, Lloyd F. "The Activities of the American Association for Labor Legislation." Ph.D. dissertation, University of Wisconsin, 1953.
Scheinberg, Stephen. "The Development of Corporation Labor Policy, 1900-1940." Ph.D. dissertation, University of Wisconsin, 1967.

INDEX

ABOUT THE AUTHOR

Bruno Ramirez, assistant professor of history at the University of Mont-
real, specializes in American and comparative labor history. His articles
have appeared in *Radical America, Relations Industrielles,* and *Critica
Sociologica.*